Participatory Visual and Digital Research in Action

Participatory Visual and Digital Research in Action

EDITED BY

Aline Gubrium, Krista Harper, and Marty Otañez

Walnut Creek, California

LEFT COAST PRESS, INC.
1630 North Main Street, #400
Walnut Creek, CA 94596
www.LCoastPress.com

ISBN 978-1-62958-054-8 hardback
ISBN 978-1-62958-055-5 paperback
ISBN 978-1-62958-056-2 institutional eBook
ISBN 978-1-62958-057-9 consumer eBook

Library of Congress Cataloging-in-Publication Data

Participatory visual and digital research in action / edited by Aline
Gubrium, Krista Harper, and Marty Otañez.
    pages cm
 Includes bibliographical references and index.
  ISBN 978-1-62958-054-8 (hardback : alk. paper) -- ISBN 978-1-62958-
055-5 (pbk. : alk. paper) -- ISBN 978-1-62958-056-2 (institutional ebook)
-- ISBN 978-1-62958-057-9 (consumer ebook)
 1. Visual anthropology--Case studies. 2. Visual sociology--Case studies.
3. Video recording in ethnology--Case studies. 4. Motion pictures
in ethnology--Case studies. I. Gubrium, Aline. II. Harper, Krista. III.
Otañez, Marty.
 GN347.P38 2015
 301--dc23
                      2015011604

Printed in the United States of America

∞™ The paper used in this publication meets the minimum requirements
of American National Standard for Information Sciences—Permanence
of Paper for Printed Library Materials, ANSI/NISO Z39.48–1992.

CONTENTS

IIIIIIIIIIIIIIIIIIIIIIIIIIIIIIIIIIIIIIIII **ILLUSTRATIONS** IIIIIIIIIIIIIIIIIIIIIIIIIIIIIIIIIIIIIIIII

Figures

Tables

Foreword

Phillip Vannini

I was profoundly surprised when I received the editors' invitation to write a foreword for this book. More than surprised, I admit that I felt like an impostor. My ethnographic work has nearly always been visual and digital. Yet, I never thought of it as sufficiently participatory or action-oriented.

For example, to generate interesting and at times even entertaining public knowledge, my hybrid media ethnographies (e.g., ferryresearch.ca; lifeoffgrid .ca) have used digital sound, photography, and video not so much as illustrations for journal articles, but rather as the narrative basis for publications in popular magazines, the Internet, TV, and newspapers. Knowledge mobilization of this kind, I have always thought, is necessary for raising awareness and molding public opinions, but perhaps it falls short of being action-oriented. Furthermore, even though I have always involved research participants in the editing of their visual representations (who would want their face or home in the national news if their depiction isn't fair or accurate, right?), I have always been cautious about calling that a form of collaboration.

But impostor syndrome or not, because I have always felt a deep antipathy toward traditional ways of doing and especially sharing research (e.g., see publicethnography.net), and a great deal of antagonism toward the structural academic bias for methodological conservativism, I agreed to write a few opening and perhaps apologetic words as I looked forward to catching up with the latest developments in this field.

As I write these words now—after having read this wonderfully thorough book—I realize that I have been conducting visual, digital, *and* action-oriented participatory research for the last few years, much to my ignorance. My feeling is that this volume will have a similar converting effect on many other readers. And indeed I can only hope that it will do so because, in all honesty, for anyone in the twenty-first century to be convinced of the value of doing inaction-oriented, analog, nonvisual, and uncollaborative research is to be trapped in a time warp of frightening proportions.

From digital storytelling and Photovoice to participatory film and collaborative mapping, and from participatory geographic information systems (PGIS) to collaborative digital archive and museum curation (and more), the contributors to *Participatory Visual and Digital Research in Action* share enough inspiring tools to convince anyone—from the already initiated to the skeptics still keen on paper-and-pencil measures—to pick up a few new skills and evaluate the potential of these evolving methodological traditions for the achievement of both old and new research objectives.

As a cynic by birthright and a critical and reflexive mind by trade, I view the immense appeal of action-oriented participatory visual and digital research strategies less in the shiny glitter that makes them new and edgy (i.e., their technological sophistication and their democratic commitment) and more in the way they allow us to take pleasure in the delight of *enchantment*.

In fact, there isn't enough enchantment in the world of research: there isn't enough respect—in other words—for the naiveté, wonder, and curiosity that drives (and should drive) all forms of inquiry in the first place. Enchantment is, regrettably, beaten out of us at every turn. Research professionals caught in the insidious mechanics of the neoliberal state have their enchantment chastised out of them every time they write a grant proposal that asks them to spell out in advance what they are going to find out, much like undergraduate and graduate students are confined to "defending" the impracticalities and romantic visions of their research designs before they embark on thesis or dissertation research. Enchantment, the institution tells us, is unnecessary, childish, biasing, impractical, and even frightening.

Disenchanted in turn by these numbing politics of bean-counting accountability, and by a myopic focus on reliability and validity-obsessed research, participatory, digital, and visual research followers want us to relearn to appreciate *creativity* and *relationality*. Creativity—the ability to envision something unique and original—and relationality—the capacity to be sensitive to others and to be open to their potential to affect us, as much as our potential to affect them—are what truly distinguish the enchanting approaches outlined in this book. Creativity and relationality are the keys to a different role for social scientific research in academia and in society. Enchantment, this book tells us, is possible, desirable, empowering, productive, and contagious. And even a lot of fun.

Acknowledgments

This project began with a conference panel at the Society for Applied Anthropology meetings in Albuquerque in 2014 and quickly grew into a wider and more interdisciplinary circle of researchers. For us as co-editors, this collection and the accompanying multimedia website has truly been a collaborative effort. We have listed our names alphabetically to reflect this.

We have benefitted from research support that helped us to develop this project. Aline received funding from the Ford Foundation to develop a digital storytelling-based research, training, and strategic communications project focused on sexual and reproductive justice, in concert with young parenting women and in collaboration with her colleague Elizabeth L. (Betsy) Krause and a number of terrific partnering organizations. Thanks to all who have fostered and supported this work. Aline also received National Institutes of Health funding to develop what she calls a "culture-centered, narrative approach" to health promotion, again centered on digital storytelling. Krista received an Instructional Improvement Grant from the College of Social and Behavioral Sciences and a Community Engagement and Service Learning Fellowship from the University of Massachusetts Amherst, both of which provided resources for research and writing. Marty received a grant from the Colorado Department of Public Health and the Environment, with a focus on viral hepatitis.

We thank Mitch Allen at Left Coast Press for his encouragement, expertise, and incredible patience in guiding us throughout the process of editing this book. Ryan Harris, Jennifer de Garmo, Michelle Treviño, Lisa Devenish, and Stephanie Adams helped us get the book in print and reaching new readers. Jennifer Collier's early feedback broadened our perspective on what we could do with this project.

We feel very fortunate to be part of scholarly communities that support our work on participatory visual and digital research. Aline thanks her colleagues in the Departments of Health Promotion and Policy and Anthropology. Krista would like to thank her colleagues in the Department of Anthropology and the Center for Public Policy and Administration (CPPA). Marty thanks his colleagues in the Anthropology Department and the Latino Research and Policy Center at UC Denver. He also thanks future storytellers who are willing to story-share and listen.

Finally, we express our deepest gratitude for our families. Aline thanks Marit, Malin, Lily, and Vince for keeping her grounded and present, especially when everything academic seems so "yet-to-come." Krista is grateful to Michael, Zeke, and Rafael for their encouragement through so many different projects. She also is thankful to her parents and the Sammet, Garner, and Ash families for always being there for her. Marty thanks his wife, graphic designer and web designer Michelle Otañez.

Introduction

Aline Gubrium, Krista Harper, and Marty Otañez

Taking the "Participatory Turn"

As social researchers, many of us were trained to focus on researcher-generated questions contributing to generalizable knowledge that might or might not be applied in community settings at some later time. Postmodern critics of the late twentieth century drew focus to issues of power in scholarly representation, leading many ethnographers to take what is now known as the "literary turn" or the "reflexive turn" (Behar and Gordon 1995; Clifford and Marcus 1986; de Groof 2013; Foley 2002). Since that time, postcolonial, feminist, and other activist scholars pushed the critique beyond scholarly texts to new forms of participatory action research (Castleden et al. 2008; Hale 2008; Harper 2012; Hemment 2007). We have moved beyond the "literary turn" and reflexivity for reflexivity's sake to a new "participatory turn" of collaborative and community-based research. At the same time, visual and digital media technologies present us with new ways to work alongside communities to produce and communicate our research collaboratively. But what does this "participatory turn" look like in action?

Participatory visual and digital research methods are changing the landscape of our work across disciplines and on the ground in collaboration with communities. Scholars in public health, anthropology, communication, environmental studies, science and technology studies, heritage studies, education and youth development, and museum studies are all taking the "participatory turn." This collection consists of six parts, each featuring contributions by experts in each of the most well-known research methods.

As in our first book (A. Gubrium and Harper 2013), where we presented key figures in the field through their "core stories," contributors recount how they came to be practitioners of emerging participatory visual and digital research and how their use of these methods changed them. Chapter authors present their own version of participation and collaboration as it plays out in action, their use of digital or visual technology, and discuss issues of power and ethics that relate to their project process or outcomes. A companion website to the book (www.pvdraction.org/) allows readers to view the research products presented in each contributor's chapter.

Part I includes two very different projects that use digital storytelling. Digital storytelling is a workshop-based process in which participants create first-person narratives about an important moment in their lives and then use digital editing software to synthesize their narrative with digital images, video, text, and sound track to create a compelling short video (Lambert 2012). Darcy Alexandra's chapter presents her longitudinal work with asylum seekers in Ireland and reflects upon digital storytelling as a way to foster "political listening," empathy, and action. Marty Otañez and Andrés Guerrero use this method to learn about the lives and challenges of people living with Hepatitis C in Denver. The chapters in Part II highlight different issues in Photovoice. Photovoice is a participatory method in which participants take photos in relation to participant-derived themes, participate in generative conversations around selected photos, and then display and dialogue around the photos in a community forum setting to address key themes for action (Wang 1999). Ciann Wilson and Sarah Flicker use the method to elicit young women's understandings of sexuality and sexual health in an African, Caribbean, and black neighborhood in Toronto, a context marked by racial, gender, and class inequalities. Cynthia Selin and Gretchen Gano harness Photovoice techniques to participatory technology assessment in the Futurescape City Tours project, in which citizens and experts explore neighborhoods as they discuss how new technologies might transform urban life in North American cities.

Part III presents the work of veteran participatory action researchers working in film and video. Charles Menzies offers a retrospective lens of his film projects with the Gitxaała Nation in Canada and his learning process as an indigenous filmmaker moving into an ever more collaborative approach. Jean Schensul and Campbell Dalglish describe their "improvisational film" technique for engaging youth in participatory action research (PAR) and communication campaigns on issues related to health and drug use.

Part IV moves into the intriguing terrain of participatory geographic information systems (PGIS). Researchers are increasingly using the cartographic techniques and sophisticated spatial analysis tools of GIS to study how maps and space matter. In PGIS projects, maps are participant-created and/or created using GIS software. Maps in either form are used as visual elicitations devices for answering four questions: 1) Where is something located? 2) Where is something concentrated? 3) What kinds of things coincide in a specific place? and 4) How is a place changing over time? (A. Gubrium and Harper 2013, 153–154). In Nick Rattray's chapter, we see people with and without physical disabilities mapping and evaluating accessibility on a university campus and revealing "invisible barriers" in the process. Simona Perry takes a participatory, qualitative GIS approach in her work with rural Pennsylvania residents, representing layers of stories associated with specific landscapes affected by shale gas exploration. Historical archaeologist Edward González-Tennant uses GIS as a starting point for grappling with multimedia research, collaborating with survivors and descendants of a massacre that took place in an African-American town in the early 1920s. His Virtual Rosewood museum uses interactive online features to engage descendant communities and the broader public in coming to terms with "difficult heritage."

Part V brings together several examples of participatory digital archives and museums. In our first book, we noted an opening up of "opportunities for the public to participate in collections and archives, not only as information consumers, but also as contributors and lay curators" (A. Gubrium and Harper 2013, 169). Heritage and digital humanities scholars increasingly see the digital archiving process as an entry point for participatory action research. Catherine Besteman gives an autoethnographic account of the development of an online archive of photographs and research materials from her fieldwork. She developed "The Somali Bantu Experience" in consultation with local Bantu refugees who were resettled in Maine after fleeing Somalia's civil war. Madeleine Tudor and Alaka Wali present their use of PAR to develop interactive, community-based exhibitions at Chicago's Field Museum, where "mixed media are the core for representing research to broader publics." Finally, Natalie Underberg-Goode examines the iterative process of developing PeruDigital, a virtual ethnographic museum created by a team of scholars, students, programmers, and artists from the United States and Peru.

Part VI marks the robust emergence of participatory design ethnography as a mode that crisscrosses social science, art, and user-focused technology. Nancy Fried Foster offers case studies of participatory design in higher-education libraries that bring together students, staff, and faculty to produce better spaces and services. She argues for the urgency of participatory design and critical design studies as harnessing research to produce "shared value." This concern runs through the chapter by Elizabeth Chin and colleagues, which follows the path of design students and homeless youth in Los Angeles as they work together to develop a multimedia installation inviting the public to "take a walk in someone else's shoes." In the final chapter, Matthew Durington and Samuel Collins take inspiration from Chin's provocative question: "Why can't design itself be a form of ethnography?" They present their team's iterative process of designing fieldwork apps as a way to analyze and reflect on the community-based multimedia materials collected over the past several years by the Anthropology by the Wire project.

Taken together, these cases present an exciting array of possibilities for engaged research, but also new tensions for scholars to navigate. Crosscutting themes emerge across the chapters in relation to theoretical and ethical issues, the research process and methods, and the products, outcomes, and "broader impacts" of participatory visual and digital research.

Theoretical and Ethical Issues

A dialectics of collaboration undergirds our contributors' research practice. Participatory work is not merely a way to gain entrée into difficult-to-access communities. Rather, the projects described here are rooted in an egalitarian ethic where the research participants and communities are first and foremost prioritized. Lying at the heart of much of this work are process questions: What good is it? Who is it good for? And who determines what good it is for?

In each contributor's core story, there comes a moment where ethical and theoretical dilemmas drive them to take the participatory turn. One turning point in many of our scholarly trajectories came when we first read the works of Brazilian educator and philosopher Paulo Freire, cited by several contributors as an inspiration behind their collaborative and social justice commitments. The methods discussed in this book all draw upon Freire's (2000) process of conscientization: a "cycle of dialogue, reflection and action [with participants in which they are] empowered via collective questioning of dominant narratives and explanations to develop critical consciousness," as Schensul and Dalglish write in their chapter. In Freire's model, inquiry is wedded to civic engagement and a vision of transforming unjust structures.

Scholars often take the participatory turn out of a commitment to "upending the political structure" of research as usual (Chalfen and Rich 2007, 63). Yet, our contributors do not romanticize the collaborative research process: they explore issues of power, particularly when working with multiple stakeholders in a project. Feminist scholar Donna Haraway's (1988) notion of "situated knowledge" is instructive as it applies to structures of power and serves as a theoretical cue for many of us going participatory. Situated knowledge, rooted in local cultural, historical, and embodied specificity, may be especially trustworthy from the vantage point of the subjugated. "Situated knowledges require that the object of knowledge be pictured as an actor and agent, not as a screen or a resource, never finally as a slave to the master that closes off the dialectic in his unique agency and his authorship of 'objective' knowledge" (Haraway 1988, 592). Rattray uses a participatory mapping process with students, some disabled and some able-bodied, to gain their "embodied expertise" on geographical barriers to ease of movement on campus. Here, participatory research serves as a "countermapping" of the usual campus map depictions, which figure as authoritative/technocratic evidence of accommodation. Participant-produced maps evoke situated knowledges and more dynamic bodies of evidence. Or, as Haraway writes: "Only partial perspectives promise objective vision" (1988, 582–583).

A number of our contributors cite the work of French filmmaker and anthropologist Jean Rouch as an intellectual inspiration. Rouch proposes a "shared anthropology," in which knowledge produced with or on a community or culture is accessible to its members (Ginsburg 1995). Similar to a Freirian emphasis on the dialogical process as critical to emancipatory research, Rouch places the collaborative process of filmmaking on equal footing with the outcome: the finished film. Collaboration serves as a "site for reflexivity and social engagement among those involved in the process" (A. Gubrium and Harper 2013, 97). A shared anthropology upgrades research participants to the position of co-researchers who are quite capable of interpreting their own experiences (Pink 2011; Rouch 1975; Rouch and Taylor 2003; Stoller 1992).

Broadening Our Spectrum of Engagement

Along with a shared research and media production process comes the idea that engagement and collaboration encompass a wide variety of roles, strategies, purposes, and outcomes. Many of our contributors position their work within the realms of PAR: some call it collaborative research, and yet others situate their work as community-based participatory research (CBPR). Some of this has to do with our theoretical influences and disciplinary conventions, as well as funding possibilities (see Peterson and A. Gubrium 2011). We do not make strong distinctions between these approaches here, but point to the common thread of scholars broadening their spectrum of engagement.

Tudor and Wali present building a museum collection as an act of community-based organizing and networking with multiple local organizations. They engage community members in the task of gathering archival material, curating assemblages of artifacts, and communicating submerged histories to the public. Besteman also frames her ethnographic work as one of "collaboration" rather than "participation," entailing the design of a digital photo archive to house her past work in Somalia and present work in Maine with resettled Somalis. The work, she notes, has promulgated a variety of encounters of engagement among multiple parties, including research (in this case photography) "subjects," students and faculty at her university, local community members in Maine where the photo archive is housed, and outside audiences viewing the photos from afar through the digital archive.

Other contributors move around within the spectrum of engagement. The specific form of participant engagement depends on the context and purpose of the particular project at hand. Flexibility in participatory strategy is exemplified by Menzies's filmmaking work. In his full-length feature film, *Bax Laansk—Pulling Together* (2011), community members provided feedback on the rough cut of the film only after Menzies has edited the film to this stage. In another film, *Gathering Strength* (2014), the entire process evolved through ongoing consultation with a community organizing team. With *In My Grandmother's Garden* (2009), he cuts a longer film into shorter pieces that he calls "video vignettes." Video vignettes are produced to serve a variety of constituencies, including outside viewing audiences and local community members, for purposes of documentation and knowledge transfer. Menzies leaves open the possibility that others may splice and repurpose his films into smaller cuts to fit their needs, which is yet another way of engaging participation.

Power Asymmetries Do Not Go Away

One may enter research collaborations intent on disrupting uneven dynamics on the research playing field. Yet, it is important to enter the game with eyes wide open to the ways that positionality continues to affect power and agency. Funders, researchers, facilitators, and participants are all involved in this negotiation. Tudor and Wali raise important questions about power dynamics:

> "Research can illuminate tensions and divides between social sectors and organizations, but can it help to address these conflicts? …Does awareness of exclusionary tendencies lead to action for inclusiveness? Do visual media provide more convincing evidence of areas of common ground between divided sectors than other ways of representing research findings?" (see page 209)

Like Tudor and Wali, we want to see how we can push participatory research further, to take these questions into deep consideration in the research process and produce richer stories of the local communities we work with and for.

Contributors also highlight the ways experience informs practice in participatory research. Newbies may come into a project with the idea in mind that power dynamics will be balanced and easily maintained. It takes experience (and/or a good bit of guidance from a practiced mentor) to realize that the imagined ideal of participation and actual practice on the ground often manifest quite differently from one another. Hierarchies and power arrangements inform the ways projects are carried out. Constraints are real. Fried Foster's chapter presents her work using participatory design to shape plans for a user-designed revamping of a university library space. While notions of the common good and benefits to wider publics undergirded the original intentions of her project, the design process sometimes strayed from this ideal due to the budgetary, structural, and technological constraints often found in a public university system. Alexandra also notes the impact of these constraints in her chapter. Writing about her longitudinal digital storytelling study, Alexandra similarly describes the impact that funders and community organizations and staff can have on the course of a collaborative project. Indeed, our interlocutors are often better attuned to these dynamics than we are, so much so that they may shape their media productions to fit the agenda of the sponsoring organization. Researchers must take these power relationships into account, too.

Logistical, ethical, and political challenges are always present in the research process, participatory or otherwise. Yet these are particularly accentuated by digital and visual methods that call for the active participation of community members to visually document their experiences. Perry's chapter evokes ways that politics complicate participation. She writes about using a participatory mapping approach to document conceptualizations of environmental justice around the controversial topic of fracking. Oppressive gender expectations (and sexism as a power dynamic in the field) are especially visible here, in terms of who participates in the work. Legal intricacies also arise, which preclude some key players (namely landowners) from participating. Furthermore, noble intentions of justice may be circumscribed by community suspicion, especially in communities that were previously exploited by or disenfranchised from the system. Perry notes that one way to disrupt the usurpation of participation by those in power is to "give back" to the community, here in the form of providing useful knowledge on policies and regulations that would help shape decision-making on fracking. While participation and power dynamics are indeed complicated matters, one can still *strive* for an ethic of equity in knowledge production.

Limits of Listening and Critique of "Giving Voice"

Haraway cautions the reader that in proposing to do emancipatory work, a danger lies in "romanticizing and/or appropriating the vision of the less powerful while claiming to see from their positions.... The standpoints of the subjugated are not 'innocent' positions" (1988, 584). Gubrium and colleagues "complicate voice," as they describe the co-created, co-mediated, and strategically authentic voicing of participants as they strive to *do something* with their digital stories (2014, 345). The stories produced are hardly value free, with language (voice) not only the speaker's, but also "ever populated with the intentions of others" (see Bakhtin 1981; A. Gubrium et al. 2014, 345). Similarly, Alexandra critiques the notion of "giving voice" to underscore the politics of listening and being heard. Rather than "digital storytelling," which might connote the idea that a person individually tells her "one truest story" to convey a most authentic voice, Alexandra reframes her process as "co-creative" and "documentary."

Audience/ing is also important. Contributors like Alexandra recognize the stagey quality of all research and keep in mind that research materials are produced with intentionality, which keys in on the idea of the "good-enough" story (J. Gubrium 2003; J. Gubrium and Holstein 2009) that is worth a listen. Several contributors explore the strategic use of emotion in stories and research. Do participants produce uplifting or tragic stories? How does this relate to one's political position and situation, as well as to that of the listening audience (Jackson 2002; Loseke 2009)? As Alexandra reminds us, it is important that we take our interlocutors seriously, as they may very well understand that by producing a certain type of story—whether it be hopeful or critical—they may increase narrative rapport with viewing audiences.

The idea of authenticity also provokes another tension: how to "authentically" represent a community and culturally centered understandings without reifying stereotypes and negative representations of the community. Might there be some value for "inauthenticity" in this regard? Sociologist Dennis Waskul (2009) takes on this challenge himself through a daylong experiment of self-imposed sincerity meant to explore "why honesty is not always the best policy." His realization: sometimes it pays to represent oneself (and others) as a "more or less" person rather than attempting to formulate an "authentic self." We see a similar approach in our own work and that of chapter contributors in terms of presentation of self and others in visual and digital media making. Schensul and Dalglish highlight this tension as they reflect on their work in a participatory action filmmaking project with urban youth in Hartford, Connecticut. Authenticity is gained through the embodied and experientially rich understanding of participants who actually have lived and researched structural constraints that shape the film script in terms of narrative arc and character motivation. Community participants are crucial in helping to define the issues, discursive strategies, and the shape of the film. Yet, the input of filmmakers and outside researchers is critical for heightening awareness among participating community members about the potential for perpetuating stereotypes that they seek to challenge. In this sense, the participatory digital and visual process is best conceived as one constituted through "strategic voicing" (see A. Gubrium et al. 2014), spoken when we witness, honor, and advocate on behalf of those who are not usually listened to or heard.

Which Stories to Tell and How to Tell Them?

As much as we may seek to amplify previously silenced voices, we must also critically examine who participates in participatory visual and digital projects and who does not. What sorts of ethical issues are raised in the process of inclusion and disclusion? Besteman homes in on ethical issues around collaboration and inclusion, as when the resettled Somalis depicted in a photo exhibition were seen as "getting all the attention" by other groups in rural Maine that perceived themselves as equally marginalized.

Not everyone wants to participate in a participatory visual and digital project. What does the absence or silence on behalf of some people signify? Wilson and Flicker write about a Photovoice/digital storytelling project focused on young black women's understandings of and experiences with transactional sex in a Toronto neighborhood. Project participants notably do not position themselves as participants in this economy, except speaking to common expectations by others (i.e., men) that they might do so. Participants instead focus on "other" young women, speaking for other women who participate in transactional sex by taking photos and producing digital stories that socially distance themselves from the practice.

Otañez and Guerrero also illustrate a complexity in voicing and representation through a case study of a digital story produced by one participant, Eric, as part of their viral hepatitis digital storytelling workshop. Strategic voicing does not just emanate from the storyteller, but is also mediated by secondary characters. The authors key in on the voice of digital storyteller Eric's father, who, though not positioned as a key actor in Eric's story, is heard throughout in the ways his voice casts shadows on his son's take of the U.S. biomedical system and its affect on his (Eric's) health-seeking practices. Other voices are also heard in the story. Eric speaks to his own small, immigrant African community members' perceptions of hepatitis as a diagnosis to be ashamed of and kept quiet. These voices mediate the narrative aesthetics, including Eric's decision not to appear in the digital story and to change the tone of voice through anonymizing software.

Our contributors wrestle with decisions about how to tell stories and which images to present. Besteman used images from her photo archiving project in an English Language Learner (ELL) book, hoping that these would resonate with the younger Somali students. Several students felt ashamed by the inclusion of old, precivil war photos, however, and some Somali community members expressed concern that photo subjects were depicted as looking "poor." They feared that these images might negatively affect public perceptions of this refugee community down the line. Besteman had to consider how images spoke to a range of potential audiences.

Ethics of Circulation

Ethical tensions arise around the circulation of media produced in collaborative research projects, especially around the repurposing, sharing, and dissemination of produced materials. Exhilaration lies in the possibility that people find the media produced in our projects *relevant enough* to repurpose and recirculate. "Wired" anthropologists Collins and Durington also signal this impulse as they note that social media is replete around us. The authors take a "networked anthropology" approach, aiming for multipurposed research products that are simultaneously media to be appropriated and used by the communities with whom we work, to connect to others (i.e., other communities, potential grantors, friends, and family), and are also research data generated in the space of an ongoing commitment to communities to assist with networking efforts to a wide breadth of audiences (Collins and Durington 2014).

The risk of breaching "internal confidentiality" was present long before the Web, but the ubiquity of social media across the world makes it difficult to guarantee confidentiality (Ellis 1995; Scheper-Hughes 2000). Even in traditional qualitative research products, knowledgeable insiders are now able to crack a pseudonym with a quick Google search. Sociologist Katja Guenther writes:

> The decision to name or not to name raises several interrelated issues, which necessitate balancing the protection of internal and external confidentiality, research goals, strategies in the field and in the presentation of data, and personal comfort. Yet conversations about these issues rarely arise (Guenther 2009, 240).

Because participatory visual research often includes identifying images or popular dissemination campaigns, scholars who use these methods are the harbingers (or alternatively, the canaries in the coal mine) of transformations in protocols for ethical research.

When the goals of a project are "broader impacts," dissemination, and reuse, traditional guarantees of confidentiality may need to be renegotiated. We have asked before, and ask here again: what is to be gained from protecting participants' confidentiality, and what is lost when their voices are kept hidden and they are not able to lay claim to knowledge production (A. Gubrium and Harper 2013)? Given the commitments of many of us to academic institutional requirements, including human subjects boards, we may need to navigate representational politics in a variety of ways, depending on the venues through which we distribute our texts. Gubrium and colleagues (2014) note this tension in their ethnographic digital storytelling work. One component of this work focused on strategic communication of new media materials from a youth sexuality project through mass and social media networks, a requirement of the foundation sponsoring the project. Yet another component centered on research output, including dissemination of research findings in peer-reviewed journals. They note the uncanny effect of meeting university human subjects board requirements to shield the identity of a research participant in a journal article, with the participant positioned as a "vulnerable research subject," while also screening the participant's digital story "full frontal" in public presentations, on the project website, and through social media after the participant provided consent for release in each of these venues. Herein lies a major strength—yet also the Achilles heel—of participatory visual and digital research. We are drawn to these methods precisely because they allow for multipurposed applications, with data collection and research interwoven with real-world activism and advocacy in the pursuit of social justice. It is often hard to harmonize formal institutional protocols with these research goals, which are also rooted in ethical practice.

Reflecting on Process and Methods

We are often asked what we have come to call the "participatory chicken and egg question": "Which comes first? The visual or digital production process, or getting to know the community context as a participatory researcher?" Our contributors offer different perspectives on how to embark on the participatory visual and digital research process. Menzies begins with participant observation, with video production coming later and serving as a complementary tool. Others, like Wilson and Flicker, argue for the visual production process as a way of gaining entrée into a community because it provides a service and engages collaborators in a common, practical mission. Later on, the process of designing digital multimedia sites and software apps can create "recursive moments" for group reflection and discussion, as Durington and Collins and Underberg-Goode argue. All contributors agree upon one thing, however: participatory visual and digital methods are not a panacea, but are best combined with engaged ethnography and a focus on process.

The Means Are as Important as the Ends

A key principle in participatory visual and digital research is that "the means are as important as the ends." Two things must happen simultaneously to build successful partnerships. Research partners develop a common understanding of the research agenda and then take the process and practical work seriously. Alexandra presents the field site in participatory visual and digital research as a "community of practice" (Lave and Wenger 1991; Wenger 1998): having a shared task to complete (such as a digital story) places the researcher alongside participants, rather than head-to-head. As Diane Austin writes: "[P]rojects are the vehicles through which we identify our strengths and weaknesses and develop trust, confidence, and direction" (Austin 2004, 422).

Paying attention to process offers insights into our partners' affective and intellectual framing of collaborative research. In Perry's chapter on PGIS, ethnography becomes a kind of "therapeutic praxis" for members of a rural community affected by shale gas exploration. Valuable knowledge emerges as participants explain their motivations and thought processes on the collaborative work in progress, as we see in diverse projects from Schensul and Dalglish's critical performance ethnography to Chin et al.'s participatory design workshops and Underberg-Goode's iterative design of the PeruDigital website.

The need for improvisation and flexibility runs through many authors' discussion of the research process. Participatory action research demands constant consideration of participants' everyday exigencies, group dynamics, anticipated audiences, and funders' constraints. Just because a project is stated as collaborative and social-justice oriented does not necessarily mean that community members will be interested in participating at all points. Participatory action researchers must pay attention to the burdens placed on individuals even as we seek to maximize the benefits to the community. Otañez and Guerrero modified their original workshop-based approach to digital storytelling to accommodate participants' work schedules by meeting one-on-one to record voiceovers between back-to-back work shifts. Flexibility meant literally meeting participants where they were at, and reflections on the research process highlighted the structural vulnerabilities faced by storytelling participants.

Many contributors discuss how the "participatory turn" has made them take the process of training novice researchers more seriously. Researchers need to prepare participants for fieldwork and media production by presenting research design, data collection methods, and ethical issues in accessible, jargon-free language. Participatory visual and digital research often involves community participants and students in the research process, potentially retooling long-standing "town-and-gown" divisions. When the research is integrated into a university course, insensitive or disengaged students may behave in a way that undermines carefully cultivated relationships with community partners. Even so, Chin and colleagues, Rattray, and Durington and Collins all note the transformative "situated/side-by-side" learning that occurs in the participatory research process (Lave and Wenger 1991).

The Role of Technology

Participatory visual and digital research can be technology-intensive relative to traditional qualitative methods, prompting new questions: What do digital technologies and environments bring to our scholarship? How do technologies relate to the theoretical insights we develop in the course of using them? We take these questions seriously. As Selin and Gano state in their chapter, "new styles of technology not only equal novel conveniences, features, and economic arrangements; they also prompt the evolution of new social forms and political arrangements." (see page 88)

Social and symbolic meanings infuse technology. Menzies points out that the technology we use communicates indexically to participants. The presence of technology signals that research is taking place and sends messages about the care and professionalism of documentation. For this reason, Menzies prefers larger, high-quality cameras to small, consumer electronics that may raise suspicions of covert research or look unprofessional. Other authors, such as Durington and Collins, revel in the democratization of mobile technologies. They prefer devices such as smartphones because these communicate that research can be "user-friendly," accessible, and integrated into everyday life.

How do we address structural issues surrounding technology without turning back to a researcher-as-expert framework? Some technologies seem ubiquitous, but several contributors faced challenges in working with people with slow Internet service and limited computer access and skills. These were obstacles for Perry's PGIS research in rural Pennsylvania. Perry readjusted her project to meet participants where they were. She asked participants to mark up laminated paper maps during focus group sessions. She then took these annotated maps back to the lab to enter the data into GIS software.

Functionally, digital platforms afford new ways to tell stories about research. Underberg-Goode suggests "understanding and exploiting characteristics of new media that can be brought to bear on narrative ethnography: interactivity, a sense of navigable space, nonlinearity, and a blurring of author/audience boundaries." (see page 218) Social scientists can leverage these qualities to reach new audiences and to break down barriers between experts and the public.

Mixing It Up and Engaging with Design

Since we wrote our first book, we have seen more and more practitioners "mixing it up" by combining different methodological techniques, disciplinary approaches, and modalities. We see Wilson and Flicker pairing Photovoice with digital storytelling and González-Tennant combining GIS, digital storytelling, and game environments. In their "Anthropology by the Wire" project, Durington and Collins began with participatory video and then added social media such as Twitter and Tumblr to foster a "networked anthropology." Now they are developing apps to "gamify" fieldwork training and create virtual tours. Rattray and Perry both mix GIS with interviews, Photovoice, and other techniques to produce maps that convey a rich, qualitative sense of place and participants' experience.

Practitioners are combining disciplinary approaches to solve problems, with the idea that the people most affected by policies and design should take part in planning. Fried Foster shows how multidisciplinary teams of ethnographers, librarians, and architects work with users to design better academic libraries that respond to student and faculty needs. Chin's team brought together design, music, ethnography, and PAR to understand and amplify the concerns of homeless youth. Underberg-Goode describes the interactions between anthropologists, Latin American studies specialists, and computer programmers to develop a bilingual, culturally appropriate digital humanities website.

Participatory visual and digital research is going ever more "multimodal": integrating visual materials and text with materials drawing upon other senses (Dicks 2014). Tudor and Wali, working in a museum setting, mix together media that participants can view and read with material culture that they can touch and manipulate. González-Tennant created a virtual environment for his Rosewood Heritage Project, allowing site visitors to wander and explore an African-American town that was destroyed by racist violence almost a century ago. Selin and Gano's Futurescape City Tours use multiple modalities to engage citizens in a discussion about how nanotechnologies and other innovations can shape and change cities. They combine urban "wayfinding" walks; conversations with a variety of citizens, stakeholders and experts; and image-based (akin to Photovoice) "deliberative" sessions. These diverse projects embrace different sensory modes to elicit participants' understandings and to engage with the broader public.

Outcomes and Audiences

Scholars are turning to participatory visual and digital methods to share their research beyond the academy and engage with multiple publics. A desire to serve the public, influence policy, and present diverse views in programming motivates them. The participatory approach reorients a sense of "broader impacts" in our research by transforming the relationship between experts and the public.

Making a Public Impact

Contributors in this volume present several cases where research outcomes directly serve the public through public institutions and programming. Tudor and Wali describe their community-based work at Chicago's Field Museum as facilitating community members as they share stories about a deindustrializing region and resist gentrification. Collaborative documentation and exhibitions support local efforts to establish the proposed Calumet Natural Heritage Area. Materials from Besteman's digital photographic archive have been integrated into teacher's guides for working with Somali refugee students in Maine. Fried Foster's "design ethnography for the public good" marshals research findings to improve libraries' layout and service provision models, enhancing work and study conditions for students, faculty, and librarians. Chin's research team stresses the importance of ethnographic listening in "design for the public good," especially when working with stereotyped groups like homeless youth.

Scholars are also making policy interventions with participatory research. Menzies, González-Tennant, and Perry used video, photography, and GIS to assist research communities in claiming land and property rights. Here, research helps to amplify the voices of less powerful groups, such as indigenous people, African-American descendant communities, and rural residents. Rattray's team used PGIS to present the situated and embodied knowledge of students with physical disabilities. Maps made a compelling case for the university to adopt a more accessible, "universal design" for campus.

Breaking Down the Fourth Wall

Participatory visual research breaks down the "fourth wall" of research, to borrow a metaphor from the performing arts. Traditionally, actors onstage perform a play as if an invisible "fourth wall" separates them from the audience. Playwright Bertholdt Brecht famously broke down the fourth wall in plays where the actors directly addressed the audience. Later, Augusto Boal developed participatory theatre, directly encouraging audience members to help solve the problems enacted on stage (Boal 1979; Quinlan and Duggleby 2009). Like actors pretending that they do not see the audience through the fourth wall, social scientists have traditionally conducted and written about their research as if it were separable from our research participants and publics. Schensul and Dalglish position their filmmaking as a form of critical performance ethnography that "engages actors in the performance of ethnographic interpretation to illustrate cultural processes or disseminate the results of research to broader audiences." In participatory visual and digital research, we move away from a model of expertise that holds up the "sage on the stage": the lecturer on the podium. Research participants are invited to go "behind the scenes" of visual research. They sometimes join us or take the lead "onstage" in presenting findings to different audiences, who in turn offer new interpretations of the issues portrayed.

Breaking down the fourth wall of research opens up the question of who is positioned as the expert, a theme running through many chapters. Fried Foster writes about participatory design as a partnership among multiple experts—including engineers and designers (in the context of this chapter), workers, and social scientists—directed at the common good. Selin and Gano attempt to upend the lay/expert hierarchy by retooling "technology assessment" as a walking tour in which citizens, policymakers, scientists, and engineers mingle and deliberate together. Yet they also caution that participants and traditional experts may still maintain the "expert/lay divide" in their interactions. Perry and Rattray's GIS projects respectively highlight participants' embodied expertise through participatory mapping. While policymakers use official maps as a static, authoritative form of evidence, participant-produced maps show barriers hidden in plain sight, "groundtruthing" more dynamic bodies of evidence (see also Maida 2013).

Material Deliberation and Materializing Knowledge

Participatory visual research uses visual and material culture to trigger public deliberation, akin to Touraine's model of a "sociology of intervention" (Touraine 1983) or Freire's "conscientization" (Freire 2000). Selin and Gano describe their work as a form of "material deliberation," with the goal of "facilitating 'reflexivity' that allows for self, community, or cultural evaluation in an iterative way." Material deliberation moves away from the two-dimensional, linear text forms common in academia to the use of artifacts as prompts for public engagement. Tudor and Wali present how their community-based museum projects use artifacts to stimulate conversations about the transformation of life in the Calumet region. Seemingly insignificant material details—such as labor union and Earth Day stickers on a steelworker's helmet—lay open more complex stories and dispel stereotypes.

In several case studies presented in this book, participants document their observations while navigating a physical space, inspired by urbanist Kevin Lynch's concept of "wayfinding" (Lynch 1960; see also the concept of "wayfaring" in Hall and Smith 2011). Selin and Gano used a walking tour to elicit people's reflections on technological change in the city. Rattray's team navigated a university campus to provide a "countermap" of physical accessibility. In Perry's work, participants took pictures of their own special places in the landscape, then came together to view the photos and discuss the transforming rural environment. Visual methods give insights into participants' routines and everyday paths and open up space for place-based stories.

Along with material deliberation, scholars in this volume describe their process of "materializing knowledge" in new formats that respond more dynamically to audience interests. Underberg-Goode's multimedia, 3D virtual museum gives users a sense of navigable space and allows them to follow multiple paths to explore interests. By "choosing their own adventure" through a body of knowledge, audiences assemble a social scientific narrative, "a kind of story world in which insights about how such complex topics as history, economics, and gender and ethnic identity play out in the context of a festival." (see page 220) González-Tennant and Durington and Collins also point to exciting possibilities for merging game formats with social scientific research and communication. Participatory design ethnography offers yet another way of "materializing knowledge." In these projects, research not only produces texts describing social practices and analyzing users' perceptions and values, it also informs the design of specific spaces, objects, and technologies.

Recontextualization and Creative Repurposing

Recontextualized documents, photos, and artifacts take on new meanings as participants and audiences encounter them in new ways (Fabian 2008). Digital storytellers gain new insights from screening their stories in a different landscape, or alongside other participants' stories, as Alexandra notes in her chapter. This allows digital storytellers to shift from participant as objectified (by experience) to material/product as object with meaning-making constituted by the participant (A. Gubrium 2009). Community-based museum research transforms exhibitions from static displays to sites where participants curate and reinterpret the significance of artifacts, as Tudor and Wali demonstrate in their chapter.

We also see a lot of creative repurposing: visual materials gain a second life when research partners reuse them. Digital technologies make it easy and inexpensive to cut, copy, and remix visual materials for multiple purposes and audiences, compared with traditional film and photography. Besteman's open access Web-based archive of photos makes it possible for the community to repurpose photos for museum exhibitions and as visual material in a textbook published for English language learners from Somalia. Otañez and Guerrero's project also allows for a multipurposed approach: digital stories are used as part of a grassroots communication campaign to promote disease testing and to inform the public about viral hepatitis as a health issue, as well as a source of research data (from the production process, digital stories, and screenings) to analyze dominant discourses about the disease.

"Remixing" research inevitably transforms the modern ideal of the scholar as *auteur* of a master narrative into a more postmodern mode of the scholar as *bricoleur* (tinkerer) assembling vignettes. Menzies's core story reflects this shift. For Menzies, digital media means "having your cake and eating it too": one can use short-format videos to make "directorial" documentary productions for one kind of audience while also retaining a collection of "video vignettes" that can be repurposed and reassembled as a video "playlist" for other audiences. Menzies writes, "[the] productive lifespan and interpretations [of these video vignettes] extend beyond the limitations of the filmmakers' specific initial intentions." (see page 109)

The PAR approach focuses strongly on outcomes, and participatory visual and digital researchers are developing new ways to evaluate the reach and reception of their projects. Durington and Collins are developing apps to track the "ripple effects" of participatory media production. They write: "As a community-based participatory project, our goal was never to go viral, simply to create a networked anthropology which participants could not only access but also creatively repurpose." (see page 262) Other scholars are taking advantage of website analytics tools to go beyond scholarly citation metrics to understand how research products are being consumed by the public.

Conclusion: Research and Action with a Human Face

Many of the forces motivating scholars to use participatory visual and digital methods are reflected in the chapters that make up this volume. Participants' narratives and media can be used to amplify previously silenced voices and perspectives; challenge dominant discourses on health, wellbeing, and society; and facilitate dialogue. The research process itself often creates a sense of solidarity among participants, bolsters and broadens social networks, and, more individually speaking, builds self-respect and confidence for resilience and coping. Research products encourage audience engagement, evoke emotional and collective responses, and can be used as materials for organizing, advocacy, and to promote change. Public screenings or exhibitions of visual and digital media provoke moments of encounter and purposeful "political listening."

Across the chapters, we sense a tension between the traditional expectation that social research be conducted in a naturalistic context and the more negotiated reality of collaborative research. Increasingly, qualitative researchers acknowledge our own role in delineating "the field" (Gupta and Ferguson 1992) and see field research as a new kind of "lab" in which more staged interactions like workshops take place alongside naturalistic participant observation. Both approaches serve as platforms for conducting meaningful research with specific publics.

All the same, while the authors acknowledge that their work is not always based on an organic approach of heading into the field and "seeing what happens," they emphasize a tactic of "letting go," in terms of relinquishing (or at least ceding) control to community member/participants. Our contributors highlight the need for improvisation and acknowledge that many of us are "learning as we go" in this work. As with the first volume, we note that many of us were not formally trained in the visual methods we have taken on, instead learning by doing. For some, this happened out of pure necessity, whether it was due to funding challenges, strategies and intended outcomes, or the realization that the method they had planned to use was not particularly collaborative or appropriate and instead served to further subjugate the voices and perspectives of participants at the expense of scholarly/authoritative knowledge.

Whether our contributors position their intellectual shifts as a lightning strike or a gradual realization in their core stories, for most of us this work has deeply transformed our methodological practice and our professional identity as researchers. This collection is a first step in creating a "community of practice" of researchers, giving our diverse practices a common name, developing a shared vocabulary for our work, and building theory and method as a joint enterprise.

REFERENCES

Austin, D. E. 2004. Partnerships, Not Projects! Improving the Environment through Collaborative Research and Action. *Human Organization* 63(4): 419–430.

Bakhtin, Michel. 1981. *The Dialogic Imagination: Four Essays.* Austin, TX: University of Texas Press.

Behar, R., and D. Gordon. 1995. *Women Writing Culture.* Berkeley: University of California Press.

Boal, A. 1979. *Theatre of the Oppressed.* London: Pluto.

Castleden, H., T. Garvin, and the Huu-ay-aht First Nation. 2008. Modifying Photovoice for Community-Based Participatory Indigenous Research. *Social Science and Medicine* 66(6): 1393–1405.

Chalfen, R., and M. Rich. 2007. Combining the Applied, the Visual and the Medical: Patients Teaching Physicians with Visual Narratives. In *Visual Interventions: Applied Visual Anthropology,* edited by Sarah Pink, 53–70. New York: Berghahn Books.

Clifford, J., and G. Marcus, eds. 1986. *Writing Culture: The Poetics and Politics of Ethnography.* Berkeley: University of California Press.

Collins, Samuel, and Matthew Durington. 2014. *Networked Anthropology: A Primer for Ethnographers.* New York: Routledge.

de Groof, M. 2013. Rouch's Reflexive Turn: Indigenous Film as the Outcome of Reflexivity in Ethnographic Film. *Visual Anthropology* 26(2): 109–131.

Dicks, B. 2014. Action, Experience, Communication: Three Methodological Paradigms for Researching Multimodal and Multisensory Settings. *Qualitative Research* 14(6): 656–674.

Ellis, C. 1995. Emotional and Ethical Quagmires in Returning to the Field. *Journal of Contemporary Ethnography* 24: 68–98.

Fabian, J. 2008. *Ethnography as Commentary: Writing from the Virtual Archive.* Durham, NC: Duke University Press.

Foley, D. E. 2002. Critical Ethnography: The Reflexive Turn. *International Journal of Qualitative Studies in Education* 15(4): 469–490.

Freire, P. 2000. *Pedagogy of the Oppressed.* New York: Continuum.

Ginsburg, F. 1995. The Parallax Effect: The Impact of Aboriginal Media on Ethnographic Film. *Visual Anthropology Review* 11(2): 64–76.

Gubrium, A. 2009. Digital Storytelling: An Emergent Method for Health Promotion Research and Practice. *Health Promotion Practice* 10: 186–191.

Gubrium, A., and K. Harper. 2013. *Participatory Visual and Digital Methods.* Walnut Creek, CA: Left Coast Press.

Gubrium, A., E. L. Krause, and K. Jernigan. 2014. Strategic Authenticity and Voice: New Ways of Seeing and Being Seen as Young Mothers Through Digital Storytelling. *Sexuality Research & Social Policy* 11(4): 337–347.

Gubrium, J. F. 2003. What is a Good Story? *Generations* 27(3): 21–24.

Gubrium, J. F., and J. A. Holstein. 2009. *Analyzing Narrative Reality.* Thousand Oaks, CA: Sage.

Guenther, K. M. 2009. The Politics of Names: Rethinking the Methodological and Ethical Significance of Naming People, Organizations, and Places. *Qualitative Research* 9(4): 411–421.

Gupta, A., and J. Ferguson. 1992. Beyond "Culture": Space, Identity, and the Politics of Difference. *Cultural Anthropology* 7(1): 6–23.

Hale, C. 2008. *Engaging Contradictions: Theory, Politics, and Methods of Activist Scholarship.* Berkeley, CA: University of California Press.

Hall, T., and R. Smith. 2011. Walking, Welfare and the Good City. *Anthropology in Action* 18(3): 33–44.

Haraway, D. 1988. Situated Knowledges: The Science Question in Feminism and the Privilege of Partial Perspective. *Feminist Studies* 14(3): 575–599.

Harper, K. 2012. Visual Interventions and the "Crises in Representation" in Environmental Anthropology: Environmental Justice in a Hungarian Romani Neighborhood. *Human Organization* 71(3): 292–305.

Hemment, J. 2007. Public Anthropology and the Paradoxes of Participation: Participatory Action Research and Critical Ethnography in Provincial Russia. *Human Organization* 66(3): 301–314.

Jackson, M. 2002. *The Politics of Storytelling: Violence, Transgression and Intersubjectivity.* Copenhagen, Denmark: Museum Tusculanum Press.

Lambert, J. 2012. *Digital Storytelling: Capturing Lives, Creating Community.* New York: Routledge.

Lave, J., and E. Wenger. 1991. *Situated Learning: Legitimate Peripheral Participation.* Cambridge, UK: Cambridge University Press.

Loseke, D. 2009. Examining Emotion as Discourse: Emotion Codes and Presidential Speeches Justifying War. *The Sociological Quarterly* 50(3): 497–524.

Lynch, K. 1960. *The Image of the City.* Cambridge, MA: MIT Press.

Maida, C. A. 2013. Expert and Lay Knowledge in Pacoima: Public Anthropology and Essential Tension in Community-based Participatory Action Research. In *Toward Engaged Anthropology*, edited by Sam Beck and Carl A. Maida, 15–35. New York: Berghahn 21.

Pink, S. 2011. Multimodality, Multisensoriality and Ethnographic Knowing: Social Semiotics and the Phenomenology of Perception. *Qualitative Research* 11(1): 261–276.

Peterson, J. C., and A. Gubrium. 2011. Old Wine in New Bottles? The Positioning of Participation in 17 NIH-Funded CBPR Projects. *Health Communication* 26(8): 724–734.

Quinlan, E., and W. Duggleby. 2009. "Breaking the Fourth Wall": Activating Hope through Participatory Theatre with Family Caregivers. *International Journal of Qualitative Studies on Health and Well-Being* 4(4): 207–219.

Rouch, J. 1975. The Camera and Man. In *Principles of Visual Anthropology,* edited by Paul Hockings, 79–98. Berlin, Germany: Walter de Gruyter & Co.

Rouch, J., and L. Taylor. 2003. A Life on the Edge of Film and Anthropology. In *Cine Ethnography: Jean Rouch,* edited by Steven Feld, 129–146. Minneapolis: University of Minnesota Press.

Scheper-Hughes, N. 2000. Ire in Ireland. *Ethnography* 1: 117–140.

Stoller, P. 1992. *The Cinematic Griot: The Ethnography of Jean Rouch.* Chicago, IL: University of Chicago Press.

Touraine, Alain. 1983. *Anti-Nuclear Protest: The Opposition to Nuclear Energy in France.* New York: Cambridge University Press.

Wang, Caroline. 1999. Photovoice: A Participatory Action Research Strategy Applied to Women's Health. *Journal of Women's Health* 8(2): 185–192.

Waskul, D. 2009. The Importance of Insincerity and Inauthenticity for Self and Society: Why Honesty Is Not the Best Policy. In *Authenticity in Culture, Self, and Society,* edited by Phillip Vannini and J. Patrick Williams, 51–64. Surrey, UK: Ashgate Publishing Limited.

Wenger, E. 1998. *Communities of Practice: Learning, Meaning, and Identity.* Cambridge, UK, New York, NY: Cambridge University Press.

PART

Digital Storytelling

Are We Listening Yet?
Participatory Knowledge Production
through Media Practice: Encounters of
Political Listening

Darcy Alexandra

Introduction

This chapter draws from research with asylum seekers and refugees in Ireland that advanced a longitudinal (2007–2010) and inquiry-based approach to digital storytelling (Alexandra 2008; Grossman and O'Brien 2011). While research findings indicate this method facilitated dynamic opportunities for engaged inquiry into asylum and migrant labor regimes, recognition of storytellers and stories, and sustained encounters of "narrative exchange" (Couldry 2010), the practice of digital storytelling raises complex questions about the "limits of listening" (Dreher 2012). Building on the recent scholarship on listening[1] (Couldry 2009; Dreher 2009; Husband 2009; O'Donnell et al. 2009), I propose that "political listening" (Bickford 1996; Dreher 2010; O'Donnell et al. 2009) not be conceptualized as something that occurs primarily after the co-creative[2] labor of image-making, script-writing, and audiovisual editing is complete. Rather, encounters of political listening occur among research practitioners and other stakeholders, and across the research site throughout production and into distribution. Attention to these encounters can serve as a means to think through the inherent complexities of participatory knowledge production through media practice and to evaluate the presence of listening in our research practice.

Research Overview

Digital storytelling (Lambert 2013) as a research methodology is a relatively new endeavor (Alexandra 2008; Burgess 2006; Brushwood Rose 2009; Gubrium 2009; Gubrium and Turner 2010; Hartley and McWilliam 2009; Hull and Katz 2006; Lundby 2008; Meadows 2003). As a doctoral fellow at the Centre for Transcultural Research and Media Practice, I designed, directed, researched, and taught a longitudinal and inquiry-based approach to the participatory media genre of digital storytelling, the first of its kind in Ireland (Alexandra 2014). The research aimed to develop a "shared anthropology" (Pink 2011; Rouch 1974; Rouch and Taylor 2003; Stoller 1992) that not only responded to the ethical complexities of research with refugees, asylum seekers, and undocumented migrants, but also created opportunities for research subjects to interpret their experiences as newcomers to Ireland. To facilitate more in-depth opportunities for research participants to analyze current circumstances and develop their craft as emergent photographers and media producers, greater emphasis was placed on audiovisual ethnography.[3] Within a community of practice (Lave and Wenger 1991; Wenger 1999), participants produced their own media to explore and document their lives as workers, parents, "cultural citizens" (Coll 2010; Rosaldo 1994), and artists simultaneously adapting to and transforming a new environment. Fieldwork occurred from June 2007 to April 2010,[4] with follow-up interviews and screenings between 2010 and 2012. During media production seminars, participants engaged with their life stories through the development of short, first-person documentary essays.[5] Seven women and six men from African, Asian, Eastern European, and Middle Eastern countries interrogated their experiences negotiating migration policy and revealed the structural violence of asylum and migrant labor regimes. They created more than 250 photographs and drawings, and produced 14 documentary essays of broadcast quality. These stories have screened before diverse audience members, including the former president of Ireland, Mary Robinson, at public forums on asylum policy and migrant rights, at the Irish Film Institute (IFI), the Guth Gafa International Documentary Film Festival, and at conferences throughout Europe and the Americas. The videos are available for viewing at www .darcyalexandra.com/practice/living-in-direct-provision-9-stories and www .darcyalexandra.com/practice/undocumented-in-ireland-our-stories.

Encounters of Political Listening

The "promise" of digital storytelling has primarily focused not on listening, or even visibility per se, but on the power and possibility of "voice." But what impact does "voice" have if no one is listening? After all, *not* listening is to exercise power (Bickford 1996, 3). Anthropologist Michael Jackson (2002) cautions against assumptions regarding any inherent "power" of storytelling, arguing that there is nothing necessarily, or automatically, transformative about speaking up and "telling your story." Jackson writes, "There is no automatic or magical efficacy in speaking one's mind unless the institutional framework of a community, a profession, or religion, contextualizes and recognizes the act" (Jackson 2002, 4). Media theorist Jean Burgess similarly argues, "The question that we ask about "democratic" media participation can no longer be limited to 'Who gets to speak?' We must also ask 'Who is heard, and to what end?'" (Burgess 2006, 203). Nick Couldry echoes this concern when he points out, "The issue is what governments *do with* voice, once expressed: are they prepared to change the way they make policy?" (Couldry 2010, 146). Of course, what is "done" with voice is not easily determined, or shaped. "Entrenched hierarchies of voice" (Dreher 2009, 446) that enable and sustain the privilege to not listen constitute a complex site of conflict. In the digital storytelling literature, conflict and adversarial communication are not associated with the critical feminist practice of reclaiming experience. Instead, gaining control over the telling of a story, and the workshop site itself, are assumed to be a supportive process and an encouraging environment. Nevertheless, the practice of producing stories unfolds within a field of diverse and, at times, conflicting interests. Participants, facilitators, researchers, and collaborating and funding agencies have different ideas about which stories to tell, who is best positioned to tell them, how they "should" and "should not" be told, and what is at stake. Within this nexus of interdependent yet unequal relationships, a methodological attention to the politics of listening offers conceptual inroads to address the power asymmetries inherent in participatory knowledge production through media practice.

Dreher employs the concept of "political listening" (Bickford 1996) to develop an agenda for listening "as a political process that is potentially difficult, conflictual and aimed at justice which sustains difference" (Dreher 2009, 448). She writes, "The interest in listening is situated and strategic, aiming to develop thinking on media change beyond increasingly predictable critiques of representation and a politics of speaking up which leaves the primary responsibility for change with those who are subjected to media racialization" (Dreher 2009, 447). For Susan Bickford (1996), thinking about listening is central to envisioning and developing democratic practices and societies. Bickford understands both speaking *and* listening as activities central to citizenship, but foregrounds the need to theorize listening as a way to address the intersubjective nature of public life. She argues, "Democratic communicative interaction depends not on the possibility of consensus, but on the presence of listening" (Bickford 1996, 18). She writes:

> Political listening is not primarily a caring or amicable practice, and I emphasize this at the outset because "listening" tends immediately to evoke ideas of empathy and compassion. We cannot suppose that political actors are sympathetic toward one another in a conflictual context, yet it is precisely the presence of conflict and differences that makes communicative interaction necessary. This communicative interaction—speaking and listening together—does not necessarily resolve or do away with the conflicts that arise from uncertainty, inequality or identity. Rather, it enables political actors to decide democratically how to act in the face of conflict, and to clarify the nature of the conflict at hand (Bickford 1996, 2).

The presence of listening and "political listening" are evocative concepts when inquiry and practice unfold within a context of oppression, surveillance, and trauma. In these cases, the workshop site and the creative inquiry involved in crafting a documentary essay can provide research participants with a sanctuary for possibility and a community of practice within which to contextualize and recognize the act of storytelling. The workshop site and, more precisely, the inquiry that is facilitated through participatory media practice can provide a space for narrative exchange in which practitioners share, analyze, re/create, and literally objectify lived experiences into audiovisual story. Given that some voices are more discursively privileged, attention to listening in the presence of conflict becomes key. Therefore, attention to the distinct dialogical moments among a community of practice within and across the workshop site also reveals complex questions in relation to the limits, controls, and possibilities of co-creative documentary practice with, for, and about "migrant voices."

A Public That Disbelieves

The claim for asylum penetrates the lives of those who seek protection. The burden of proof is carried on the migrating body, located in the asylum story,[6] and scrutinized for credibility by state apparatuses that increasingly disbelieve the very legitimacy of the international right to asylum (Fassin 2011). At the time of research, asylum adjudicators in Ireland mostly did not believe the asylum-seekers' claims to protection. Based on Eurostat online data, between 2008 and 2012 Ireland had one of the lowest recognition rates of claims to protection in the European Union (European Commission n.d.). For example, as reported to Eurostat, for the third quarter of 2010, 1.3% of asylum applicants received refugee status (Albertinelli 2011).[7] In the workshop seminar, two of nine research participants had received refugee status. That is to say, the asylum claims of two participants had been formally recognized by the state as meriting refugee status; all other participants were in different stages of appeal and feared losing legal status and, ultimately, deportation.

In and out of the workshop site, participants were aware of potential disbelief and restrictions on their stories. Participants expressed worry about how collaborating partners might respond to the digital stories, repeatedly asking if their story was "okay," if they could "really" tell it, and if the collaborating agencies would approve of their stories. Furthermore, research subjects demonstrated an understanding of the strategic and symbolic positioning and significance of their stories; they did not want to appear dangerously "ungrateful," or to be seen as "complaining" or "giving out" (author's field notes,[8] November 19, 2008). This discursive complexity undergirded the entire production cycle.

When the veracity of one participant's story was questioned during a workshop session, it brought the issue of truthfulness, and the weight of disbelief, to the surface. During this workshop we were discussing the possibility of holding a "story circle"[9] (author's field notes, September 29, 2009). Rebecca[10]—the only Nigerian woman in the workshop who had received refugee status—offered to go first. Her story, she told the group, was about "crossing the desert without food or water, hungry and thirsty, risking life at sea, suffering and crying, and coming at last to Ireland." Ogo immediately questioned the veracity of her story, wondering if it had "really" happened. Rebecca hesitated, and responded that it hadn't happened to her directly, but that it happens to many. Ogo insisted that the story needed to be about the storyteller, and something he or she had directly experienced.

Susan agreed with Ogo: it needed to be something known from experience. If not, people would wonder if it "really" happened. I confirmed the assertion regarding the storytelling research guidelines: the audiovisual story did need to be self-narrated, and based on something the storyteller had personally experienced or witnessed firsthand. Conscious of the end result, Ogo nodded to Susan, and raised the question of audience.

"People will see these stories," he noted.

I reminded the group that this would happen only if participants granted permission for the stories to be publicly screened. I asked if anyone else wanted to share a story or idea. Abazu agreed. He told a humorous story about a music tour he organized for his son, whom he described as a successful musician back home. In his story, Abazu faces logistical nightmares, difficult club managers, and endless red tape, but in the end, he perseveres, and everything works out. Participants shifted in their seats. No one said anything. Finally, Rebecca responded, "But what does that have to do with anything?" Abazu shrugged his shoulders. I reiterated that each person would have the choice, and final say, about whatever story they wanted to tell, and whether or not they wanted to screen that story beyond the seminar setting.

"But if we tell about our lives in Ireland," Omar asserted, "they must be positive stories." He repeated they must be positive stories, added that it was important to show how grateful they were to be in Ireland, and concluded that they shouldn't tell "the sad stories."

"If people are indeed grateful and have a positive story to tell, yes, certainly," I interjected. I suggested that peoples' stories might be more complicated, and those stories were appropriate to tell as well. Everyone would have different perspectives. The workshop was a chance to consider which story they wanted to share, and to produce that story. As media practitioners, it might be the first story they create, but hopefully not the last. Ogo, Mona, Susan, Farrokh, and Adrian nodded their heads in the affirmative. Omar seemed uncomfortable with my idea. I suggested that Omar's approach—to focus on the positive and demonstrate gratitude—was one important representational strategy among many. I explained that for the research, and as the facilitator, it was important not to impose any particular feeling or idea. Everyone would have their own perspective, and it would probably be more nuanced than "good," "bad," "happy," or "sad."

I asked if anyone else had a story idea. No one volunteered. I suggested we not hold a "story circle." Instead, if they preferred, we would take more time, give people a chance to make images, and consider narratives. When they were ready they could share these images and scripts with the group, or not. This would provide a chance to experiment in and out of the workshop setting, and explore different approaches to their audiovisual compositions. Participants appeared to like this idea. Next, I outlined the workshop method (author's field notes, September 29, 2009).[11]

Did That Really Happen?

Ogo's question regarding the veracity of Rebecca's story provided an opportunity to critically discuss the labor and potential impact of social documentary practice, consider the contours of the methodology, and make adaptations: in this case, the decision to not facilitate a standard story circle. But what would have happened if I had not contradicted Omar's strategy to focus on the positive? If I had agreed with him that yes, it was indeed best (and perhaps strategically imperative) to focus solely on "happy" stories? Might the finished stories have had wider viewership among "mainstream" Irish audiences? In my mind, my intervention was necessary both for the research (to learn from research participants about their diverse experiences as newcomers), and for my position as an educator (to facilitate an inquiry process in which participants could engage with those experiences). It served to support the aim of learning from and through the stories participants created, and affirmed a commitment to participants' rights to tell heterogeneous stories.

The interaction regarding the veracity of Rebecca's story points to the larger tension of widespread disbelief of asylum seekers and their claims (Fanning 2002; Lentin and Moreo 2012; Loyal 2011). Ogo's questioning of the truthfulness of Rebecca's story could be understood as a small-scale reproduction of this disbelief. Alternatively, it could be interpreted as a way in which he enters into dialogue with her: by questioning the "veracity" of her story, and defending the boundaries of his own "truthful" claim. I felt uncomfortable with Ogo's question—what I interpreted as disbelief— essentially a man asking a woman, "Did this really happen?" I followed Rebecca's lead, and checked in with her after the workshop. The question gave her pause, but she did not appear troubled by it. She revealed that she was indeed telling a metaphorical story. Importantly, in that moment of telling, Rebecca resisted the "personal" story approach. Instead, she presented a kind of "Every Asylum-Seeker's Story" (author's field notes, September 29, 2009).

Brushwood Rose (2009) addresses the question of disbelief when she writes:

(W)e might understand the digital story not primarily in terms of its accuracy or authenticity in representing experience, but as an intermediate area of experience in which the story we tell can contain both what we know and what we imagine. Put another way, we might understand the digital story as a space in which the storyteller risks their connection to the world by finding and creating useful objects—in this sense, it is up to the researcher never to ask "is it the truth, or did you make it up?" (Brushwood Rose 2009, 219).

Theorizing the digital story as a useful object and intermediate space for the storyteller to contain what he/she knows and imagines is helpful, perhaps especially when working with people who are disbelieved, or whose stories have been silenced. Instead of asking, "Is it truth?" we might ask instead: In what ways is it true? What does this story mean to the storyteller and the viewer? What does this story do? As Schaffer and Smith argue, the "truth" of a story cannot be read "solely or simply [as] factual. There are different registers of truth beyond the factual: psychological, experiential, historical, cultural, communal, and potentially transformative" (Schaffer and Smith 2004, 7–8).

Discussion

Revelation and concealment are central to the act of storytelling. What should be shared? What cannot be told or shown? How should the author position her or himself in relation to the audience? Literally visualizing the voice—crafting the audiovisual narrative—brought these questions to the forefront as participants considered what to reveal and how to maintain their anonymity. Within a community of practice, participants debated decisions regarding participation, images, scripts, and stories. The development of a co-creative documentary practice, significant attention to media production values, and consistent mentoring in photography and audiovisual editing constituted productive ways of taking storytellers, their stories, and the labor of documentary story production seriously. This in itself was a form of political listening. Subsequently, the media production site grounded ongoing dialogue and debate about the politics of voice and listening. Encounters like the one with Rebecca revealed power asymmetries as well as definitive moments of listening and being heard. From one-on-one discussions with research participants about the potential implications of speaking visibly to discussions with institutional gatekeepers about possible legal implications of the documentary essays, the production process over time and across sectors offered opportunities to question assumptions about what constitutes a "migrant" story and how "best" to tell these stories throughout the academic, nongovernmental, and professional media settings that enable and restrict voice and listening.

Media production and the dialogue it necessitates provided opportunities for learning about participants' everyday circumstances as asylum seekers and refugees in Ireland. In and out of the research site, practitioners discussed and interrogated the asylum system through their image making, creative writing, and audiovisual editing. The documentary essays that participants produced detail the vulnerable circumstances they endured and continue to endure while living in the asylum system. The conversations facilitated through the artifacts revealed a debilitating lack of autonomy for individuals and families living in conditions of internment; a sense of imprisonment within a system that seemingly disregards the safety, wellbeing, and dignity of asylum seekers; concern for how living in direct provision[12] was affecting the lives of young family members spending significant portions of their childhood and adolescence in state institutions; and a pattern of intimidation against—and fear of—speaking out and organizing for change.

The documentary essays premiered to an audience of decision-makers, scholars, community workers, and family members at a historically Irish cinema in Dublin. Evelyn, one of the research practitioners, welcomed the audience with the following statement:

> These are our stories, written from the heart, with no guards on our emotions, our experiences, or our ideas as single women, fathers, mothers, Asian, African, non-English speaking, Christian and Muslim people living in direct provision centers across the country. Our stories might be different, but the frustrations are the same. Dreams have been shattered, self-esteem destroyed, talents wasted, the steam and fire of our labor years put out, except for that familiar label: "a bunch of asylum seekers." We did not participate in this project to evoke sympathy, but to remind this society that the mental health of every individual, even that of an asylum seeker, is an important decimal in the economic data of any society. I could go on and on, but our images and sounds will do the job. On this note, I leave the stage for our films to speak our words (*Living in Direct Provision: 9 Stories* premiere, Dublin, Ireland, May 28, 2009).

Evelyn recognized the heterogeneity of the stories and the commonality of a systemic problem. The reason for participation in the research, as she defined it, was to invite the viewer to listen beyond categorical assumptions and to seriously consider the human cost of an asylum policy has failed and is failing significant numbers of individuals and families who seek international protection. In that moment, research participants—storytellers and practitioners—crossed a border. It marked the end of the participatory inquiry and production process and a potential beginning: the reception of the stories beyond the workshop seminar.

Attention to encounters of political listening, from conceptualizing and mentoring research participants as emergent media practitioners to understanding media production as both a site of collaboration and contestation, could provide a framework for theorizing the contradictions of developing shared practices within proprietary contexts and societies that disbelieve asylum seekers. Purposeful attention to encounters of political listening might help us to "decide democratically how to act in the face of conflict" (Bickford 1996, 2).

Acknowledgments

Research was supported by an ABBEST doctoral fellowship and a Fiosraigh Research Scholarship. Sincere thanks are due to the Forum on Migration and Communications (FOMACS), Integrating Ireland, Refugee Information Service, and the research practitioners who opted to collaborate in the study.

REFERENCES

Albertinelli, A. 2011. Asylum Applicants and First Instance Decisions on Asylum Applications in Third Quarter 2010. *Eurostat: Data in Focus,* January 19. http://ec.europa.eu/eurostat/en/web/products-data-in-focus/-/KS-QA-11-001, accessed April 5, 2015.

Alexandra, D. 2008. Digital Storytelling as Transformative Practice: Critical Analysis and Creative Expression in the Representation of Migration in Ireland. *Journal of Media Practice* 9(2): 101–112.

———. In press. More than Words: Listening and the Visual in Co-Creative Documentary Practice. In *Deep Stories: Practicing, Teaching and Learning Anthropology with Digital Storytelling,* edited by A. Thornburg, A. Booker, and M. Nunez-Janes. Warsaw, Berlin: De Gruyter Open.

————. (2014). Visualising "Migrant" Voices: Co-Creative Documentary and the Politics of Listening [Doctoral dissertation]. Dublin Institute of Technology, Dublin, Ireland.

Angel-Ajani, A. 2006. Expert Witness: Notes Toward Revisiting the Politics of Listening. In *Engaged Observer: Anthropology, Advocacy and Activism,* edited by V. Sanford and A. Angel Ajani, 76–89. New Brunswick, NJ, and London: Rutgers University Press.

Bickford, S. 1996. *The Dissonance of Democracy: Listening, Conflict and Citizenship.* Ithaca, NY, and London: Cornell University Press.

Brushwood Rose, C. 2009. The (Im)Possibilities of Self Representation: Exploring the Limits of Storytelling in the Digital Stories of Women and Girls. *Changing English* 16(2): 211–220.

Burgess, J. 2006. Hearing Ordinary Voices: Cultural Studies, Vernacular Creativity and Digital Storytelling. *Continuum: Journal of Media & Cultural Studies* 20(2): 201–214.

Coll, K. M. 2010. *Remaking Citizenship: Latina Immigrants & New American Politics.* Stanford, CA: Stanford University Press.

Conlon, S., S. Waters, and K. Berg. 2012. *Difficult to Believe: The Assessment of Asylum Claims in Ireland.* Dublin: Irish Refugee Council. http://www .irishrefugeecouncil.ie/wp-content/uploads/2011/08/Difficult-to-Believe-The -assessment-of-asylum-claims-in-Ireland.pdf, accessed April 2, 2015.

Couldry, N. 2009. Commentary: Rethinking the Politics of Voice. *Continuum: Journal of Media & Cultural Studies* 23(4): 579–582.

————. 2010. *Why Voice Matters: Culture and Politics After Neoliberalism.* Los Angeles, CA: Sage.

Dreher, T. 2009. Listening across Difference: Media and Multiculturalism beyond the Politics of Voice. *Continuum: Journal of Media & Cultural Studies* 23(4): 445–458.

————. 2010. Speaking Up or Being Heard? Community Media Interventions and the Politics of Listening. *Media, Culture and Society* 32(1): 85–103.

————. 2012. A Partial Promise of Voice: Digital Storytelling and the Limit of Listening. http://ro.uow.edu.au/cgi/viewcontent.cgi?article=2548&context=artspapers, accessed November 20, 2014.

Edwards, E. 1997. Beyond the Boundary: A Consideration of the Expressive in Photography and Anthropology. In *Rethinking Visual Anthropology,* edited by M. Banks and H. Morphy, 53–80. New Haven, CT, and London: Yale University Press.

Edwards, E., and J. Hart. 2004. Introduction: Photographs as Objects. In *Photographs Objects Histories: On the Materiality of Images (Material Cultures),* edited by E. Edwards and J. Hart, 48–64. London and New York: Routledge.

European Commission. n.d. Eurostat Database. http://ec.europa.eu/eurostat/data/
database, accessed April 8, 2015.

Fanning, B. 2002. *Racism and Social Change in the Republic of Ireland*. Manchester,
UK, and New York: Manchester University Press.

Fassin, D. 2011. Policing Borders, Producing Boundaries: The Governmentality of
Immigration in Dark Times. *Annual Review of Anthropology* 40: 213–226.

Gavan, R. 2013. Ireland Rejects More Asylum Seekers than Most EU Countries.
The Journal.ie, June 18. http://www.thejournal.ie/ireland-asylum-seekers-eu-
955725-Jun2013/, accessed April 2, 2015.

Grossman, A., and A. O'Brien. 2011. "Voice," Listening and Social Justice: A
Multimediated Engagement with New Immigrant Communities and Publics in
Ireland. *Crossings: Journal of Migration and Culture* 2: 39–58.

Gubrium, A. 2009. Digital Storytelling as a Method for Engaged Scholarship in
Anthropology. *Practicing Anthropology* 31(4): 5–9.

Gubrium, A., and K. C. N. Turner. 2010. Digital Storytelling as an Emergent Method
for Social Research and Practice. In *Handbook of Emergent Technologies in
Social Science Research*, edited by S. N. Hesse Biber, 469–491. Oxford, UK:
Oxford University Press.

Harper, D. 1987. The Visual Ethnographic Narrative. *Visual Anthropology* 1: 1–20.

———. 2003. Framing Photographic Ethnography: A Case Study. *Ethnography*
4(2): 241–266.

Hartley, J., and K. McWilliam. 2009. *Story Circle: Digital Storytelling Around the
World*. Hoboken, NJ: Wiley Blackwell.

Hull, G. A., and M. L. Katz. 2006. Crafting an Agentive Self: Case Studies of Digital
Storytelling. *Research in the Teaching of English* 41(1): 43–81.

Husband, C. 2009. Between Listening and Understanding. *Continuum* 23(4): 441–443.

Jackson, M. 2002. *The Politics of Storytelling: Violence, Transgression and
Intersubjectivity*. Copenhagen, Denmark: Museum Tusculanum Press.

Lambert, J. 2002. *Digital Storytelling: Capturing Lives, Creating Community* (first
edition). Berkeley, CA: Digital Diner Press.

———. 2013. *Digital Storytelling: Capturing Lives, Creating Community* (fourth
edition). New York and London: Routledge.

Lave, J., and E. Wenger. 1991. *Situated Learning: Legitimate Peripheral Participation*.
Cambridge, UK: Cambridge University Press.

Lentin, R., and E. Moreo, eds. 2012. *Migration, Diasporas and Citizenship*. London:
Palgrave MacMillan.

Loyal, S. 2011. The Direct Provision Regime. In *Understanding Immigration in
Ireland: State, Capital and Labour in a Global Age,* edited by S. Loyal, 101–121.
Manchester, UK, and New York: Manchester University Press.

Lundby, K. 2008. *Digital Storytelling, Mediatized Stories: Self-Representations in New Media*. New York: Peter Lang.

MacDougall, D. 2006. *The Corporeal Image: Film, Ethnography, and the Senses*. Princeton, NJ: Princeton University Press.

Meadows, D. 2003. Digital Storytelling: Research-Based Practice in New Media. *Visual Communication* 2(2): 189–193.

Melgar, F., director. 2008. *La Forteresse* [documentary]. Switzerland: Climage.

———. 2011. *Vol Spécial* [documentary]. Switzerland: Climage.

O'Brien, C. 2014. Lives in Limbo. *The Irish Times*, August 8. http://www.irishtimes .com/news/lives-in-limbo, accessed April 2, 2015.

O'Donnell, P., J. Lloyd, and T. Dreher. 2009. Listening, Pathbuilding and Continuations: A Research Agenda for the Analysis of Listening. *Continuum: Journal of Media & Cultural Studies* 23(4): 423–439.

Pink, S. 2011. Images, Senses and Applications: Engaging Visual Anthropology. *Visual Anthropology* 24(5): 437–454.

Rosaldo, R. 1994. Cultural Citizenship in San Jose, California. *PoLAR* 17(2): 57–64.

Rouch, J. 1974. The Camera and the Man. *Studies in the Anthropology of Visual Communication* 1(1): 37–44.

Rouch, J., and L. Taylor. 2003. A Life on the Edge of Film and Anthropology. In *Ciné-Ethnography: Jean Rouch*, edited by S. Feld, 129–146. Minneapolis: University of Minnesota Press.

Schaffer, K., and S. Smith. 2004. *Human Rights and Narrated Lives: The Ethics of Recognition*. New York: Palgrave MacMillan.

Smyth, J. 2010. State Has EU's Lowest Rate of Granting Refugee Status. *The Irish Times*, July 10. http://www.irishtimes.com/news/state-has-eu-s-lowest-rate-of-granting-refugee-status-1.619864, accessed April 2, 2015.

———. 2011. Irish Acceptance of Asylum Claims Lowest in EU. *The Irish Times*, January 21. http://www.irishtimes.com/news/irish-acceptance-of-asylum-claims-lowest-in-eu-1.1278606, accessed April 2, 2015.

Spurgeon, C. L., J. E. Burgess, H. G. Klaebe, J. A. Tacchi, K. McWilliam, and M. Tsai. 2009. Co-Creative Media: Theorising Digital Storytelling as a Platform for Researching and Developing Participatory Culture. Paper presented at the Australian and New Zealand Communication Association Conference, July 8–10, Queensland University of Technology, Brisbane, Queensland, New Zealand.

Stoller, P. 1992. *The Cinematic Griot: The Ethnography of Jean Rouch*. Chicago and London: University of Chicago Press.

Wenger, E. 1999. *Communities of Practice: Learning, Meaning and Identity*. Cambridge, UK: Cambridge University Press.

NOTES

1   See Volume 23, Issue 4 (2009) of *Continuum: Journal of Media & Cultural Studies*. For discussion on listening within ethnographic labor, see Angel-Ajani (2006).

2   Media scholars studying digital storytelling initiatives in Australia (Spurgeon et al. 2009) propose the term "co-creative media" as a concept more precise than "digital storytelling" to describe "the ways in which participatory media are facilitated by people and organisations, not just technology" (Spurgeon et al. 2009, 275) The authors write that the concept of co-creative media "seeks to remind us that participatory new media culture is socially produced, and to acknowledge the difficulties that can be associated with achieving participatory culture" (Spurgeon et al. 2009, 275).

3   Images were not understood as tools for eliciting information, or as data and evidence to represent "what really happened." Instead, images were conceptualized as mediational objects (Edwards and Hart 2004; Harper 1987, 2003) that facilitate inquiry (MacDougall 2006) and allow for more poetic and analytical engagements with experience (Edwards 1997).

4   Fieldwork involved collaboration with 14 research practitioners, three nongovernmental organizations (NGOs), and the Dublin Institute of Technology (DIT), and the development of two longitudinal digital storytelling seminars. Research participants were recruited through collaborating NGO partners. Each longitudinal media production and research seminar lasted between five and six months. Seminars occurred weekly in the college media lab and lasted between two and five hours. Research and media production continued outside of the lab in the asylum hostels where participants documented their living circumstances and further developed their images and scripts.

5   Given the significant adaptations to the standard Center for Digital Storytelling model, documentary essays best describe the labor at hand. For a detailed account of the methodological adaptations initiated in this research see, Alexandra in press).

6   For documentary treatment of asylum policy in Europe, see *La Forteresse* (Melgar 2008) and *Vol Spécial* (Melgar 2011), directed by Fernand Melgar.

7   Irish media reported on the low acceptance rates for asylum seekers; see, for example, Gavan (2013), O'Brien (2014), and Smyth (2010, 2011). For an assessment of the low acceptance rates, see Conlon et al. (2012). Since 2014, there has been a noticeable increase in acceptance rates.

8   As an ethnographer and educator I consistently took detailed field notes of every seminar and interaction with practitioners and collaborators. Most often, I wrote down observations and participant quotes from discussions and media production interactions at the time of the seminar or during the conversation. I would then develop and expand these notes. Research participants did not agree to audio and video recordings of our interactions, but were comfortable with

my consistent note taking. Finally, research participants released all scripts and images, and 12 of the 14 digital stories, for discussion, analysis, and publication. Ten stories are currently available for viewing online.

9   In the Center for Digital Storytelling model, the audiovisual production most often begins with a "Story Circle" in which participants tell a spoken-word story, read from a prepared script, or share ideas about a particular experience or issue they would like to develop into an audiovisual story. More recently, some facilitators have introduced the idea of sharing a photograph as a story starter as well.

10   Pseudonyms are used to protect research participants' identities.

11   The original "7 Steps" method promoted by the Center for Digital Storytelling included point of view, dramatic question, emotional content, the gift of your voice, the power of the soundtrack, economy, and pacing (Lambert 2002, 45–60). In the latest digital storytelling "cookbook," the steps are listed as follows: owning your insights; owning your emotions; finding the moment; seeing your story; hearing your story; assembling your story; and sharing your story (Lambert 2013, 53–69). In this digital storytelling research project I did not teach the "7 Steps." Instead, participants kept writing and image journals, and workshop periods began with a creative writing or image-making activity. Writing prompts were based on the images people photographed in the asylum hostels, and on selected entries participants chose to share from their journals. In addition, participants wrote in response to selected digital stories, film clips, and photographs from international and local photographers. Invited documentary photographers visited the seminar to discuss their practice, and filmmakers collaborated with participants during the final editing phase. In this way, workshop inquiry, participants' ethnographic and creative labor outside the workshop site, and the gradual development of a community of practitioners served to support research participants as they authored their stories.

12   In the Direct Provision system, individuals and families seeking international protection are placed in accommodation centers, the majority of which are privately run and located in isolated, rural areas. Asylum-seekers receive full board and a weekly allowance of $20.75 per adult and $10.43 per child per week, a figure established in 2000 that has not changed to reflect the current cost of living. While awaiting a decision on their application, adult asylum-seekers are not allowed to work or travel freely outside the country. Asylum-seekers also cannot access free third-level education or social assistance. Direct Provision has been widely criticized as detrimental to the mental health, physical wellbeing, and economic security of families and individuals who are legally present in the country. For further consideration, see The Asylum Archive, an online resource concerning the asylum system in Ireland that is curated by a former asylum-seeker and photographer (http://www.asylumarchive.com).

Digital Storytelling
and the Viral Hepatitis Project

Marty Otañez and Andrés Guerrero

Digital storytelling is an elixir for researchers and community members who wish to make their work more relevant for broader audiences. It is used to increase project participants' control of their lived experiences that researchers seek to collect and represent, helping to redefine traditional notions of academic work as a knowledge production enterprise controlled by university representatives. Storytellers engage in collaborative activities with project leaders in a workshop format or one-on-one approach to humanize people's experiences; in the process, storytellers develop basic proficiency in story sharing and video-making and receive a DVD copy of their video. In this chapter, an anthropologist (Otañez) and health worker (Guerrero), who partnered in a viral hepatitis project, seek to boost the power of digital storytelling as a research method and a co-creative media technique that crosses boundaries in academic work (Spurgeon et al. 2009; Underberg and Zorn 2013).

The exercise in co-authorship is consistent with the digital storytelling approach, with its focus on collaborative work in the service of social justice. During my (Otañez's) doctoral research and with virtually no formal training in visual strategies, I turned my anthropology dissertation on tobacco farm workers in Malawi into a documentary video (http://tinyurl.com/kbcso38). In my subsequent video projects in Malawi, I began to feel dissatisfied with the traditional interview approach to storytelling that appeared superficial and impersonal. I wanted to work more closely with individuals to get at the essence

Marty Otañez and Andrés Guerrero, "Digital Storytelling and the Viral Hepatitis Project" in *Participatory Visual and Digital Research in Action,* Aline Gubrium, Krista Harper, and Marty Otañez, eds., pp. 57-70.

of their social situation and misfortune through storytelling. During a later project to produce a documentary video about men in nursing in California in 2009 (http://tinyurl.com/lvt4mhu), I worked with a videographer with expertise in digital storytelling and realized that digital storytelling might be a more optimal production method than ethnographer-based video making. I continued my work with digital storytelling in Colorado.

In 2010, as a public health professional in the Viral Hepatitis Program at the Colorado Department of Public Health and the Environment (CDPHE), I (Guerrero) received an email from Otañez regarding a digital storytelling workshop aimed at addressing health disparities. Working in hepatitis prevention, I was aware of the effects of health disparities. The populations most at risk of contracting viral hepatitis tend to be the same groups that society often ignores: drug users, prisoners, sex workers, and the homeless. After watching some digital stories in preparation for the workshop, I was struck by the stories' honesty. Their authenticity led me to believe that digital stories could potentially be useful in disseminating health prevention messages. Through funding from CDPHE specifically earmarked for raising awareness of viral hepatitis, we created the Viral Hepatitis project to explore the possibilities of using digital stories for public health purposes.

During the workshop, I (Guerrero) became more convinced that this form of communication could be useful in public health as I began to understand that the process of creating the digital story itself could be an opportunity for marginalized populations to share stories with each other and, in doing so, to find support. In collaboration with Otañez, we co-facilitated the production of 10 videos (http://tinyurl.com/p43erxh) with themes of disease prevention and treatment. In this chapter, we discuss the use of digital storytelling to reveal social experiences with hepatitis and increase disease awareness.

The project was part of a landscape in which up to 5.3 million persons are living with viral hepatitis in the United States, and millions more are at risk for infection (U.S. Department of Health and Human Services 2014). Because viral hepatitis can persist for decades without symptoms, 65 to 75% of infected Americans remain unaware of their infection and are not receiving care or treatment. Most morbidity and mortality result from the chronic form of viral hepatitis caused by hepatitis B virus (HBV) and hepatitis C virus (HCV) infection. In Colorado, approximately 70,000 people have ever been infected with HCV (Colorado Department of Public Health and Environment 2012a) and 220,022 people have ever been infected with HBV (Colorado Department of Public Health and Environment 2012b). The goals of the Viral Hepatitis project were to use digital storytelling to humanize individuals infected and/ or affected by viral hepatitis, to inform the public about the ways people make sense of hepatitis infection and how they can protect themselves from the virus, and to analyze the power of hepatitis-related discourses. Finally, we were also interested in assessing the influence of first-person-produced videos on peoples' intentions to get tested for the disease.

Dominant discourses tend to criminalize infected individuals (Davis et al. 2014) and take a paternalistic tone to people infected with viral hepatitis (Fraser 2004). The project was framed to promote innovative, policy-relevant, and culturally centered digital stories about viral hepatitis to help educate the public. During the digital storytelling process, 10 participants each created a video. Nine of the videos featured experiences with hepatitis C infection and one featured hepatitis B infection. The project prioritized individuals with hepatitis C because of program priorities within the Colorado Department of Public Health and the Environment.

Along with digital storytelling, we also collected data using pre- and post-surveys completed by the 10 project participants, a Web survey with embedded digital stories directed toward online viewing audiences, pre- and post-surveys completed by 28 audience members in a community screening of videos, and video recordings of a discussion among storytellers and audience members after the community screening. In this chapter, we discuss the digital storytelling approach used in the Viral Hepatitis project and then present one of the videos, produced using a one-on-one digital storytelling production model.

Digital Storytelling: Creating and Sharing Visual Narratives

Our approach to visual story sharing comprises a multiday workshop model with 24 hours of instruction modeled on the format pioneered by the Center for Digital Storytelling (CDS). The CDS approach includes seven story-sharing components: self-revelatory, personal or first-person voice, a lived experience, photos more than moving image, background music and sound effects, economy in length and design, and intention (Lambert 2013). The components are guidelines as opposed to rigid rules in the creation of first-person videos that tend to generate personal transformation among some storytellers through sharing, often for the first time, a lived experience

(Otañez and Lakota, 2015). Personal photos or royalty-free images from websites such as Unsplash.com are optimal for individuals in the process. Single images, more than video excerpts that comprise 30 still images for each second of video, are easier for new storytellers to use in video-editing software applications. The simplicity of still imagery is consistent with the digital storytelling ethos to draw the attention of viewers to a compelling narrative, with imagery a secondary concern. Instrumental music and sound effects are additional characters in a story that may enhance messaging and draw viewers into the story. These characteristics are highly personal and reflect the emotive impact and pacing of a video that a storyteller seeks to achieve. A digital story is two to three minutes long; storytellers are challenged to identify one memory or encounter and develop it into a narrative, while recognizing that it is nearly impossible to share every aspect of a story in truncated form.

A professional facilitator from CDS was retained for the Viral Hepatitis project to assist participants with the process. Ten videos were created with themes such as intravenous drug use, the immigrant experience, stigma, and disease diagnosis. Here we focus on one digital story (*Doctors in America: They Just Want Your Money*, http://tinyurl.com/m2orked) to illuminate our encounters in the one-on-one approach and argue that digital storytelling creates opportunities to communicate public health issues in a resonant way to broader audiences.

While digital storytelling developed separately from ethnographic filmmaking and visual ethnography, it emerged when anthropologists and other social scientists that applied visual strategies were becoming self-reflective on the politics of representation and imbalances of power in the construction of images of nondominant cultures (Hall 1997). The CDS model appeared to derail practices that insufficiently interrogated meanings of cultural representation and how ethnographic visual practices perpetuated a western fetishization of marginalized cultures (Raheja 2007; Rony 1996). Scholars and practitioners interested in making anthropological praxes transparent and increase parity in researcher-participant relationships applied digital storytelling to a range of social and wellness concerns. Studies that illuminate applications of digital storytelling as an innovative method examine identity formation (Bigalondo 2012; Davis and Weinshenker 2014), gender and gender justice (Gubrium and DiFulvio 2011; Hill 2010), policymaking (Freidus et al. 2013), the material practices that surround personal photographs (Vivienne and Burgess 2013), and ethics associated with participatory visual research (Gubrium et al., 2014; Hill 2014). Our work in viral hepatitis shows that possibilities exist to more systematically understand digital storytelling's communicative power.

The Viral Hepatitis Project

As we started to recruit participants and schedule the workshop, we recognized that our shared interest in the model applied to viral hepatitis was in the humanizing element of digital storytelling: the manner in which a visual story draws so much focus from viewers that people tend to not even notice that they received information about disease prevention and transmission, but still retain information in the context of a story and become engaged, to varying degrees, in public health communication. We shared the view that digital storytelling is a platform for others to share their stories of health (in) equities that may be used to hold economic and political leaders accountable for behavior that partly generates hepatitis and other issues of inequity.

Our recruitment plan involved Hep C Connection, a community-based agency that focuses on education, support, and prevention for individuals affected by, or at risk for, hepatitis C. Also, we used new and existing contacts to disseminate a recruitment flyer. Selection criteria for participants were willingness to participate; infected or affected individuals; aged 18 years and older; and commitment to 1) produce a 300- to 500-word draft script describing their personal experience with hepatitis one week prior to the digital storytelling workshop, and 2) attend all three days of the workshop. We requested that individuals share a meaningful experience, good or bad, with viral hepatitis that they believed could be a resource for other infected persons, health providers, decision-makers, and community members. No previous experience in video production was required. Storytellers were recruited from infected, at-risk, and affected populations, including injection drug users, ethnic minorities, immigrants from countries where hepatitis B is endemic, those who are co-infected with hepatitis C and HIV, and spouses or family members of individuals with symptoms of acute and chronic hepatitis. Participants each received a copy of their video and a $50 gift card after completing a workshop.

The goal was to recruit 10 people for the workshop, but we only recruited three for the group workshop. Difficulties recruiting participants may have derived from the model of digital storytelling used in the project. The consecutive three-day workshop (eight hours each day) was not compatible with the schedules of the prioritized population due to work schedule conflicts, transportation issues, and other barriers. Individuals faced job responsibilities, health issues, financial problems, or prior commitments that made it difficult for them to devote three full days to a workshop. In addition to the relatively great time commitment, other explanations may have been insufficient time for recruitment and general lack of interest in the project. We spent approximately three weeks recruiting individuals prior to the beginning of the workshop. From our experience and through discussions with community members and academic researchers, we learned that two months of recruitment is an optimal target for future projects.

Outside of the group workshop, seven more participants developed story scripts working closely with Otañez and the CDS facilitator in one-on-one meetings and through an online platform. The work included script development, voiceover recording, selection of imagery and background music, and administration of pre- and post-tests. One-on-one work involved three or more meetings between individual storytellers and Otañez or the CDS facilitator to develop scripts and videos. Each meeting lasted approximately two hours. All storytellers approved the final versions of their digital stories.

Doctors in America: They Just Want Your Money: A One-on-One Produced Digital Story

Doctors in America: They Just Want Your Money is presented here as an exemplar story to show how digital storytelling as a method contributes to public anthropology and a "new" health communication focused on culture-centered approaches. These approaches acknowledge the diversity of understandings of health, what it means to stay healthy, and the range of assumptions about experiences with illness and disease (Dutta 2008). The story is also representative of a one-on-one process to address hepatitis B through digital storytelling. *Doctors in America* and other videos created in the project reveal the lived experiences of often marginalized populations that lose, to varying degrees, their right to health as a result of an imbalance in the distribution of power in the United States and elsewhere (Navarro 2009).

In *Doctors in America*, Eric, the storyteller, discusses the cultural stigma of having hepatitis B and how regular clinical check-ups are required for treatment. He shares an anecdote in which his father and friends within his West African immigrant community tease him for multiple visits to a doctor to check his viral load. When his friends call him "clinic guy," Eric informs them, "Well, I take care of myself and I don't sit for years complaining about the same problem." He defies social pressure by visiting a clinic every six months to manage his infection and eliminating fast food from his diet. Without prompting, Eric put the following text on screen at the end of his story, before the credits: "I hope that immigrants, especially Africans in Colorado, make visiting a doctor a part of living. Please don't abuse your health." English subtitles are used when Eric speaks of his father chiding him, saying, "Doctors in America, they just want your money. They know nothing." Eric conveys his story with a series of video clips of him walking near a lake and sitting on a pier with his feet dangling above the water. For the storyteller, the lake symbolizes a place of wellness where he takes leisurely walks by himself and with friends. His video features a song from a popular West African musician, representing a link to his homeland and cultural belongingness.

One year prior to the project, Otañez had collaborated with Eric on a different visual project focusing on the immigrant experience in the Rocky Mountain region. After Otañez explained the hepatitis project to Eric, Eric revealed his hepatitis B status and said that he wanted to share his story with others. He developed his script in consultation with Otañez via telephone conversation and email exchange. Eric recorded his story voiceover with Otañez in the front seat of a rental car during a break in between his multiple jobs, highlighting the insecurity of his life circumstances. Eric was unsure about which images to use in his video. In a conversation that followed the audio recording session, Eric and Otañez agreed to capture video clips of Eric walking along a beach and pier at a lake near his apartment. He selected the location because he enjoyed visiting the lake during his time off from work. As requested, the video shots with Eric were framed to ensure that his identity was concealed. Eric feared that members of his West African community in the small Colorado mountain town where he lived would shun him if they learned about his disease. At the end of our session, Otañez agreed to return to Denver to assemble Eric's digital story, applying an audio filter to disguise Eric's voice and selecting background music for the video.

In *Doctors in America*, Eric parlayed multiple public health messages. The underlying message of the digital story is that Eric is a positive role model among his family, friends, and coworkers. Yet he also addresses the problem of stigma associated with hepatitis B in the script line, "[N]o one in my family knows about it. I only told my close friends, who are American. People in my community, if they knew about my condition, might look at me as someone who people need to be careful with, or treat me as an outcast." Negative beliefs about certain diseases, especially those that people perceive to be linked to sexual behavior such as HIV/AIDS, run deep among West Africans and many others. The story indicates generational tensions when Eric's father, who is not aware of Eric's health status, shows his disdain that his son has "fallen for" the U.S. medical system, believing it to be profit-driven and ineffectual along health lines. In addition, when he mimics his father saying, "Doctors in America, they just want your money," the storyteller reveals social divisions and political commentaries on health care services, which serve as powerful subtexts for the situation of secondary characters in first-person videos.

Eric refuses a stigmatized status generated by his roommates, who do not know his health status and tease him for visiting health clinics. Name-calling is only a minor obstacle that Eric confronts as he seeks treatment, removes fast food from his diet, and exercises. However, there are limits as to how far he can influence change among his West African community members. During one digital storytelling production meeting, Eric asked that we conceal his identity to prevent community members who viewed the piece from stigmatizing him. As a result, the strength of Eric's message is only partially conveyed to those who may need it the most. Possibly, if Eric chose to not disguise his voice and show personal identifiers, community members who watched the video may have felt that it was also safe for them to come forward to talk about their health experiences with hepatitis and other wellness issues. We honored Eric's request and were required to do so based on the options for confidentiality and protection of human subjects as one of the core ethics of the project.

Despite his relative anonymity in the digital story product, Eric actively participated in the co-creative process when (unprompted) he inserted an on-screen text public health message at the end of his video. His explicit recommendation to members of the West African immigrant community in which he belongs communicates culturally appropriate information that prioritizes members of his community, who are typically disenfranchised from the U.S. medical system due to cultural beliefs, stigma associated being infected with hepatitis, lack of resources for high-quality health care, and structural racism (Williams and Mohammed 2009).

Local and Global Implications of Digital Storytelling

The Viral Hepatitis project reveals how people may make sense of hepatitis infection. The value of the project lies in the power of visual media to illuminate discourses of risk knowledge and illness management. The video discussed here is representative of the 10 videos produced in the project that present human experience with viral hepatitis infection and the ways individuals visualize their wellness situation with personal stories, photographs, and video excerpts. Furthermore, the digital story itself serves as a form of informational intervention among those infected and affected. It is a useful mechanism for informing health professionals, researchers, and policymakers about the lived realities of infection and for showcasing the voices of people with hepatitis, which need to be heard at the decision-making table where priorities are set and resources are allocated. Eric's story directly speaks to the landscape in which hepatitis treatment and prevention receives relatively few dollars in the U.S. public healthcare system (Centers for Disease Control and Prevention 2014; Li et al. 2009). Eric presents a personal journey of being unaware of his infection, learning about his condition, following up on blood tests, and presenting messages to his social group to counter stereotypes that belittle health-seeking behavior. Our project intent was not to produce visual representations of existing public health information in pamphlets and websites, but rather to draw attention to the lived experiences of people who encounter viral hepatitis in their own lives, families, or social networks.

Several key method-related points arose from our flexible approach to digital storytelling in the Viral Hepatitis project. First, our approach was not limited to a traditional group workshop format, which would have limited participation and would not have easily accommodated participant needs. The traditional method of a three-day workshop was impossible for most of the project participants, and we quickly realized that the CDS digital storytelling model is highly adaptive. In our project we truncated most of the didactic training in story writing and video editing, for example, to allow more one-on-one work, even in the group workshop, to accommodate varying degrees of computer skills among participants. Seven videos were produced using a completely one-on-one model. Second, by providing minimal guidance on the content of stories, we were able to glean a variety of stories that more likely resonated with participant concerns and conveyed a breadth of lived experience. Even though we never specifically asked storytellers to talk about viral hepatitis risk factors, treatment, stigma, or protective behaviors, many stories touched on these key topics because these themes had a significant influence in their experiences with the infection. As a result, we received stories that were "from the heart" but still conveyed important information for public health applications.

We did learn a few lessons during the project. We felt a heavy burden of bureaucratic red tape as a result of working with two state agencies—a university and a public health department—that increased our workload over the several months of project activities. Furthermore, academic researchers and public health workers involved in participatory digital media projects must jump through a number of hoops compared with those who work with more tried and tested, traditional text-based projects, because institutional administrators such as state health departments and university human subjects committees are still trying to understand the complexities of evidence-based research that uses participatory, visual, and digital methods. Others interested in engaging in this type of research endeavor should be advised to allocate enough time (e.g., four or more months) to sort through the maze of rules and regulations that such methods and collaborations produce. Researchers should see themselves as educators responsible for teaching review boards about the details of protocols for multipurposed participatory visual and digital research projects (Gubrium and Harper, 2013). Essentially, as researchers and practitioners in this capacity we have become what we call "über obligantus," scholar-activists who mix ethnography, public health promotion, participatory research, and policymaking, such that they become over-obligated to all. We feel responsible for conceptualizing novel designs for research that engage participants on a more level playing field while navigating our own and our institution's human subjects board ethical frameworks, and then actually doing something with the data—here digital stories—whether for health communication messaging or for advocacy purposes, to promote social justice by circulating the digital stories in diverse social media environments.

Digital storytelling is not a new means of communication, but it is still relatively new to public health and the social sciences as a method for data collection, intervention, and advocacy. As public health practitioners seek out new dissemination channels for messaging, digital storytelling should not be overlooked. The relatively short video format (two to four minutes) is useful for opening community dialogue by using a digital story to present a human story and to ensure that meeting participants are on the same page in terms of agenda. The dissemination of personal videos by uploading to websites and sharing through social media platforms such as Facebook and Twitter, can increase dialogue beyond traditional health communication means while adding to the resources available for individuals who are increasingly obtaining health information from online sources. The integration of short health videos in online surveys is another strategy we implemented in the Viral Hepatitis project.

While many health communication benefits may be realized from digital storytelling, we note challenges to the process. Recruitment and retention of participants to the Viral Hepatitis project was difficult. We faced low participant turnout for the group workshop and felt compelled to use a hybrid digital storytelling approach in which individuals worked independently with the facilitators, instead of in a group setting. We have realized the need for flexibility in these endeavors, adjusting the digital storytelling method to suit our needs, as well as those of the participants, while recognizing that storytellers in a one-on-one production context may have missed out on the strong sense of collective solidarity and group support that sometimes develop in the story circle and group screening of digital stories (Gubrium and Harper 2013; Otañez and Lakota 2015). Furthermore, given that there is virtually no evidence for the impact of digital stories on health policymaking, researchers may want to create a research design that assesses their impact by using social media metrics (i.e., Google Analytics) and collects data on the number of supportive letters and statements submitted to project leaders from policymakers and other key stakeholders who participate in video screenings (Rockefeller Foundation 2014). Additional visual-based research is needed on how individuals who share their stories in projects such as this one can more directly contribute to social movements that hold economic and political leaders accountable for practices that generate viral hepatitis and other issues of health inequity in the first place.

Acknowledgments

The viral hepatitis project was supported by the Colorado Department of Public Health and Environment. We thank MaryAnn McNair and Daniel Weinshenker with the Center for Digital Storytelling (www.storycenter.org) for their involvement in the workshop and creation of the visual narratives. The project team is grateful to Debe Wise for providing audiovisual recording services during the public screening and to Yvonne Kellar-Guenther for assisting with data collection and analysis. We appreciate Katrina Greschner's statistical analysis of project data. We are indebted to the individuals who shared their stories and to the community members who participated in the community screening (www.hepatitiscolorado.info).

REFERENCES

Bigalondo, A. 2013. Hello, I Am what You See: A Chicano/a: Digital Storytelling and the Construction of an Emergent Chicano/a Identity. In *Experiencing Digital Storytelling*, edited by M. Alcantud-Diaz and C. Gregori-Signes, 116–131. Valencia, Spain: JPM Ediciones.

Centers for Disease Control and Prevention. 2014. HIV/AIDS, viral hepatitis, sexually transmitted infections and tuberculosis. http://tinyurl.com/oufcgh8, accessed October 1, 2014.

Colorado Department of Public Health and Environment. 2012a. *Hepatitis C in Colorado 2011 Surveillance Report: Cases of Acute and Chronic Hepatitis C in Colorado.* Denver, CO: Viral Hepatitis Program in the Disease Control and Environmental Division.

———. 2012b. *Hepatitis B in Colorado 2011 Surveillance Report: Cases of Acute and Chronic Hepatitis B in Colorado.* Denver, CO: Viral Hepatitis Program in the Disease Control and Environmental Division.

Davis, C., J. Johnston, L. de Saxe Zerden, K. Clark, T. Castillo, and R. Childs. 2014. Attitudes of North Carolina Law Enforcement Officers Toward Syringe Decriminalization. *Drug and Alcohol Dependence* 144: 265–269.

Davis, A., and D. Weinshenker. 2014. Digital Storytelling and Authoring Identity. In *Learning in Doing: Social, Cognitive and Computational Perspectives*, edited by C. Ching and B. Foley, 47–74. New York: Cambridge University Press.

Dutta, M. 2008. *Communicating Health: A Culture-Centered Approach.* Cambridge, UK: Polity Press.

Fraser, S. 2004. "It's Your Life!" Injecting Drug Users, Individual Responsibility and Hepatitis C Prevention. *Health: An Interdisciplinary Journal for the Social Study of Health, Illness and Medicine* 8(2): 199–221.

Freidus, N., S. Schromen-Wawrin, S. Benson, N. Sadow-Hasenberg, and A. Rahimian. 2013. Mapping Our Voices for Equality: Stories for Healthier Policies, Systems and Environments in King County, Washington. In *Experiencing Digital Storytelling*, edited by M. Alcantud-Diaz and C. Gregori-Signes, 98–115. Valencia, Spain: JPM Ediciones.

Gubrium, A., A. Hill, and S. Flicker. 2014. A Situated Practice of Ethics for Participatory Visual and Digital Methods in Public Health Research and

Practice: A Focus on Digital Storytelling. *American Journal of Public Health* 103(10): e1–e9.

Gubrium, A., and K. Harper. 2013. *Participatory Visual and Digital Methods*. Walnut Creek, CA: Left Coast Press.

Gubrium, A., and G. DiFulvio. 2011. Girls in the World: Digital Storytelling as a Feminist Public Health Approach. *Girlhood Studies* 4(2): 28–46.

Hall, S. 1997. The Work of Representation. In *Cultural Representations and Signifying Practices*, edited by S. Hall, 1–74. London: Sage.

Hill, A. 2010. Digital Storytelling for Gender Justice: Exploring the Challenges of Participation and the Limits of Polyvocality. In *Confronting Global Gender Justice: Women's Lives, Human Rights*, edited by D. Bergoffen, P. R. Gilbert, T. Harvey, and C. McNeely, 126–140. London: Routledge.

———. 2014. Digital Storytelling and the Politics of Doing Good: Exploring Ethics of Bringing Personal Narratives into Public Spheres. In *Community-Based Multiliteracies and Digital Media Projects: Questioning Assumptions and Exploring Realities*, edited by H. Pleasants and D. Salter, 21–44. New York: Peter Lang.

Lambert, J. 2013. *Digital Storytelling: Capturing Lives, Creating Community* (4th edition). New York: Routledge. Companion website available at www.routledge .com/cw/lambert-9780415627030/#&panel1-1, accessed April 1, 2014.

Li, K., J. Xing, M. Klevens, R. Jiles, J. Ward, and S. Holmberg. 2012. The Increasing Burden of Mortality from Viral Hepatitis in the United States Between 1999 and 2007. *Annals of Internal Medicine* 156(4): 271–278.

Navarro, V. 2009. What We Mean by Social Determinants of Health. *Global Health Promotion* 16(1): 5–16.

Otañez, M., and W. Lakota. 2015. Digital Storytelling: Using Videos to Increase Social Wellness. In *Video and Filmmaking as Psychotherapy: Research and Practice*, edited by J. Cohen and L. Johnson, 119–130. New York: Routledge.

Raheja, M. 2007. Reading Nanook's Smile: Visual Sovereignty, Indigenous Revisions of Ethnography, and Atanarjuat (The Fast Runner). *American Quarterly* 59(4): 1159–1185.

Rockefeller Foundation. 2014. *Digital Storytelling for Social Impact*. http://tinyurl .com/ng6394y, accessed August 11, 2014.

Rony, F. 1996. *The Third Eye: Race, Cinema and Ethnographic Spectacle*. Durham, NC: Duke University Press.

Spurgeon, C., J. Burgess, H. Klaebe, J. Tacchi, K. McWilliam, and M. Tsai. 2009. Co-Creative Media: Theorising Digital Storytelling as a Platform for Researching and Developing Participatory Culture. Paper presented at the Australian and New Zealand Communication Association Conference, 8–10 July, Queensland University of Technology, Brisbane, Queensland.

Underberg, N., and E. Zorn. 2013. *Digital Ethnography: Anthropology, Narrative and New Media*. Austin, TX: University of Texas Press.

U.S. Department of Health and Human Services. 2014. *Action Plan for the Prevention, Care and Treatment of Viral Hepatitis: Updated 2014–2016*. Washington, D.C.: U.S. Department of Health and Human Services.

Vivienne, S., and J. Burgess. 2013. The Remediation of the Personal Photograph and the Politics of Self-Representation in Digital Storytelling. *Journal of Material Culture* 18(3): 279–298.

Williams, D., and S. Mohammed. 2009. Discrimination and Racial Disparities in Health: Evidence and Needed Research. *Journal of Behavioral Medicine* 32: 20–47.

PART

2

Photovoice

A

Picturing Transactional $ex:
Ethics, Challenges, and Possibilities

Ciann Wilson and Sarah Flicker

Introduction

The Jane-Finch neighborhood is located in northwest Toronto, Canada. Nearly a quarter of the population is African, Caribbean, and black (ACB), and the community is much younger (Richardson 2008) and faces higher rates of unemployment (Green 2006) than the rest of Toronto. Jane-Finch is often characterized as an immigrant enclave synonymous with poverty and crime (Richardson 2008).

The larger context of inequality and racialized poverty is exacerbated by the fact that black women remain one of the most socially, economically, and politically excluded groups in Canada (Williams et al. 2009). Challenges are compounded for young ACB women who regularly experience the trifecta of discrimination: racism, sexism, and classism. For many, this context results in poor sexual health outcomes. The neighborhood experiences some of the highest rates of unplanned pregnancies, sexually transmitted infections (STIs), and HIV in the city of Toronto (Robertson 2007). Nevertheless, despite the odds, some young ACB women in Jane-Finch flourish. Our research and experience in the community tells us that some are able to maintain their sexual health and feel in control of their sexuality.

The goal of the Let's Talk About Sex (LTAS) research project was to explore how young, racialized women in Jane-Finch negotiate sexual agency in this context of risk. Specifically, we wanted to understand the individual, community, social, and/or structural factors that might support

Ciann Wilson and Sarah Flicker, "Picturing Transactional $ex: Ethics, Challenges, and Possibilities" in *Participatory Visual and Digital Research in Action,* Aline Gubrium, Krista Harper, and Marty Otañez, eds., pp. 73-86. © 2015 Left Coast Press, Inc. All rights reserved.

youth resiliency. We also wanted to choose methods that would help us understand how young women make sense of their own sexual health choices, as well as celebrate their agency in hostile, structurally inequitable environments. Finally, we wanted our methods to reconcile with our values of supporting youth to become active partners in the health of their community by catalyzing thoughtful reflection and informed action (Barndt 2008). For this reason, we selected Photovoice and, subsequently, digital storytelling.

Photovoice is a community-based research (CBR) approach, advocacy tool, and health promotion strategy pioneered by Wang and Burris in research with village women in rural China (Wang and Burris 1997). It has been used in research and community development interventions with various marginalized populations (Castleden et al. 2008; Hergenrather et al. 2009). Participants are given cameras to visually and narratively represent their perspectives on a question or community concern. Through individual and group discussions, participants engage in critical dialogue and reflective writing about their photos, and produce exhibits and other knowledge exchange strategies (Catalani and Minkler 2009; Wang and Burris 1997). Digital stories are short, audiovisual narratives that synthesize images, video, audio voice recordings, music, and text to create compelling accounts of experience (Gubrium 2009). Approaches such as Photovoice and digital storytelling are a part of the growing body of literature that incorporates a range of communication tools (e.g., photography, video, music) to promote community development, capacity building, artistic expression, and social activism (Boydell et al. 2012; Hergenrather et al. 2009).

Research and other forms of dominant discourse (such as the media) tend to present ACB youth as occupying pathological and problematic positions in society. Young ACB voices are consistently muted (Wright 2011). Participatory arts-based approaches can help youth "speak up," while encouraging them to critically research their worlds, building on their assets and talents (Wright 2011). In representing their lived experiences, youth can challenge dominant culture and its inherent power relations (Barndt 2008). These approaches can facilitate dialogue about difficult topics (Flicker et al. 2013) and support youth in developing strategies for change (Flicker et al. 2010). By taking concrete steps towards improving their communities, youth can build their self-respect and confidence to cope with other life situations while becoming better connected to their communities, their cohort, and caring adults (Flicker et al. 2008). The products of arts-based approaches can also be used to transmit information, raise awareness, and convey emotion (Flicker et al. 2014). Moreover, incorporating history as well as critical race and class perspectives into arts-based approaches may help to disrupt racist stereotypes. Such efforts have the potential to diminish the stigma, fatalism, and self-blame that negatively affect racialized youth (Larkin et al. 2007; Larkin and Mitchell 2004).

In this chapter, we explore the engagement of an iterative approach to participatory visual methodologies, which produced both qualitatively rich insights and unique ethical challenges around the issue of transactional sex among young people.

Methods

Our project used an iterative data collection and analysis process (Table 4.1). At each step, we engaged in a variety of participatory arts-based data collection strategies to explore adolescent girls' sexual health in the context of structural inequality. As we proceeded, we refined the questions we were asking to develop more nuanced and situated understandings. In particular, we became increasingly interested in the ways that research participants were depicting and talking about transactional sex. As we dug deeper into the issues, we continued to reflect on the ethical implications of our work.

TABLE 4.1: An iterative data collection and analysis process

Photovoice
What are young women saying?

⬇

Member Checking
How do we want to share this?

⬇

Digital Stories	
Why here? Why now?	What ethical issues arise as we share our work?

⬇

Community Conversations	
What can we do about it?	How do we expand the conversation?

LTAS was done in collaboration with representatives from York University, Northwood Community Centre, and Black Creek Community Health Centre. It was initiated and led by Ciann Wilson as part of her master's degree. As a young black woman, she was keen to choose methods that would be fun and amplify the voices of her peers in conversations about their sexual health. She had already been working in Black Creek as a youth program instructor for six years when she began the project. In the fall of 2011, members of the research team involved in Jane-Finch youth programming recruited interested participants from local high schools, malls, youth-based programs, and organizations. Participants were screened (via a telephone interview) and 20 were selected to ensure a diverse representation of ages, knowledge of sexual health, and ethno-racial backgrounds (African, Caribbean, black-Canadian, and/or mixed). Fifteen young (14- to 18-year-old) ACB women ended up actively seeing the project to completion. We attribute the high retention rates to the entertaining and engaging nature of the program.

That winter, three members of the research team (all women of color) coordinated and co-facilitated nine three-hour sessions, all part of one Photovoice workshop. Participants were instructed to take photos that spoke to their perspectives on each of the following simplified research questions:

- What is sexual health?
- How can I be "sexually healthy"?
- What help or support do I need to make sexual decisions?
- What makes it hard to make healthy sexual decisions?
- What are some stereotypes about girls who live in my community?
- How can I challenge these stereotypes?

We started with Photovoice because we wanted to give the young women an opportunity to respond to the ways in which they were represented in the media and speak to the issues that were important to them through the use of their own images and narratives. During each session, participants chose their favorite photos and used the SHOWeD framework (Text Box 4.1) to write about them (Hergenrather et al. 2009; Wang and Burris 1997). Then, they collectively discussed the meaning of their images.

Over the course of the nine sessions, the quality of the photos improved and ensuing discussions deepened as the girls became more familiar with the technique, each other, and the topic. In the final session, facilitators conducted one-on-one semistructured interviews with each participant to

TEXT BOX 4.1: SHOWeD Prompt Questions

What do you **S**ee here?

What is really **H**appening here?

How does this relate to **O**ur lives?

Why does this concern, situation, strength exist?

How can we become **E**mpowered through our new
understanding?

What can we **D**o?

garner her reflections. To honor their participation, participants received a $100 digital camera, 30 community service hours towards their secondary school diploma prerequisite, nutritious meals, and transit tokens.

In the spring, five of the Photovoice participants engaged in a group member-checking session during which they were presented with the study findings and had an opportunity to reflect on whether results adequately represented their perspectives. This session provided a pivotal moment to unpack the issues represented by the photos and narratives.

Some participants expressed challenges and frustrations with the writing process; these young women wanted to share their photo narratives orally. We applied for further funding to collaborate with a small group to create digital stories using the images collected. Through digital storytelling, participants could verbally, textually, and musically narrate the photos they created through Photovoice, as well as reach a broader audience through the appeal of this multimodal approach. Youth orally told their stories and worked with facilitators (who helped to transcribe or take notes) to refine their scripts. During recording sessions, some youth read their scripts out loud, while others improvised from their notes.

Three of the four digital stories created touched on issues surrounding transactional sex. Since the Photovoice and digital storytelling workshops, the research team has had several opportunities to present findings and products at community and university forums across Toronto and at international conferences. These discussions have been central for raising awareness of, and expanding the conversations about, North American youth engagement in transactional sex.

Data for this chapter are drawn from audio-recorded Photovoice workshop sessions, individual interviews, member-checking sessions, video-recorded audience responses at community forums, the Photovoice pictures and narratives produced by participants, the digital stories created, and our reflections and field notes. NVivo 9 software was used to code and qualitatively manage the dataset using a grounded theory approach.

Results

Photovoice participants shared that young women in the community regularly engaged in three types of relationships where material resources were exchanged for sex: 1) "loving relations," 2) those with much older men (i.e., "boopsies" or "sugar daddies"), and 3) casual encounters in hotel rooms. Below are some accounts of the range of economically motivated relations the young women identified.[1]

Several participants described the material motives behind "loving relationships" among their peers. Participants emphasized that, even in a "loving relationship," a man's appeal is often his money. "Men have to take the girl out and buy her stuff," said one participant. Meanwhile a girl's "selling point" is her "vagina, sex, and good looks." One of the photo-narratives, *The Perfect Couple* (Figure 4.1), depicts two pairs of Air Jordan basketball shoes: one presumably worn by a girl, and the other by her male partner. The participant who produced this photo-narrative stated that for youth, expensive clothing and shoes made members of the opposite sex more appealing or attractive when it came to dating.

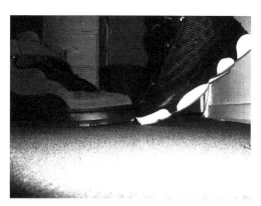

FIGURE 4.1:
The perfect couple

Some of the participants described how "other" girls engage in transactional sex with significantly older men to secure material goods. In her photo-narrative, one participant stated that these girls are easily recognized in the community because they have the latest designer clothes and other expensive items. In contrast to the social acceptance of the material motives for "loving relationships" with men their own age, participants were especially critical of transactional relationships involving older men. One participant used the term "boops" to describe a man who pays a young woman for sex; young women who get money from guys for sex engage in "boopsing."[2] These young women often receive admiration from their peers for the material possessions they receive from their partners. According to this narrative, some girls even shared their "boops" with their friends.

> [The girls] are having sex with guys for money (they are boopsing guys). This happens A LOT because there is nowhere else to make money and they have to have material things or they're not going to be popular....
> [T]he guys they are boopsing take them on shopping sprees. Not all of this is legal. You have young girls and there is like a 10-year age difference between her and the guy. ...[G]irls are lazy. They don't want to get a job when a guy can just come by and give them things.... The girls brag to their friends, they aren't considered whores. They will pass the guy's number along to their friends. They are gold diggers. (Photovoice participant)

Named *Paradise* after the strip club next to a church depicted in the photograph, the image (Figure 4.2) infers the moral view the participant had of transactional sex. This photo-narrative also touches on the illegality of some of the transactional sex that is occurring in the community. Some of the men in these relationships were often significantly older than the young women, qualifying these relationships as statutory rape.[3]

During the member-checking session, participants discussed receiving frequent text, Instagram, and Facebook invitations to "come out and make some money." Participants went on to share how men—some not much older than they were—would book a hotel room and invite girls they knew. These girls would then invite their friends, and groups of girls would go to a room where several johns would pay a fee to receive sexual favors. The rooms were described as stocked with alcohol and drugs to facilitate the orgy. The organizers would then split the profits with the girls. However, one of the young women reported that one of her girlfriends who participated in these orgies did not think she was being paid fairly.

FIGURE 4.2: Paradise

I get so much messages that say "you wanna come bone [and make some money] this weekend?" ...People don't hide it anymore it's so common (Member-Checking Session).

I have a friend (who) every once in a while feels she is down on some money and they are like, "we will rent the room for you and you will have to split the profits" (Member-Checking Session).

One participant depicted many of these issues in her digital story, *Sex, Money and Religion*. In it, she captures the disapproving sentiments regarding transactional sex that were echoed by her peers throughout the study, and socially distances herself from the issue.

Community forums were held across Toronto to share the project findings. Photos were displayed and digital stories were screened, followed by facilitated discussions. They were well attended by a broad spectrum of community members, from toddlers to senior citizens. While many enjoyed looking at the Photovoice exhibit and reading the narratives in groups and alone, it was the digital stories that evoked emotional and collective responses from the audience. Attendees between the ages of 10 and 30 tended to have some knowledge of the existence of economically motivated sexual relationships within their communities. In one forum held in the Jane-Finch community, a young woman in her twenties shook with emotion as she recounted the horrifying experience of being approached by an older man for transactional sexual relations in front of her daughter. "I was so violated and my daughter had to witness that creep; I dunno, lately it just grew in Jane and Finch." Two young boys, not much older than 11, recounted seeing young women negotiating money and drugs in exchange for sex. A man in his mid- to late twenties said with a sly, knowing smile, "We call that a boopsie. Everyone knows what that is," in response to the discussion of older men having relations with younger women. In a forum held in a sister community, a coordinator of a local community health center said that he was aware of young women who would regularly leave school during their lunch breaks with men in cars to exchange sexual favors for money. At another forum held at York University, a student who self-identified as white recounted the existence of transactional relationships among other young, white women in her high school in an affluent area in downtown Toronto. Meanwhile, a local theatrical group at the Jane-Finch forum responded to our findings by performing an entire play about economically motivated sexual relationships.

By contrast, participants older than 30 were shocked, and many were outraged by the existence of sexual exchange for money among "their young women":

> The moral values are not instilled in the family home.... [W]here's the family structure in the community?... You want the biggest this and the Gucci that, but guess what, you ain't working to afford it...so you selling yourself (Community Forum).
>
> It goes back to self-image and self-love.... I'm a Christian...so I don't go after the Gucci bags...[designed] to take my money from me.... [I]t all goes back to how you see yourself, what is your self-image? Where does your value come from? (Community Forum).

As these quotes demonstrate, many invoked moralistic arguments and cited the importance of parenting, family, and re-establishing self-esteem, dignity, and self-worth among young women. Others, outraged, called for the police to arrest predatory men.

This rhetoric of powerlessness victimizes the young women involved, particularly those engaged with much older men and in casual sexual encounters. Meanwhile, some adult participants took a different tone:

> We have no clue what our young people are going through right now....
> The system keeps the adults so busy, we have no time for our youth....
> Wow, our young girls are going through this and where are we mothers?

Even if you're not my daughter, when I'm walking past you on the street please don't frown at me, don't roll your eyes, don't have a strong stare face like you're angry at me because I want to be there for you.... [A]dults that are in this room…we need to listen to the youth (Community Forum).

They stressed the need for adults to listen to young people and understand, as well as question and criticize the behavior of other adults, not young people, when it comes to circumstances involving transactional sex.

Discussion

Despite the financial hardships faced by participants, none self-reported engaging in transactional sexual relationships. All reports were of friends or peers who had "made these choices" or who had "succumbed" to economic reality. This lack of self-reporting may result from the social taboos associated with engaging in transactional relationships, a demonstration of the resistance of some of the young women in this community, or from selection bias. Many of the participants were community leaders. Despite the various recruitment strategies used, there remain many harder-to-reach youth within the Jane-Finch community who choose not to engage in these sorts of extracurricular opportunities. In particular, youth who are "boopsing" may be too busy to participate in other recreational activities and don't need the small honorarium participants received. Noting their absence or silence is important.

Given how widespread transactional sex appears to be, this absence of girls who self-identify presents several ethical and methodological challenges. In their photo-narratives and digital stories, participants not only socially distanced themselves from personal knowledge of transactional relations (by depicting the issue in an impersonal way), they often "othered" the girls who were engaged in them, deeming their actions morally inferior. One wonders whether (and how) the choice of participatory visual methods may have affected potential disclosures. Because so much of the work happened in groups for public consumption, the risk of admitting transactional activity to their peers in a close-knit community may have been too great. While confidentiality was always an option offered, and participants could decide whether or not to share their work publicly, participants were extrinsically rewarded for owning their work at community forums and contributing to public discussions with others about their art. Most of the girls wanted to be credited for their work. As such, there were inadvertent incentives for participants to publically perform the role of "good girls," presenting themselves in the best light for their communities and families. The social distancing engaged in by participants may have been a strategy for affirming their own agency, in opposition to dominant stereotypes (Wright 2011). This posturing, however, unintentionally reinscribed stereotypes that vilified or shamed other young women in their community for making different choices.

It also raised questions about who has the right to tell which stories. What does it mean for girls to tell the story of "the other girl" rather than focusing on their own narratives? How does Photovoice, as a form of "documentation," contribute to the "othering" of young women and serve dominant judgmental interests? In an effort to help girls think more broadly about community concerns, many of our "prompted" Photovoice questions (e.g, "What is sexual health?") allowed for impersonal responses. This may have inadvertently encouraged girls to tell the stories of "the other." By contrast, in creating their digital stories, girls were more explicitly asked to think about narrative and their relationship to it. As such, the digital stories became personal accounts of their relationship to the topic (as opposed to simply documenting the issues). Still, because none of the young women in this project spoke from the perspective of personal experience, questions remain about the agency of young women engaged in these relations: to what extent is this a "real issue," and for whom? What stories might young women who were engaged in transactional sexual activities tell?

Participants perceived and postulated that young women engaged in transactional sexual relations did not do so just to "get by." Instead, these activities afforded them access to luxury items that were seen as desirable markers of social status among their peers (Ankomah 1999; Kuate-Defo 2004; Poulin 2007; Rosenbaum 2011). What is evident from the range of transactional relations in participant narratives is that there are nuanced differences and overlaps between transactional and loving relationships that need to be unpacked. Photovoice and digital stories provide abstract text with multiple layers of meaning and symbolism that can encourage rich discussion. They both reflect and evoke multiplicity and contradiction. There is also the potential that many more messages are created than originally intended by the artists. Questions arise about the normative rules surrounding male-to-female gifting within society more generally, and the conflated space between these socially acceptable relations and transactional sex (Wilson, in press). Further questions arise about the more nefarious predatory nature of relationships in which there are wider economic, age, or power imbalances.

Whether or not there was a real or imagined difference between the young women in the study and those they depicted through their work, their art demonstrates that participants have internalized dominant "slut-shaming" ideologies. Despite being able to describe various types of widespread transactional sexual typologies, participants (and the wider community) were universally critical of these practices. At the same time, they felt that many of the young women engaged in these relations do not see themselves as victims. These findings suggest that the varied dynamics of economically motivated relationships complicate the ready rhetoric of powerlessness and victimization on the part of the young women involved. As a result, we must exercise extreme caution to avoid generalizations that reinforce hegemonic gender norms and reinscribe stereotypes about women's lack of agency in transactional relations while promoting and honoring sexual subjectivity (Kuate-Defo 2004).

Using iterative approaches to participatory visual methodologies helped us complicate our understandings of various types of sexual transactions and challenge dominant discourses. This approach allowed us to clarify the nuances of the issue, engage in richer conversation by asking deeper questions, and strategize with the participants on the best way to further interrogate and share our findings in a step-wise fashion, ensuring the young women consented to what and how things were shared with each step as well as involving communities and stakeholders in critical discussions. This careful control of how the information was shared helped to desensationalize the subject matter and broaden the discussions beyond race and space. In unpacking these findings, we struggled with thinking about how to contextualize them in ways that do not perpetuate stereotypes about young black women, but instead get at the underlying issues and promote self-determination and health. In our roles as researchers and organizers, we actively wondered how we could help communities to "see" or "hear" these reflections in ways that might support more productive dialogues. Although these works were originally intended for "public consumption," we ultimately decided that they were best taken up in spaces of facilitated dialogue, where the nuances could be unpacked, sensitive issues interrogated, and the myths around sex, race, and geography could be challenged.

REFERENCES

Ankomah, A. 1999. Sex, Love, Money and AIDS: The Dynamics of Premarital Sexual Relationships in Ghana. *Sexualities* 2(3): 291–308.

Barndt, D. 2008. Touching Minds and Hearts: Community Arts as Collaborative Research. In *Handbook of the Arts in Qualitative Research*, edited by J. Gary Knowles and Ardra L. Cole, 352–364. Thousand Oaks, CA: Sage Publications. Retrieved from http://srmo.sagepub.com/view/handbook-of-the-arts-in-qualitative-research/n29.xml.

Boydell, K. M., B. M. Gladstone, T. Volpe, B. Allemang, and E. Stasiulis. 2012. The Production and Dissemination of Knowledge: A Scoping Review of Arts-Based Health Research. *Forum Qualitative Sozialforschung/Forum: Qualitative Social Research* 13(1). Retrieved from http://www.qualitative-research.net.ezproxy.library.yorku.ca/index.php/fqs/article/view/1711.

Castleden, H., T. Garvin, and Huu-ay-aht First Nation. 2008. Modifying Photovoice for Community-Based Participatory Indigenous Research. *Social Science & Medicine* 66(6): 1393–1405.

Catalani, C., and M. Minkler. 2009. Photovoice: A Review of the Literature in Health and Public Health. *Health Education & Behavior* 37(3): 424–451.

Flicker, S., J. Danforth, E. Konsmo, C. Wilson, V. Oliver, R. Jackson, et al. 2013. Because We Are Natives and We Stand Strong to Our Pride: Decolonizing HIV Prevention with Aboriginal Youth in Canada Using the Arts. *Canadian Journal of Aboriginal Community-Based HIV/AIDS Research* 5: 4–23.

Flicker, S., J. Danforth, C. Wilson, V. Oliver, J. Larkin, J.-P. Restoule, et al. 2014. "Because We Have Really Unique Art": Decolonizing Research with Indigenous Youth Using the Arts. *International Journal of Indigenous Health* 10(1): 16–34.

Flicker, S., A. Guta, J. Larkin, S. Flynn, A. Fridkin, R. Travers, et al. 2010. Survey Design From the Ground Up: Collaboratively Creating the Toronto Teen Survey. *Health Promotion Practice* 11(1): 112–122.

Flicker, S., O. Maley, A. Ridgley, S. Biscope, C. Lombardo, and H. A. Skinner. 2008. e-PAR: Using Technology and Participatory Action Research to Engage Youth in Health Promotion. *Action Research* 6(3): 285–303.

Green, Gary. 2006. United We Stand: Jane & Finch. http://www.greenforcouncil.ca.

Gubrium, A. 2009. Digital Storytelling: An Emergent Method for Health Promotion Research and Practice. *Health Promotion Practice* 10(2): 186–191.

Hergenrather, K. C., S. D. Rhodes, C. A. Cowan, G. Bardhoshi, and S. Pula. 2009. Photovoice as Community-Based Participatory Research: A Qualitative Review. *American Journal of Health Behavior*, 33(6): 686–698.

Kuate-Defo, B. 2004. Young People's Relationships with Sugar Daddies and Sugar Mummies: What Do We Know and What Do We Need to Know? *African Journal of Reproductive Health/La Revue Africaine de La Santé Reproductive* 8(2): 13–37.

Larkin, J., S. Flicker, R. Koleszar-Green, S. Mintz, M. Dagnino, and C. Mitchell. 2007. HIV Risk, Systemic Inequities, and Aboriginal Youth: Widening the Circle for HIV Prevention Programming. *Canadian Journal of Public Health/Revue Canadienne de Sante'e Publique* 98(3): 179–182.

Larkin, J., and C. Mitchell. 2004. Gendering HIV/AIDS Prevention: Situating Canadian Youth in a Transitional World. *Women's Health and Urban Life: An International and Interdisciplinary Journal* 3(2): 34–44.

Poulin, M. 2007. Sex, Money, and Premarital Partnerships in Southern Malawi. *Social Science & Medicine* 65(11): 2383–2393.

Richardson, C. 2008. "Canada's Toughest Neighbourhood:" Surveillance, Myth and Orientalism in Jane-Finch [doctoral dissertation]. Brock University, St. Catherines, Ontario. http://jane-finch.com/articles/files/Richardson_Thesis.pdf.

Robertson, S. 2007. *Who Feels It Knows the Challenges of HIV Prevention for Young Black Women in Toronto.* Black Coalition for AIDS Prevention. http://accho.ca/pdf/BCAP%20Report%20on%20Young%20Black%20Women%20-%20Who%20Feels%20It%20Knows.pdf.

Rosenbaum, J. 2011. Condoms, Jobs, and Sugar Daddies: Sexual Bargaining about Condom Use Among Low SES Women. *Journal of Adolescent Health* 48(2): S2.

Wang, C., and M. A. Burris. 1997. Photovoice: Concept, Methodology, and Use for Participatory Needs Assessment. *Health Education & Behavior* 24(3): 369–387.

Williams, C. C., P. A. Newman, I. Sakamoto, and N. A. Massaquoi. 2009. HIV Prevention Risks for Black Women in Canada. *Social Science & Medicine* 68(1): 12–20.

Wilson, C. In press. Let's Talk About Sex and Money: An Exploration of Economically Motivated Relationships Amongst Young Black Women in Canada. In *Legacy of the Crossing: Life, Death and Triumph Among Descendants of the World's Greatest Forced Migration,* edited by T. A. LaVeist. Baltimore, MD: Claybridge Media.

Wright, C. Y. 2011. Visual Research Methods: Using Cameras to Empower Socially Excluded Black Youth. *Sociology* 44(3): 541–558.

NOTES

1   For a more detailed account of study findings around transactional sex, see Let's Talk About Sex and Money: An exploration of economically motivated relationships amongst young Black Women in Canada, (Wilson, in press)

2   According to UrbanDictionary.com, "Boopsie is a guy who is a woman's toy or fool. He gives her anything she wants and receives nothing from her" (urbandictionary.com). The term's origins come from Jamaican Creole. It is interesting to note that participants used the term to describe relations where the men do benefit from relationship as girls traded sexual favors with older men in return for material goods.

3   Under the Criminal Code of Canada, persons under the age of 16 cannot give consent to any form of sexual activity, from kissing to intercourse.

Seeing Differently: Enticing Reflexivity in the Futurescape City Tours

Cynthia Selin and Gretchen Gano

Nowhere else in modern life are technological systems, artifacts, and tangled skeins of social relationships so brashly intertwined than in cities. Technology underpins the urban experience in both obvious and subversive ways: underground heating and cooling systems feed skyscrapers hundreds of feet high, and emergency response systems lay coiled in wait. Technologies big and small color our collective experience and, in turn, reflect our social values in delicate and not-so-delicate ways. As Science and Technology Studies (STS) scholars, we are sensitized to the ways in which science and technology relate to social and political values and priorities. We have become convinced that to produce scientific and technical innovation in the service of societal needs, increased and more sophisticated public vigilance is needed.

We come to this view because we observe that while technology informs contemporary existence in dramatic ways, citizens severely lack the access to spaces and information necessary to find contestable moments to intervene. Too often scientific and technological processes are obscured from public scrutiny or "black boxed" (Latour 1999), and decisions that ought to involve public deliberation are made behind the scenes by a smaller subset of experts. Instead, rigorous and influential public deliberation should occur around big questions such as: Which investments need to made to alleviate climate change in big cities? How should surveillance systems be knitted into the urban infrastructure? Where should new transportation networks

Cynthia Selin and Gretchen Gano, "Seeing Differently: Enticing Reflexivity in the Futurescape City Tours" in *Participatory Visual and Digital Research in Action,* Aline Gubrium, Krista Harper, and Marty Otañez, eds., pp. 87-100. © 2015 Left Coast Press, Inc. All rights reserved.

be routed through a city? We see the city as a ripe site for interrogation and a good locus for engaging the public in conversations about emerging sociotechnical issues. Most recently, our work has involved engaging publics in examining how nanotechnology, a set of technological innovations just on the horizon, may affect urban social life and infrastructures.

Underpinning this work is the idea that technologies either mundane or enchanted are substantial features of the urban experience. We thus turn our gaze to explore the ways in which technologies structure contemporary experience and actually help formulate our sense of agency. Architectural and technology critic Lewis Mumford attests that we live in the era of the "megalopolis": a new urban order that is the "relentless extension and aggrandizement of a highly centralized, super-organic system, that lacks autonomous component centers capable of exercising selection, exerting control…and answering back" (Mumford 1961, 567). As few life choices and daily habits are now *not* informed by the technologies that we have created, technologies around us can be thought of as springing up from a powerful collective capacity to make new things that, in turn, capture and refocus our attention and energies. In other words, new styles of technology not only equal novel conveniences, features, and economic conditions; they also prompt the evolution of new social forms and political arrangements. It is this broad, politically charged manifestation of technology that is important for the public to grapple with in a deliberative fashion.

It is in this context that we take up and adapt participatory digital and visual methods to support public engagement that connects the collective experiences of urban sociotechnical systems with rigorous debate about the role and desirability of new technologies. Our case for this chapter, a large-scale public deliberation designed by the Center for Nanotechnology in Society at Arizona State University, is called Futurescape City Tours (FCTs; see http://www.futurescapecitytours.org/brochure-1/). Nanotechnology—a form of interdisciplinary science and engineering that blends a host of familiar materials, from gold to titanium dioxide, to new uses by manipulating them at the scale of the impossibly small (as small as one-billionth of a meter)—is expected to be a persistent, pervasive, and powerful force in reshaping the urban environment. Today there are skyscrapers sheathed in pristine self-cleaning glass and parking lots that defuse urban heat islands with nanomaterials that deflect rather than absorb the afternoon sun. Nanotechnology is said to be making our cities "smart" by rejuvenating subterranean water, waste, and energy infrastructures (Wiek et al. 2012).

As technologies in the urban environment evolve, it is important to create democratic spaces for diverse publics to inquire critically into the benefits, risks, desirability, and impacts of these technologies (Barben et al. 2008; Guston and Sarewitz 2002). Thus, the conceptual frame for conducting FCTs is to examine, through collaborative inquiry, how nanotechnologies and other new innovations might change cities.

The FCTs involve a constellation of civic engagement events composed of an urban walking tour; varied interactions between citizens, stakeholders, and experts; and image-based deliberative sessions. These methods were developed against the backdrop of STS and our own applied research. We assert that new methods are needed to connect direct, public experiences of the sociotechnical systems wiring the city that embrace diverse ways of knowing and seeing while also cultivating a critical imagination about the future. In 2011, the Center began experimenting by using walking tours, autoethnography, and photography in public engagement and developed the concept of "material deliberation" (Davies et al. 2012, 2013). These experiments and conceptual developments led to a pilot FCT conducted in Phoenix in the fall of 2012 and culminated in a coordinated national implementation of the FCTs in 2013 in six North American cities.

In this chapter, we situate our work in STS, describe the methods of the FCT, and demonstrate how the approach makes visible seemingly invisible urban sociotechnical systems and draws on diverse ways of knowing to open collective urban imaginaries for inquiry. We explore how the digital and visual methods work to cultivate reflexivity among the participants. As applied social scientists intimately involved in designing and implementing the FCTs, we draw on our experiences as well as the data (field notes, interviews, transcripts of meetings, and post-tour evaluations) from the coordinated national implementation in 2013.

Triggering Reflexivity in Public Deliberation

Our research brings diverse groups together to debate science and technology issues of public concern. We generate what Touraine (1983) and others have called a "sociology of intervention" to aid public consideration of often hidden scientific and technical issues. Our recruitment of diverse members of the public, our notions of how participants confront unfamiliar topics and interact with one another, and the desired outcomes of these interventions reflect this stance.

At the heart of this intervention is the idea that to take seriously some of the obvious and not-so-obvious impacts of technology in society, an otherwise disinterested member of the public experiences a perspective shift that allows her or him to recognize the impact of systems that often escape scrutiny. Therefore, our efforts have been to design and conduct deliberation that cultivates a perspective shift among publics. We refer to this change in vantage point as facilitating "reflexivity" that allows for self, community, or cultural evaluation in an iterative way.

By building reflexivity, we aim through the methodological design of the FCT to enable participants to unhinge habitual ways of thinking, establish new vantage points, and discover the pervasive influence of socio-technical systems. What causes FCT participants to shift their perspective? We specifically want to better understand how the integration of participatory visual and digital deliberative mechanisms mattered in this pursuit of reflexivity. How do the different settings and modes of communication enable or constrain collective, critical reflection? How did the mix of media mingle with the physical instantiation of a walking tour of a familiar city to foster social learning?

Many modes of engaging experts, stakeholders, and publics fail to capture alternative ways of knowing or account for spatially and temporally situated experiences of technological change in a way that builds reflexivity. Most rely on assembling people in a standard workshop setting and talking about the pros and cons of a particular technology. What is often missing is what Miller and colleagues (2008) refer to as "epistemological pluralism" that honors multiple ways of knowing. This more inclusive "way of knowing" goes beyond the inclusion of different disciplinary perspectives to include diverse modes of expression. In other words, following Young (2001), public engagement exercises often privilege a stale style of discourse that is decidedly rational and too hygienic. We capture a richer approach to the kinds of knowledge relevant for reflexive public participation as "material deliberation," which points to the import of visual and discursive storytelling, place-based reflections, and the study of material objects in citizen engagement (Davies et al. 2012).

Thus, with the FCTs, we investigate how to move "beyond discourse" within deliberation so as to incorporate the material, visual, and affective. The FCT methodology helps in this regard because it brings the technologies of a city into clear view and supports a more reflexive approach to technology assessment by enabling participants to generate rich visual and narrative data.

Interrogating the City through Visual and Digital Methods

As a research project, Futurescape City Tours seek to better understand the value and functionality of public engagement activities that integrate diverse stakeholders and publics, tend to the politics of place, rigorously trigger imagination, and creatively use multimedia tools. The FCTs involve four interactive sessions with a group of between 10 to 15 citizen recruits who are natives in their respective cities. In selecting participants we sought to create a balance in the group in terms of age, education, income, gender, and ethnicity.[1]

The goal of the first session is to identify a pressing question related to urban sustainability by eliciting the curiosities and concerns of participants. From these participant-led ideas, the Center researchers then designed and conducted a walking tour of the city, visiting places and meeting individuals resonating with the citizens' elicited "concerns and curiosities." During the tour, participants wrote reflections and took photographs to document, observe, question, and point out the places in their city that struck them. They then tagged the photographs as linked to the past, present, or future. Along the way, participants interacted with a variety of guest scientific experts and civic stakeholders that we, as organizers, arranged to meet with the tour group due to their connection to the citizens' agenda. During the third phase, participants selected photographs (from the lot they took during the tour itself) to anchor a three-part deliberative exercise where they negotiated the past, articulated the present, and envisioned the future of their city. Some of the national tours held in 2013 closed with a public gallery displaying of the citizens' images and responses to questions about the role of emerging technologies in the city.

Within this basic structure, there were several digital and visual mechanisms built in to encourage critical reflection that involved integrating experts, visiting diverse places, mobilizing different interaction spaces, and using photography as a tool of documentation and deliberation. For instance, we coached the participants in writing captions for their photographs, which they then tagged and shared on an online photo-sharing site. In the third session, we invited participants to build a timeline into the future using the photographs that they took on the tour. While there is more to be said about the specific formats of the sessions (Selin and Banks 2014), here we pluck out the methods that best exemplify how reflexivity was cultivated.

Seeking Evocative Places

A key way to encourage layered modes of reflection is to diversify the places visited and types of settings where conversations happened during the tour. The citizens' interactions with stakeholders and scientific experts took place in a variety of locations and formats: the dynamics between strolling along a canal talking about water quality with environmental scientists differed from visiting a solar rooftop installation with an energy company representative. In designing the stops, organizers also worked to include a diverse array of indoor and outdoor settings (e.g., a farmer's market, (re)industrial zones, hidden infrastructures) and modes of interaction (some active and energizing, like participant-led interviews, some pensive and slow, like observing behavior on a metro and free-writing).

As researchers, we also paid attention to including unique sites that the participants would not otherwise have access to. Inspired by urban spelunking, we sought to offer citizens looks into hidden places. For example, in the Phoenix edition of the FCT, the group visited a heating and cooling facility that offered a particular ambience to the start of the tour. As described by FCT researcher Jathan Sadowski:

> On an unseasonably brisk Saturday morning in October, I met up with a group of almost 20 other people in front of downtown Phoenix's convention center. Soon, out of a locked metal door tucked back away from the street—one composed by hashmarks that only barely conceal what lies behind—emerged a man. He greeted us, said his name was Rick, and ushered us through the door, which opened up to the top of a set of concrete and steel-lined stairs that descended underground. The group made their way, zigzagging down the stairs—three stories, 40 feet—below the earth. We reached the bottom and pushed open another door, this one heavier, solid. "Welcome to Phoenix's underground district cooling system," Rick said. Once we all donned hard hats, earplugs, and safety goggles, we would be venturing into the city's guts.

In addition to the different settings visited, the FCTs also experimented with different interaction environments. Some interactions were reminiscent of traditional learning settings (an expert panel and question-and-answer sessions), while others were less so. In the 2012 FCT Pilot, citizens were shown a do-it-yourself (DIY) biofuels demonstration in a vacant lot in downtown Phoenix. In the 2013 Phoenix tour, participants were dropped off at a farmer's market and conducted impromptu interviews with the vendors and patrons about the future of the city. These different atmospheres were intentionally designed to trigger different ways of knowing, with the hope to generate a more diverse assemblage of perspectives. Participants found the ways they were encouraged to engage in these new interactional spaces helpful; for example, one participant noted (in the evaluation survey): "Forcing me and others to speak was very useful and comforting."

Seeing Differently through Photography

Our use of photography as a tool for dialogue in FCT is akin to the Photovoice technique. Photovoice has been used in health care contexts and with vulnerable populations as a method for drawing out sensitive concerns and sociocultural values in direct reference to on-the-ground living conditions (Gubrium and Harper 2013; Wang and Burris 1997). Practitioners put cameras in the hands of people as a participatory action research technique that empowers marginalized communities. Similarly, in the FCT, we sought to amplify participant voices with the goals of enabling broader expression and prompting reflexivity through the use of photography. The process of taking photos gives people another sort of canvas to articulate, share, and contest the values revealed through the images.

All of the FCT participants used digital cameras to track their intrigues during the tour; after the tour, they selected 20 photos to post on a shared site. Each photo was accompanied by a caption meant to articulate what they were thinking about when they snapped the shot. They were also asked to tag each photo "past," "present," or "future," adding a layer of analysis and reflection to the task. The invitation to make choices about what to capture, how to frame the shot, and what to write as a caption involved cognitive and emotive processing that surpasses—or is at least profoundly different from—engaging in critical debate. Photography directs attention to the external world: it invites looking, noticing, and analyzing. The act of then selecting photographs provides opportunity to probe another analytical vantage point on the experience and its intellectual or affective resonances. In this way, different features of the city were first observed, then made meaningful through the captions, later to become empirical evidence equal to the scientific and technical information provided by FCT organizers and experts.

After the tour, during the third gathering of the participant group, the hundreds of photos were printed out and placed around the meeting room. Over the course of three hours, the citizens worked on three different tasks with the photos. First, they were asked to select three photos tagged "past" that mattered most to them, and then discuss in small groups how they see that past persisting. Next, all of the photos tagged "present" were stuck to a large wall and the participants were instructed to select one "positive" and one "negative" image and then explain, in writing, their choices. Finally, participants were invited to select several photos from the "future" pile, and then place them on a wall overlaid with a matrix (time × desirability). The matrix ran on the x-axis from now to 50 years, and on the y-axis from desirable to undesirable. Thus, the participants were asked to select, from the hundreds of photos tagged "future," those images that resonated most with them, and then give their reasoning or feeling about when the representation crops up and with either desirable or undesirable implications. The resulting timelines offered a collage of their collective imagination about the future of their city.

Encountering Diverse Perspectives

Another important feature of the tour is the varied interaction that the citizens have with community leaders, prominent stakeholders, and scientific experts in nontraditional settings to encourage shared inquiry. Prior to the tour, we identified, recruited, and coached at least one expert and one stakeholder who met the citizen group at each of the tour stops. Across the 2013 national sites, citizens visited people at scientific laboratories, maker spaces, heating and cooling facilities, freeway underpasses, and community gardens and had the opportunity to pose questions, initiate discussions, and offer their critiques, hopes, and fears to the engineers, policymakers, or scientific guides specially invited to interact at each location.

In addition to the live interactions with others, the participants also confronted each other's viewpoints in a wide variety of ways. For instance, the use of photography enabled a means to share perspectives, both in terms of which sights prompted a shot to the captions crafted to express the reasoning behind the shot. In the deliberative session, organizers created an opportunity to juxtapose differing viewpoints. For example, participants drafted a reflection—either positive or negative in tone—in relation to a "present" photo of their choosing. Their reflections were then posted on a common wall where the photographs all hung so that multiple interpretations of a single image could coexist. Ambiguities were left in place, and the whole group could observe how a single image can evoke hopes and fears, disappointment or pleasure.

Power in Participatory Digital and Visual Methods

We now turn to a discussion of how well the FCT methods functioned to build reflexivity through an examination of the nature of participation enabled throughout the project, and of our use of digital and visual techniques with attention to issues of power and ethics. Our goal in using these methods has been to disturb routine habits of mind and perception and to bring participants into closer contact with material aspects of their cities as a means to spark new agenda setting and fresh conversations about public needs and priorities. We wish to explore how these different experiences and modes of communication function in this context of technology assessment, and to especially focus on the use of photography as a deliberative prop.

The Nature of Participation in the FCTs

The tour format enables both formal and informal mixing of our invited experts and recruited citizens, with much of the informal occurring in interstitial moments when no expert was "on stage." Walking about allows for both conversation and the more solitary act of photography. Since the scientists or other guests were invited to join the subsequent tour stops, there was ample opportunity for further exchange, unscripted conversations, and joint inquiry. To give a sense of the nature of participation during the tour, consider a moment during the tour in Springfield, MA:

> Late in the afternoon, a school busload of participants and graduate student organizers emptied out into the courtyard of a nearly abandoned mill compound. We cast back the sash of a sliding industrial door and followed one another up three concrete flights of stairs. One student hung behind to help a participant brandishing a cane, letting him know that he was not required to make this last stop, but he insisted on climbing down and meeting the others. One by one we crowded into a dimly lit space, a haphazard machine shop with three large rows of steel industrial tables covered in circuitry, machine tools, and gadgets. We were greeted by a handful of women and men in rolled shirtsleeves who stood at the ready in the shop by instruments, poised to explain how each worked. A tall, casually dressed African-American man stood in the middle walkway with his arms crossed. As we approached, he turned his head toward us in welcome and seemed to brighten in a certain way from the moment before as he talked to one of the machinists. This

man was a material scientist from UMass Amherst who researches the design and use of high-performance polymers that impact advanced microelectronics. He had arrived at our stop early and was meeting the machinists for the first time. We had landed at our last stop on the tour among the Geek Group of Western Massachusetts, a local maker space owned and maintained by local Springfield residents who share a love of machining and making. Our material scientist host had come to talk with us about a cutting-edge technique for roll-to-roll manufacture, a way of making low-cost, large-area nanomaterials and devices for applications like water purification and filtration, batteries, and thin film photovoltaics. While the crowd stood around patiently as the engineer finished his talk, scattered talking and laughing broke out just as the Geek group began to demonstrate their own inventions, including a handmade 3D printer and a Van de Graaff generator. People milled about the space every which way and our engineer stayed too, strolling casually among the tools and excitement.

These seemingly impromptu gatherings were the types of joint inquiries that organizers sought; yet, the significance of this sort of fluid exchange is difficult to quantify. In post-survey data, participants reported that they valued having access to knowledgeable people whom they might not have a chance to meet and in places they rarely visit.

Intervening as participatory action research, the FCTs consciously construct a public around specific staged interactions rather than becoming involved with an existing social or political group or community. Most technology assessment involving the public takes the disinterested citizen as its most valued participant. FCT broadens the conception of the ideal participant by taking a "hybrid forum" (Callon 2009) as its model, where both knowledgeable experts and lay participants learn together and identify issues of mutual concern. The FCTs attend to social power differentials in this hybrid public by organizing information and expertise to support citizen-set agendas. This type of exchange is a foundation for what Guston has called "capacity building," a civic sensitivity that is "not about scoring political points or winning elections, but…understanding what's important for ourselves, our fellow citizens, and our communities" (Guston 2014, 57). The Springfield example demonstrates how this technique works well to mix the group.

However, traditional power relationships did crop up, due perhaps to personality differences among lay and expert participants, experts' comfort levels at communicating specialist information to general audiences, and the expectations of participants themselves. As Davies (2011) diagnoses in her review of engagement practices, participants tend to maintain an expert/lay divide. For example, during a site visit on one of the Phoenix tours focused on nanotechnology and water filtration, we met several scientists on the banks of the canal system that runs through the city. We were surprised to note that as the scientists began to share their stories about how nanotechnology might change how we process gray water, the participant group took several steps back and became an impromptu audience in a semicircle around the speakers, remaining silent until the remarks concluded.

Photography as Reflexivity

The use of photography in the FCTs revealed influential power dynamics. On the one hand, the use of photography is liberating in that it brings into the conversation thoughts or ideas that might not be readily expressed. Values rise to the surface as renewable energy options or farmer's markets are explored. Yet on the other hand, one could argue that photography relies too heavily on what can be seen and imaged in the environment. In a sense, the visual becomes authoritative knowledge; what is seen becomes the evidence. If there are no drones in downtown Portland, does the military industrial complex get discussed? Some topics that cannot be summoned from the environment might be left unexamined.

In other words, images have sway and are directly linked to what can be observed. Yet underneath the images shot by participants are loaded meanings and memories. One photograph may reveal a little-remembered detail about the former use of a now-abandoned building, leading to a creative discussion that recovers a potentially robust repurposing of the space. But the photographs can also constrain creativity. For example, in Springfield, MA, images of the city's derelict train station recurred and bounded discussions of transportation in the city more generally. It was difficult for the participants to shift their thinking beyond the relics of a system that had long since ceased to serve them. In this sense, it is fair to say that photography can raise *and* ruin reflexivity. While photography in the dialogue setting can be very powerful in amplifying the concerns of underserved, quiet, or overlooked community members, it can also continue to lend legitimacy to longstanding discourses in the city, or even relevant national issues, that should instead be challenged or reimagined.

Conclusions

The chief goal of the Futurescape City Tours is to experiment with participatory visual and digital methods to enhance the quality and depth of citizen engagement in relation to questions about the role of nanotechnology and other emerging technologies. Our higher-order goal is to amplify citizens' skills to engage with complex technological subjects and to develop and articulate their own views. This aim connects with Langdon Winner's (1986) suggestion that to live well in this technologically mediated "megapolis," it is crucial to trigger collective reflection on the subaltern desires and designs of our sociotechnical system. Asking questions publically about, for instance, how the existence of surveillance systems subtly changes our behavior on the streets (perhaps even without us noticing) is an important role for the engaged citizen. Winner (1986) warns that since technology acts as a sort of legislation, shaping many aspects of contemporary existence, reaching from our civil liberties at the voting booth to end-of-life choices in the hospital, being socially responsible means being alert to the relationship between technology and our freedom and wellbeing. There is a new necessity to be reflective, to question routines, and to make serious inquiries, rather than to merely observe and react to the ebb and flow of the technological mediations in daily life.

As a practice-based research project, the FCT experiments with both digital and analog media to support civic reflexivity and public engagement with emerging technologies. In doing so, it responds to STS approaches to public engagement and models a methodology that more effectively harnesses the collective imagination to make transparent, share, and hopefully subvert business as usual. In participatory technology assessment, where events are more rare and contrived around elusive issues of scientific and technological impact, as well as in community engaged research, where knowledge develops iteratively through long term relationship building, new techniques are needed for revealing community assumptions and cultivating critical reflexivity. In our example of FCT, techniques for subverting routine perceptions of how the city and its technologies work provide an example for how participatory visual and digital methods work. At heart, they are about noticing differently and sharing fresh perspectives through collaborative inquiry.

REFERENCES

Barben, D., E. Fisher, C. Selin, and D. Guston. 2008. Anticipatory Governance of Nanotechnology: Foresight, Engagement, and Integration. In *The Handbook of*

Science and Technology Studies, edited by E. J. Hackett, O. Amsterdamska, M. E. Lynch, et al., 979–1000. Cambridge, MA: MIT Press.

Davies, Sarah R. 2011. The Rules of Engagement: Power and Interaction in Dialogue Events. *Public Understanding of Science* 22(1): 65–79.

Davies, Sarah R., Cynthia Selin, Gretchen Gano, and Ângela Guimarães Pereira. 2012. Citizen Engagement and Urban Change: Three Case Studies of Material Deliberation. *Cities* 29(6): 351–357.

———. 2013. Finding Futures: A Spatio-Visual Experiment In Participatory Engagement. *Leonardo* 46(1): 76–77.

Gubrium, Aline, and Krista Harper. 2013. *Participatory Visual and Digital Methods*. Walnut Creek, CA: Left Coast Press.

Guston, D. H., and D. Sarewitz. 2002. Real-Time Technology Assessment. *Technology in Society* 24(1–2): 93–109.

Guston, David H. 2014. Building the Capacity for Public Engagement with Science in the United States. *Public Understanding of Science* 23(1): 53–59.

Latour, Bruno. 1999. *Pandora's Hope: Essays on the Reality of Science Studies*. Cambridge, MA: Harvard University Press.

Miller, Thaddeus, R. Timothy, D. Baird, Caitlin M. Littlefield, Gary Kofinas, F. Stuart Chapin III, and Charles L. Redman. 2008. Epistemological Pluralism: Reorganizing Interdisciplinary Research. *Ecology and Society* 13(2): 46.

Mumford, Lewis. 1961. *The City in History: Its Origins, Its Transformations, and Its Prospects*. New York: Harcourt, Brace and World, Inc.

Selin, Cynthia, and Jennifer Banks. 2014. *Futurescape City Tours: A Novel Method for Public Engagement. Guidebook for Practitioners*. Tempe, AZ: Center for Nanotechnology in Society, Arizona State University.

Touraine, Alain. 1983. *Anti-Nuclear Protest: The Opposition to Nuclear Energy in France*. Cambridge, UK, Paris: Cambridge University Press, Editions de la Maison des Sciences de l'Homme.

Wang, Caroline, and Mary Ann Burris. 1997. Photovoice: Concept, Methodology, and Use for Participatory Needs Assessment. *Health Education & Behavior* 24(3): 369–387.

Wiek, Arnim, Rider W. Foley, and David H. Guston. 2012. Nanotechnology for Sustainability: What Does Nanotechnology Offer to Address Complex Sustainability Problems? *Journal of Nanoparticle Research* 14(9): 1–20.

Winner, Langdon. 1986. *The Whale and the Reactor: A Search for Limits in an Age of High Technology*. Chicago, IL: University of Chicago Press.

Young, Iris Marion. 2001. Activist Challenges to Deliberative Democracy. *Political Theory* 29(5): 670–690.

NOTE

1 While we explored the notion of "competent outsiders" (Feinstein 2011) and considered recruiting highly involved civic leaders, we decided to prioritize demographic balance instead. We noticed that many of our applicants were those who regularly engage in civic life.

PART

Participatory Video

In Our Grandmothers' Garden: An Indigenous Approach to Collaborative Film

Charles R. Menzies

Digital image technologies have swept across all sectors of our society. In a few short years technologies once beyond the technical and financial reach of most people have become ubiquitous. The camera in my iPhone takes a higher resolution image than my first "high-res" digital camera did at a fraction of the cost. Having always had an inclination toward the visual, I too took the plunge into digital video production. The ability to link active research with community through a tangible and understandable research output was beguiling. Yet my initial attempt is, I think, a great example of why enthusiasm and enterprise are no substitution for knowledge and expertise.

I very much like my first film, *Working in the Woods* (2002), even though it is a thoroughly bad film. In fact, I would suggest it is a textbook case of bad filmmaking: poor framing of subjects (most of which are talking-head shots), horrible sound quality, terrible color composition…the list goes on. The only redeeming qualities are the artful editing of my collaborator Jennifer Rashleigh and the endearing commentary by the film's key character, Dorothy Anderson.

The experience of making *Working in the Woods* taught me several important lessons that have come to guide my subsequent forays into digital film production. At the heart of this realization was a recognition that 1) film technique is critical and 2) simply translating the research interview to digital videotape misses the potential of the digital medium. Too often social science researchers pick up digital equipment and proceed as though it is simply a multimodal audio recorder or, worse, a pen and notebook. Big mistake.

That said: I have learned my lesson, and the films I now produce prioritize a collaborative perspective. This is especially critical given my work with and for indigenous communities.

My approach is a combination of the longstanding Canadian tradition of documentary filmmaking established by the mid-twentieth century National Film Board of Canada and digital pastiche. The first approach locates my take within a well-established tradition of filmmaking, an approach that conceives of film as having a clear narrative structure with a beginning, middle, and end. This is an approach driven by a filmic aesthetic that relies upon a directorial attention to detail within the domain of an overarching vision. But, given the technological flexibility of digital media we can, as it were, have our cake and eat it too. That is, we can maintain the directorial view and disarticulate and segment the medium into pieces that can live outside of—even in opposition to—the director's vision. We achieve this through the combination of distributing video vignettes via online platforms and by producing longer, classically structured documentaries.

As an anthropologist, my interest in filmmaking emerged from my focus on collaborative research projects. My focus on collaboration arises out of my subject location as a person of indigenous descent.[1] The camera, as described earlier, was an addition to the process, not the starting point. This sets me apart from the dominant trend in North American visual anthropology. Whereas a great many other visual anthropologists begin with the idea of film as central to their work and production, the camera has been an adjunct to my own research, and its value lies in its capacity to reach a more general public. This does create some problems in which the "theoretical" aspect of my work focuses upon collaboration rather than discursive and self-reflexive nods to postmodernist anthropology, thus rendering my films less comprehensible to mainstream North American visual anthropologists. That is, some mainstream visual anthropologists have criticized my work and see a naive realism at the core of my films in my assertion of the importance of a directorial vision routed in a fidelity to the reality that I observe. I have more to say on this later, but let me turn to what I see as the significance of this approach to a social anthropology that matters.

Since the so-called crisis of representation in anthropology (Marcus and Fisher 1986), anthropologists have fretted with a dual concern: How do we attend to the voice and desires of those we study while simultaneously asserting a constructivist and "fictive" (à la Geertz) antirealist approach to writing up our ethnographic research? This is, to a certain extent, a false duality that has led mainstream anthropology down a cul-de-sac of self-indulgence and flights of representational fancy. As the mainstream academy attacks the principles of reliable and robust social science, a minority of scholars has followed a different path rooted in collaborative, community-based research.[2]

My primary field research involves working with, and on behalf of, indigenous peoples of the Pacific Northwest. The questions that I address, while mundane in terms of the dominant tendencies of the discipline, are of critical importance for the peoples I work with: How long has a particular community lived within its traditional territories? What types of resources were harvested, and are they still being harvested? How were goods transported, how far, and for what purpose?

Answering these types of questions requires more than critical theory: it requires solid, empirical research methods. My work is tied to a documentary style of ethnography in which I write empirically grounded reports that are linked to defending and advancing the rights and title of indigenous communities. This is not an a-theoretical enterprise. In my academic work I make a point of drawing upon relevant theoretical models and approaches (see, for example, Menzies 2013). I am not adverse to a reflective style in prose when warranted. Nor am I saying there is no place for textual exploration or high theory: indeed there is. My point is that given the type of research that I do, I need to be able to ensure a reasonable fit between my reports and comments and an observable reality. I need to be reasonably certain that another observer reviewing the same materials as I have will come to a similar conclusion. That requires a kind of empirical groundedness that has been lacking of late within mainstream anthropology and cultural studies. Film production is a central aspect of this endeavor.

My film work encompasses three general facets: 1) traditional narrative documentary; 2) community video; and 3) video vignettes. Traditional documentary should require little elaboration. It is, simply put, my voice and storytelling of the social worlds that I film. The community videos are designed much in the same manner as my documentaries, but their primary audience is the subject community and the process is far more collaborative and consultative. Finally, the video vignettes are movie snapshots destined for the realm of digital ephemera. They are loosely edited, cut from the cloth of the more elaborate documentaries and community videos and sent "out there" via online platforms that allow each piece to take on a life of its own. The vignettes arise out of the process of making documentaries and community videos, but are adaptable to the frenetic pace of the consumer download. Sometimes we package the vignettes as teaching aids; other times they are simply addressed to the growing global corpus of public videos.

Case Studies

I have selected three examples that highlight the three facets of my work: *Bax Laansk—Pulling Together* (2011), *a Story of Gitxaała* (a documentary); *Gathering Strength* (2014; a community video); and the YouTube video playlist *In My Grandmothers' Garden* (2009; vignettes).

Bax Laansk—Pulling Together

Bax Laansk (https://vimeo.com/charlesmenzies/baxlaansk) is a classic documentary. I shot this film with my colleague Jennifer Rashleigh. Together we worked out the story arc, Jennifer did the editing, and I facilitated community reviews and discussions of the film (including initial permissions to produce the film). The ultimate directorial decision-making rested with me.

Initially we had planned on a more collaborative approach. We floated ideas of involving youth, setting up community advisory boards, reviewing footage as it was shot. At one point a cousin, who was involved on the research committee, put a stop to all of that. "You do your film," she told me. "What we need are movies of people doing things. We can add our own explanation when we use it." She went on to explain that collaboration takes a lot of time from community. There are moments when those with the skills should just get going and do what needs to be done. So that's what we did.

In this film we use filmic devices to signal key points in the story arc. The opening is a montage overlaid with community voices that declare that the land and water belong to Gitxaała. The tone shifts as a litany of complaints against colonialism are laid out. Then everything slows down as we move through a series of vignettes spotlighting the contemporary community of traditional producers. Midway through the film the tone, pace, and imagery again shift. A voiceover comes in, and we move back to the theme of colonial disruption and industrial resource extraction. Here we learn that even as Gitxaała society was disrupted, there was pride in the community's resilience and adaptability in the face of significant disruption. The film is brought to a close with a future-facing, optimistic vision that emphasizes the importance of cultural rediscovery and growth. Thus we have a statement, a director's vision of being contemporary and indigenous: while much has changed, we remain here and we remain Indians.

Gathering Strength

Gathering Strength (https://vimeo.com/charlesmenzies/gathering) is a community video shot specifically for and at the request of Gitxaała's health agency. The film documents Gitxaała youth's participation in an annual long-distance canoe journey. Prior to the journey I met with the community organizing team to determine their objectives and expectations for the film. These discussions laid the basis of the instructions for the videographer, Maryel Sparks-Cardinal (at the time, a recent University of British Columbia [UBC] graduate). Following the trip I reviewed the footage with Maryel and then consulted again with the community organizing team once I had an impression of the nature of the footage collected from the journey. From there, my colleague Jennifer Rashleigh began the process of logging, assembling, and editing a rough cut of the film, drawing upon the discussions that I had had with the community organizing team. The community organizing team and canoe journey participants then screened a series of rough cuts. Their critiques were ultimately used to fashion the final version of the film.

The canoe journey itself is an explicit act of cultural rediscovery and an assertion of cultural continuity. This film was designed to tell the story of the youth as they learned, played, and struggled, but, most importantly, to highlight their potential for personal growth and wellbeing through a grounding in one's own culture. The film begins with the youth preparing to depart from Gitxaała. We see them being recognized by community elders and leadership. We then follow them as they travel from one coastal community and camping location to another until they finally arrive at their final destination: Metlakatla, Alaska. Along the way we use recorded narratives, speeches, and campfire storytelling to carry the primary narrative of growing through adversity and cultural awareness. The film ends with a montage of the youth participants. Because the audience is primarily local, there is little contextualizing information embedded in the film. The tone is generally upbeat and optimistic.

Our Grandmothers' Garden

This group of four video vignettes (www.youtube.com/playlist?list=PLDC4D 420B4DC80761) is adapted from our documentary *Bax Laansk*. The vignettes live in several different virtual locations: a research website hosted by UBC, YouTube, and Facebook. In each setting they have taken on a somewhat different social life with differing collective and individual impacts and histories of use. On the UBC site, the primary user (identified via site-tracking software) is based at a research institute or government agency. The usage was higher during the initial six months of posting and has generally tapered down to practically nil after three years online. With the exception of one video vignette about smoking fish, the YouTube videos circulated primarily within a Gitxaała online community. The one exception, with more than 20,000 individual views, was picked up and linked to a wider online community interested in the processing and consumption of wild meats. As posted via Facebook, the videos stayed closely linked within a Gitxaała online community, with wider circulation following social links outward to other indigenous communities and people. With both YouTube and Facebook, the videos had an intense use over their first several weeks to six months online that rapidly (again with the exception of the fish-smoking video) fell off to rare visits after a couple of years. The DVD versions of the videos circulate locally in Gitxaała and find use in the school and health center.

The underlying idea of the video vignette is to break down the master narrative of our documentary form and allow segments to be sampled and repurposed in ways that as digital authors we may not have originally considered. At the most basic level, we produce vignettes like this to support teaching and knowledge transfer in Gitxaała and through my own university-based teaching. In more complicated ways the vignettes, especially via the YouTube platform, are picked up and recirculated through networks not immediately intended.

The four short films that comprise the *Our Grandmothers' Garden* playlist focus on contemporary enactments of traditional knowledge and practices. One follows Myrna Robinson as she walks through a forested area near Gitxaała village explaining and describing plant resources to two UBC graduate students. A second follows Myrna, Annabelle Woods, and several other women as they explore an island garden that their grandmothers used to garden. Incidentally, the garden rests on top of an ancient Gitxaała habitation site. While at the garden, Myrna and Annabelle talk about the traditional gardening practices that included indigenous cultivars as well as new plants brought by Europeans. Cyril Astor narrates the third film as he demonstrates peeling cedar bark from a living tree that will be used later to weave baskets and traditional regalia. The fourth film, which has a YouTube view count of more than 20,000, shows Ernie Bolton smoking fish aided by his sister, the late Alberta Jackson, and his wife, Merle Bolton. The fish-smoking video intersects with a wider wild food and meat subculture beyond the local audience, lending to the film's unique popularity. All of these films are designed with a primarily local, Gitxaała audience in mind. The topics emerge out of direct community-level interactions. While these films are a type of visual ephemera, their productive lifespan and interpretations extend beyond the limitations of the filmmakers' specific initial intentions.

Discussion

The case studies I present here reflect separate, but interconnected, aspects of my approach to film. Each case study reflects a different degree of community participation and collaboration, a different approach to the deployment of visual technology, and different ethical considerations. Taken separately, none of the case studies fully meets with my sense of an appropriate approach to film within my sense of what it means to be both anthropologist and indigenous.

Participation and Collaboration

Collaborative research is a guiding principle that underwrites much of my approach to research. Yet, there are gradients of collaboration: there are times when one needs to take instruction (essentially to act as directed), and others when one needs to express one's own point of view. Approaches that try prioritizing one extreme over the other are, in my opinion, impoverished research approaches. We need both. This does require that one's corpus be considered in its totality, rather than piecemeal, something that as a creator one can't always control.

Of the three case studies, the video vignettes are the most collaborative in terms of selection, production, and ultimate use. Community participation was present from the initial inceptions through to the final use. The idea behind the video vignettes is for the filmmaker to relinquish control and draw upon the power and inspiration of collaborative participation. While some of our video vignettes are drawn directly from longer documentaries, most are produced first as vignettes with direct community input and then later integrated into the larger film project. During production, discussions were held with participants and local knowledge holders to identify what would have most value locally as vignettes. Once we had collaboratively decided that, our production team did the filming and editing and then posted to the specified online platforms. From the online platforms, those who linked, shared, sampled, and recirculated the videos on their own transformed the use and interpretation of the vignettes.

Bax Laansk was the least collaborative in terms of filming, writing, and editing. Though we began with an idea that it would be an explicitly collaborative project, we came to the realization that it made more sense to use it as a vehicle of our own directorial voice and then pull out separate video vignettes that appealed more directly to community interests and desires. First, researchers often overlook the community effort required to be collaborative. It might seem like a great idea to fully engage community members in all aspects of film production. However, community members often do not have the time available to devote to such a project, whereas the researchers are typically being paid by their university or through the deferred payment of earning a graduate degree that will, they hope, lead to their ultimate employment. Second, video vignettes are a more flexible and malleable medium, shorter (both in full-length and production input) and thus more amenable to collaborative community involvement. *Bax Laansk* was thus a film defined by our vision as directors.

Gathering Strength, however, was the opposite of a director-led film. While not specifically a commissioned film (we had a degree of license not typical for commissioned films), we were producing a video on behalf of and for Gitxaała. In that sense our specific filmic interests were less important than cultivating community sentiments and desires through the film.

As a group of interrelated film projects, these projects allow for a more holistic and sincere filmic view of Gitxaała. Varying degrees of collaboration and community participation allow for a creative intermix of points of view linked through a common corpus of film and textual materials. If I had relied upon only one approach—say, a community-based method—and had silenced my own voice in the process, I fear the films would have been deficient. Better to have a diversity of perspective, however dissonant the outcome, than a false uniformity of view.

Visual Technology

The core tool that we use in our filmmaking is a high-definition digital video camera. Whereas some collaborative film projects deploy small, handheld consumer devices or high-end digital SLRs, my preference is for using a camera that "looks" like a video camera and that also provides a high-quality output. This is consistent with my approach to anthropological fieldwork. The anthropologists should, I believe, ensure that those one is studying know they are being studied and observed. This is an ethical principle for me. Too often anthropologists have been accused of (and found out to be) engaging in surreptitious research, which is almost never appropriate to do. Clearly, surreptitious research is inappropriate in an indigenous context, where it is akin to theft. Using cameras that cannot be confused with cell phones or retail devices is the technical parallel to holding a pen and notebook obviously in one's hands while doing research. Using high-quality cameras also provides a quality output, which gives us more flexibility in output and final use when it comes to editing and producing our films.

The camera and editing suite is not my central instrument of research, but rather a complementary tool that comes later in the process and in such a way as to extend the potential of the moment of research. I begin with observational research directly: no camera. I participate, talk, engage, and watch as things unfold through the normal course of life. Then, once I have developed an understanding of what is taking place, I start working with the camera. This allows me to identify people who have a certain presence, a comfort working in the research moment and on camera. I also find it important to begin filming from a perspective of understanding rather than using the camera to accumulate images and moments out of which to build a filmic understanding. I firmly believe that technological processes should be adapted to the underlying research approach, not the other way around.

My filmmaking and deployment of visual technologies is adapted to my idea of an observational mode of research. I need to understand the context, the people (their culture and personality), the problems, the processes, and the minutiae of daily life *before* I can begin to film. Some filmic approaches (anthropological and documentary) combine observing with filming. For me, I want to construct a film that resonates with the reality that I wish to represent, but I would rather do my initial observations without the camera in hand. I like to be able to identify people who will have a presence in the frame and who will be able to convey the essence of their world without seeming forced or contrived in the way that most talking-head interview styles do. This approach underlies all three of the case studies described in this chapter.

Where my deployment of visual technologies diverges in these case studies is in the domain of distribution and dissemination. Clearly, in our contemporary context all of these films are displayed online through various platforms. However, as the audiences for each film product are slightly different, I deploy different means to distribute the products described in the case studies. The approach to the documentaries and the community videos are similar: packaged DVDs are sold. Yet, the documentary is targeted to an audience wider than just Gitxaała. The community videos are solely distributed within the community of account, here being Gitxaała. The video vignettes are the most different in this sense.

For the video vignettes, I purposefully distribute them through a range of online platforms. *Our Grandmothers' Garden* is broadcast via YouTube and a UBC website. But other video vignettes have been distributed through sites as diverse as 4chan, bebo (nonexistent today), Twitter, Facebook, or Vine (very, very short vignettes). The idea is to disseminate these products as widely as is conceivable.

In the community of account (in this case, Gitxaała) we distribute by whatever means is possible: VHS, DVD, mp4, and so on. The idea is to release the material so that it can take on its own life within the community. I have seen our video vignettes played on phones, passed around on CDs, and sampled and inserted (sometimes with credit, sometimes not) into home videos that are then posted onto YouTube. It's a chaotic deployment of techniques, but one that ensures that I can hold onto my own voice while simultaneously relinquishing control to others as they express their own sense of indigeneity.

Ethical Considerations

My ongoing research in collaboration with Gitxaała Nation has its formal roots in a research agreement in 2001 (Menzies 2004). The crux of the agreement was that my research team and I were effectively licensed to use the data that we collected (be it oral, documentary, or video) for the production of research reports, papers, films, and so on. However, the data itself—the knowledge, information, histories, and images—belong to Gitxaała and can be used by Gitxaała members according to internal culturally appropriate protocols. This approach undergirds all of my subsequent research with Gitxaała and informs my approach to research with other communities, be they indigenous or not. This meta-level ethical approval does not obviate the need to pay attention to ethical considerations in the context of each particular project, nor does it relieve one of the need to consider the ways in which differing levels of collaboration shape ethical concerns in practice.

At a starting level, every project is guided by a multilayer approval process: approval of the community decision-making authority, approval of an individual (or group as appropriate) for filming and interviewing, approval from the individual for the manner in which they are represented in the film, and finally approval by the community decision-making authority.

This ensures a continuous interactive process of review and consent as the film project is being developed.

Some might criticize this approach as limiting or restricting independent scholarship. I suppose they may be right if they consider that the right of the researcher supersedes all other concerns. However, ethical research practices have long since established some very basic guidelines that all social science research must adhere to, primarily cause no harm and the idea of prior informed consent. Our protocols are not just compliant with the form of respectful ethical research, but they also embody the content of ethical research. It has been my experience over more than two decades of research that embodying respectful research practices enhances the ultimate outcomes. It is slower, more time consuming, and at times fraught with what feel like setbacks in the moment. However, the quality of our outcomes makes it clearly worthwhile.

The ethical concerns that most concern me relate to the circulation of information that occurs through the use of online platforms. There is much benefit in these technologies of distribution. Yet, the very aspects of the technologies that inspire me to use them also trouble me: widespread, indiscriminate distribution. I have no solution to this particular dilemma other than to withhold my final judgment, to observe, and to consider the risks and benefits of diving into the great ocean of Internet distribution.

Final Words

As an indigenous scholar and filmmaker, I want my works to speak to a social reality that is observable. I insist on a fidelity to a reality that is clearly out there. For me, this is a world in which my uncle can jokingly light a smokehouse fire in a pink ceramic bathtub with a propane lighter and call it "an Indian match." This is a world in which the histories of lineage groups of the millennia-distant past intertwine in the world of contemporary village basketball. This is a world that can only reveal itself through the artful use of life, observation, patience, and the desire to return home over and over again.

Not every researcher can pick up this sort of approach. To a certain extent this is an approach that is idiosyncratically rooted in my own life experience and professional practice. I would caution others from trying to use my reflections and ruminations as a blueprint for their own work. Rather, I would ask that you consider my words, view my films, and then develop your own approach. Borrow, sample, rearrange as you find appropriate. Ultimately, my desire is to inspire in others a similar love and appreciation of creative possibility.

My films and my written works are stories rooted in real lives and real events. They emerge from the colonial entanglements and encounters that litter human history. The power of film is that it allows us a creative intervention into storytelling that helps address the problem of information and reports that Walter Benjamin so eloquently noted in his paper about the storyteller (1969). Film, in its multitude of forms, returns the power of storytelling to both audience and filmmaker, especially when one can cut and recut and distribute pieces and vignettes of our work. Writing as though telling stories has been at the heart of my work for many years. Yet it is only in the filmic genre that I believe the storytelling mode can truly take on its full potential.

REFERENCES

Benjamin, Walter. 1969. The Storyteller: Reflections on the Works of Nikolai Leskov. In *Illuminations*, edited by Hannah Arendt, 83–109. New York: Schocken Books.

Marcus, George, and Michael Fischer. 1986. *Anthropology as Cultural Critique: An Experimental Moment in the Human Sciences.* Chicago, IL: University of Chicago Press.

Menzies, Charles R. 2004. Putting Words into Action: Negotiating Collaborative Research in Gitxaała. *Canadian Journal of Native Education* 27(3): 15–32.

———. 2013. Standing on the Shore with Saaban: An Anthropological Rapprochement with an Indigenous Intellectual Tradition. *Collaborative Anthropologies* 6: 171–199.

NOTES

1   I am a member of Gitxaała Nation. I am also, due to the quirks of colonial history, an enrolled member of the Tlingit and Haida Tribes of Alaska.

2   I am here referring to three strands or paradigms within social science research: a reflexive postmodernist stream; a mainstream social science as "science" stream; and an approach that prioritizes collaborative community-based research models. There is more that could be said, but this is not the best forum to elaborate. I outline my specific approach in more details in a paper called "Standing on the Shore with Sabaan" (Menzies 2013).

A Hard Way Out: Improvisational Film and Youth Participatory Action Research

Jean Schensul and Campbell Dalglish

Most anthropologists who publish on educational topics are employed by schools of education to train students in the use of ethnography to improve educational practices. They also may contribute to curricula and educational policy. There is, however, a vast arena of applied educational work conducted by anthropologists and educational ethnographers that falls outside of these pursuits. This includes the invention and implementation of curricula for out-of-school learning, museum exhibits and other interactive displays, innovative ways of representing research results to the public, and new ways of engaging publics in conducting their own research for interventions and advocacy (Schensul 2011). In this chapter we focus on the relationship between youth participatory action research (YPAR) and improvisational filmmaking as a pedagogical approach to increasing public voice among youth experiencing social, economic, and educational disparities by offering them a unique means of engaging different publics with their research and lived experience.

Youth Participatory Action Research and Transformational Curricula

Anthropologists and critical educators have described transformational approaches to education of young people designed to address justice and equity at the individual, group, and social levels. YPAR is an often-cited approach, and critical pedagogy is the most coherent framework through

Jean Schensul and Campbell Dalglish, *"A Hard Way Out:* Improvisational Film and Youth Participatory Action Research" in *Participatory Visual and Digital Research in Action,* Aline Gubrium, Krista Harper, and Marty Otañez, eds., pp. 115-128. © 2015 Left Coast Press, Inc. All rights reserved.

which to frame transformational curricula (Berg et al. 2009; Schensul 2011, 2012; Schensul and Berg 2004; Schensul et al. 2004). Darder and colleagues have noted that critical pedagogy directs youth to recognize that their beliefs about what is normative and unchangeable are culturally/socially constructed, as are their responses to it, and that they have the right to act in an informed way to bring about changes in undemocratic structures and practices (Darder et al. 2003, 9). Through a cycle of dialogue, reflection, and action youth can become empowered via collective questioning of dominant narratives and explanations to develop critical consciousness (Freire 1970). This process is essential for involving youth in civic engagement through transformational change to address unjust circumstances (Freire 2008). A rounded approach to critical pedagogical practice includes a careful analysis of all sources of inequality, including race, ethnicity, gender, age, political hegemony, and other forms of power and dominance (Giroux 1989).

While much is written about the potential for critical pedagogical practice, the methodology for bringing about these processes through YPAR remains opaque. Cammarota and Fine's edited collection on YPAR is a significant exception (Cammarota and Fine 2010). None of the authors in this volume, however, introduces participatory filmmaking or performance improvisation as methods for critical YPAR. YPAR as practiced by the Institute for Community Research (ICR) is a transformational approach to education in and out of school (Berg et al. 2009; Schensul 2012; Schensul et al. 2004). Using constructivist facilitation approaches, group problem-solving, and unique applications of ethnographic methods attuned to youth, ICR produces critical consciousness, youth voice, collective efficacy, and ongoing incremental social change while developing basic skills in reading, writing, communications, mathematics, and social development among youth participants.

Critical performance ethnography (Denzin 2003) engages actors in the performance of ethnographic interpretation to illustrate cultural processes or disseminate the results of research to broader audiences. Performance ethnography is inconsistent in its engagement of the audience either in dialogue or to generate additional data. Within the domain of critical performance, the best known approach is the Theatre of the Oppressed (TO), which involves creating a theatrical piece that addresses contradictions or structural/social issues and offering the audience an opportunity to engage by improvising alternative endings (Boal 1992). Filmmakers have also used this approach (Rothschild 2014), and it is not uncommon in classroom settings (Howard 2004). The TO approach is based on principles similar to critical pedagogy:

participation of the group affected by structural inequities in theatre as authentic actors and reflectors based on their lived experience; group definition of the narrative through dialogue; continued dialogue with the audience as a means of reflection; and movement toward action. Most examples of TO, however, are derived primarily from the lived experiences of the actors and do not include activist-engaged research through YPAR.

In our approach, filmmaking using participatory improvisational techniques integrates critical pedagogy, performance ethnography, and critical theatre. The addition of youth-driven ethnographic research through interviewing and observation introduces differences of perspective and enriches the story narrative by integrating participant-actors' learned and lived experiences. The research process engages youth with others, building their social skills and critical analytic capacity. Filmmaking increases the potential for disseminating the message to multiple audiences while still integrating dialogue, reflection, and action. Further, participatory filmmaking based on critical research, analysis, and improvisation can be integrated into social media approaches to mobilizing public attention to the issue and consequent action both on the ground and via the Internet (cf. Cohen et al. 2013). The links among social media, popular education, audiovisual products, participatory action research, and social movements are nascent in educational anthropology and need to be nurtured to result in transformational change within schools and communities. Below we provide a case example that moves in this direction.

A-Ha Moments: YPAR and Improvisational Filmmaking

One of us (Jean Schensul) is an applied medical anthropologist with a methodology and educational background. She is based at ICR, an organization she founded in 1987 and built with others to use the "tools" of research (theory, methods, results, dissemination) in collaboration with communities and organizations to promote justice and equity in a diverse world. ICR is unique in representing a crossroads for university-trained researchers working for community change and community stakeholders and residents who share the same goals. ICR is located in Hartford, Connecticut, a city of about 120,000 residents, with an economy in steady decline stemming from the demise of industry in the northeastern United States. YPAR has been an important part of ICR's work since its inception. Using a "multiple intelligences" framework

(Gardner 1999), we integrate various art forms into the research process and as a means of disseminating results. The film project we describe in this chapter was ICR's first attempt at using participatory improvisational film in moving the ICR YPAR transformational agenda forward.

The Teen Action Research Project (TARP), a five-year program funded by the Center for Substance Abuse Prevention, arose as a response to drug-related violence rampant in Hartford's neighborhoods in the early 1990s. A collaboration of ICR and three youth-serving community organizations reached African-American, Latino, and other youth in three different areas of the city. In a yearlong prevention program, youth learned about the drug trade and drug abuse, and to view themselves as change agents in their communities. Each group was required to conduct a YPAR project. The overall intervention was theoretically grounded in social learning and self-efficacy theory (Bandura 1994), as well as theories of empowerment (Watts et al. 2011) and community organizing (Christens and Dolan 2011). It was based on the idea that collective youth involvement in research and action on substance use were more likely to develop antidrug norms and reduce their own drug risk behavior (Berg et al. 2009).

TARP youth carried out mapping exercises, observations, and in-depth interviews with their peers and adult allies on the history of violence, instances of community violence, and exposure to and fears about experiencing violence associated with the burgeoning drug trade in their neighborhood. Beyond their own personal experiences, they learned from these data how the drug/violence interface was affecting other youth and adults. They were intent on using their knowledge to reduce gang- and drug-related violence.

At the point where they were considering their actions, Schensul met Campbell Dalglish, a filmmaker and graduate of the Yale School of Drama, then teaching filmmaking at New York University (NYU). Similar to Schensul's perspective on research and voice, Dalglish believed that, as actors, youth could perform their roles more deeply if they created the storyline and script themselves based on their data and their personal and community experiences. Chowdhury and colleagues (2010) confirm that improvisation may produce a less-polished result but gives actors more voice in the process and product. Together, Schensul and Dalglish created a plan to work with youth researchers to produce a film based on research, collaborative scriptwriting, and improvisation.

Campbell, an activist educator and filmmaker, had a background in theatre skills: improvisation, mime, voice, modern dance, theatre, and songwriting. He honed his conflict resolution skills in Connecticut by working with youth in prisons, juvenile delinquent centers, inner-city schools, and many different K-12 programs in New Haven. In doing so he found that youth expressed their stories by acting out characters that were at once real, entertaining, and informative. One of his early "a-ha" moments was recognizing the importance of getting the youth as actors in front of an audience. Skilled in coordinating with other resources, he linked with public access television, which is mandated to provide workshops for public programming. His students recounted how they were deeply affected by seeing their lives, communities, and even relatives' stories reflected on public TV, and he was able to connect students' stories to a way of conveying their characters and voices through film programming. The work was inspired by Boal's Theatre of the Oppressed, and by Tevocoyani, a Nicaragua activist actors group (Weiss 1989) that based their community stories on immersion in the community, thereby impassioning the audience and provoking action. His encounter with Tevocoyani convinced him of the deep significance of participant observation (immersion experiences) for film scripting and directorship.

A Hard Way Out: An Improvisational Film

A Hard Way Out was filmed in 1992. The story was based on the realities of life in a large public housing project, Charter Oak Terrace (COT). COT is a community rich in history and cultural heritage, and rife with conflict. It was created to respond to the post–World War II housing needs of white veterans and later to inmigrating African Americans and Puerto Ricans (Radcliffe 1998). The housing project was affected by the discriminatory policies that led to the decline and demise of American public housing from the 1980s to the turn of the century. Neglect, disinvestment, lack of health, and transportation facilities, social isolation, and internalized stigma resulted in residents feeling conflicted about their community, and at the same time very much attached to it.

At the time of the project, the community was home to a number of older African-American and Latino gang members, imprisoned for drug dealing in the late 1970s. While in prison, they became members of larger gang networks. Newly released a decade later, these men began recruiting youth to participate in a revitalized nationally linked illicit drug trade. Youth felt compelled to join a gang for protection. Conflict between different gangs often resulted in violence, shootings, and killings. Drive-by shootings were not uncommon, and civil strife between gang rule and community resistance was ongoing. It was in this environment that our project was forged to provide an alternative for youth who wanted to avoid drug use and keep their peers from joining gangs and becoming involved in the drug trade.

With support from Schensul and the team, Dalglish began meeting with the TARP youth during their regular after-school meeting time. The goal was to enable youth to use their knowledge and experience to further explore gang violence and drug issues and craft a dramatic story to be videotaped with the assistance of Ron Gould of Connecticut Public TV (CPTV) and with video equipment and talent from NYU. The situation could not have been more volatile: one member of the TARP group had been executed in a drive-by shooting on Thanksgiving Day, and on another occasion, a drive-by shooting took place seconds before students were picked up from their homes and rushed off to the safety of the workshops.

Our method for filming included 20 sessions, broken up into five parts. In sessions 1 through 3, we explored improvisation techniques. Activities focused on character development and were based on the assumption that everyone is an actor performing their lives (i.e., performative ethnography). By understanding how one acts, one can choose to change one's actions. By exploring selves and each other through improvisation, youth created a list of "premises" for our story. Every story has a premise, and every premise represents a "changing truth." We called these "a message in a bottle." If we could tell the outside world one changing truth about ourselves, who we are and what's going on, what would that be? Youth participants were asked to respond to several questions that prompted them to analyze the interaction of causal factors and effects and their interaction in their own lives and communities. The process is consistent with YPAR's use of a research-based technique called "modeling," a process that involves youth in diagramming perceived causes of issues affecting them and their communities. In response to these questions, the group came up with many premises. We combined three of the premises for *A Hard Way Out*: 1) gang rule leads to death; 2) the only way out is to work hard and work your way out; and 3) to do this it is necessary to change one's attitude about who is control of your life. These premises created a theoretical model for the film.

In sessions 4 through 8 we developed characters to represent different aspects of the premises. The characters were a mother who would be killed by a drive-by shooting at the story's start, leaving her teen children to take control of their own destinies; a son influenced by gang activities, drugs, gang rules, violence, and selling drugs, but diverting money owed to his gang to pay the bills after his mother's death; a sister going to school to gain a future for herself and her family; a social worker who tries to take control of the siblings' future as wards of the state; and gang members taking advantage of the new situation by claiming to protect the teens while controlling the brother by making it risky for him to leave the gang and his drug business.

In sessions 9 through 12, we developed the premises, along with characters, into a story structure filmed in three locations. The story begins as the mother is killed in front of her apartment. Brother and sister make efforts to recover from their grief and remain in their home. Gang members arrive and, seeing an opportunity to take over, try to do so by involving the brother in the gang. A social worker arrives from the state to enforce the rule that an underage girl cannot live in a home with an underage guardian. She tries to separate the siblings who refuse. They discover they must have an income to stay where they are (pay the rent). The sister decides to return to school and finds a job to pay their way. The brother agrees behind the sister's back to continue selling drugs and turning income over to the gang. The sister discovers her brother's continued involvement with the gang when she finds gang members in the house partying. She begs her brother to get a legitimate job. The brother refuses to work at McDonald's and continues his involvement as a gang member. He is asked to make a drug delivery.

His sister tries to talk him out of it, arguing that he must work hard to get out of the fix they are both in. Meanwhile, he owes money to the gang that he has diverted to pay for household needs without telling his sister. Because he has not returned the income from his drug-selling activities, his gang brothers hunt them down to seek their money and keep him from running away. The brother and sister go into hiding in a vacant apartment. The gang members arrive at the door of the apartment and pound on the door; the film ends with a barrage of gunfire.

Later sessions involved rehearsing the piece from beginning to end; finding locations for filming, including a front stoop, an abandoned apartment in COT, drive-by locations, and a cemetery; and constructing a set for a day of shooting at the CPTV location. In the first three sessions, the rehearsed story was videoed at the various locations and on set at CPTV.

Dalglish completed the editing of the scenes and produced the film at CPTV with contributions from colleagues as well as TARP staff and teens. The project team arranged to release *Hard Way Out* (20 minutes) at a grand opening in Hartford, sponsored by a local insurance company. The public audience included more than 400 people, including parents, teens, community leaders, congregations, the YMCA and Boys and Girls club organizations, and the general public. Introduction and recognition of the actors, producers, the director, and colleagues was followed by an hour-long, open-ended question and answer session. Everyone had the opportunity to express their opinion about the accuracy and familiarity of the story as portrayed by the actors.

The film subsequently was shown in youth programs throughout the city. Almost all the youth involved in making the film went on to college. Dalglish continues to screen this project at the Media and Communication Arts Department at City College of New York as a model effort, illustrating the engagement of youth in research and actor improvisation to produce a culturally centered film about youth life. ICR continues to screen the film to youth living in urban Connecticut, who are still vulnerable to recruitment into drug dealing and other illegal activities. The methodology for creating film is replicated in ICR YPAR programs.

TARP was ICR's first large-scale effort with urban teens. It was based on ICR's principles of collaboration with multiple sites and community participants (Schensul 1998). ICR provided the Prevention and Action Research staff, curriculum, training sessions, and production program. The three youth-serving organizational partners provided a base for the program, supervisory support, wraparound services, materials and supplies, and transportation. The teens from the COT arm of the TARP program were fully engaged in scripting and performing the film, and in speaking about it at various showings once the film was completed. The Hartford Housing Authority provided a base for the COT TARP program and a vacant apartment for filming the final scene. CPTV was an ICR partner and offered full access to its studios. The TARP program alliance was well networked with other urban resources, including the insurance company that provided the location for a public screening.

Despite deep interest, ensuring youth participation was a challenge. Participants' lives and responsibilities sometimes interfered with work on the film. However, adult allies were committed to supporting the work and the youth participants during the research and filmmaking process. Collaborations such as this one require money, human resources, and networking to forge a common agenda.

Visualizing Local Truths

When deciding on approach, we discussed the value of theatre performance rather than film. Theatre, a more flexible medium, is not readily transferable, and repeated performances are difficult to organize, especially when youth participant/actors have busy schedules. Filming made it possible to rehearse roles and to show the film in perpetuity. Most of the filming took place at the ICR facilities and at CPTV. Street scenes were limited because of the risks associated with filming in gang territory.

Youth did not do the filming. For this effort, youth *were* centrally involved in production: in creating and setting up the scenes, deciding on props, and creating and giving life to their characters with feedback from the other members of the group. Mosher argues that some or all group members should have a chance to see multiple versions of a film as it is being edited (Mosher 2012). Campbell completed post-production at CPTV in Hartford, with an original music score, sound mix, and color, where students had the opportunity to view the film and make editing decisions. Editing had an impact. One of the actors broke down watching the piece: "I had no idea this was the life I was living! I just accepted it as the way things are!" By participating in the creation of the film, she was able to visualize a "changing truth" in her own life.

The final film represented the first time that a group of Hartford youth had demonstrated their capacity to conduct research and reflection, create a scripted and improvised narrative, and transform it into a film, recording their own commentary on life in Hartford's public housing projects during a heightened period of gang activity.

Ethical Issues

The production of the film and research that supported it raised many ethical issues related to confidentiality, risk, and stereotyping. The teen actors were well known in the community, and some had been targeted for gang recruitment. Participation in the filmmaking effort presented a strong anti-gang statement. Thus, it was extremely important that the youth NOT act out moments from their own lives, or the lives of their interviewees, but instead develop fictional characters based on real-life experiences and narrative interview summaries. Hence, the stories cobbled together to create the narrative for *A Hard Way Out* were based on real situations that had affected real people in the study community, but the facts, events, names of characters, and locations were constructed and fictitious, thus protecting the privacy and the lives of those involved.

In a city intentionally segregated by an informal coalition of business and "downtown" interests after the 1960s urban protests, Hartford's public housing, built to house returning veterans, became largely African American and Latino. By the time of the project, national policies favored disinvestment in public housing with consequent increasing concentrated disadvantage. In this environment, the general public held racist and stereotyped views of the community where the filming took place, seeing it as a negative space filled with violence, crime, drugs, and abuse. The residents were ambivalent about their community, sharing the wider view of its negative qualities but at the same time recognizing its cohesion and shared identity. TARP was therefore challenged to represent these contradictory positive and negative views of the community without contributing to negative stereotypes. Thus, the resilience of young people stands as a contrast to negative structural factors, even in the face of negative outcomes. We discuss this when showing the film.

ICR staff maintained constant vigilance over potential conflicts and flashpoints to address any gang intrusions. The research strategy was risky because youth who were not engaged directly in substance use and drug selling interviewed their friends who were. To protect both youth researchers/actors and ICR staff from any risks, youth always interviewed other youth in pairs in a program-designated location with a program adult available nearby. To avoid misidentification, they carried badges identifying their program and used a script to explain their purpose. At the same time, since information traveled rapidly through COT, the program and filming were widely recognized as positive influences. ICR program people were representative of and familiar with the areas in which the project was located and tried to foresee problems as they arose. Following institutional review board (IRB) protocol to ensure confidentiality, interviews were anonymized, and material used from the interviews was pooled to avoid any possible identification with individuals.

For filming, we also took many precautions. Though much of the production was conducted indoors either at ICR, CPTV, or at another offsite home to protect youth and staff from the possibility of exposure to violence, the last scene had to be filmed at COT, and an incident Dalglish recalls illustrates the ways in which risks were both taken and averted in protecting all participants:

It's the final scene, and our two characters, the brother and the sister, are hiding down below a window in a COT vacant apartment, hoping against hope to avoid being found out by the gang. They both know that once you join the only way out is death by execution. Dr. Schensul discovered at the last minute that a local chapter of one of the national gangs had learned about our project and were on their way to shut us down. I am inside the room with the two brave TARP actors, the sound person and other NYU personnel. Dr. Schensul starts knocking at the door. "Campbell. This is not safe. I have to get the teens out of here immediately. You have to stop recording, now!" I begged for five minutes to get the shot. We turned the camera on the door and asked her to bang a little harder, and that is what we recorded—Dr. Schensul banging on the door, playing the part of the gang members who were at that very minute walking up the street to stop our shoot. The moment could not have been more real. We completed our shot, and released the actors to safety. My DP [director of photography], sound person, and I walked out of the building as calmly as we could as we watched a group of young men walking up the street looking for us.

Overall, great care was taken to film only those street and backyard scenes open to the public; no specific residences were identified. All rehearsals, improvisations, and video recordings were conducted in locations with permission and approval from the owners of the locations. Any public footage gathered to represent the setting was in the public domain.

Concluding Thoughts

This project was ICR's first attempt to introduce YPAR as a means of increasing youth voice and organizing around drug violence. It was also the first effort to translate data and lived experience into a participatory film project based on improvisation that could be used to disseminate youth perspectives about a devastating situation to a wider audience, as a stimulus for action. Ethnography is essentially improvisational. The fundamental tools of ethnography can be combined in different ways and shaped to setting, user, audience, and purpose at any moment. Improvisational filmmaking is flexible in much the same way. The rules of representation for an ethnographically based improvisational film require that the elements of the composite narrative (language, storyline, setting, actors and their appearance, props) are authentic to the setting and historical moment, and achieved through the active participation of young people from the setting. A filmed critical drama must be rooted in the actors' embodied and intellectual understanding of the structural factors that give rise to the narrative and what might be done to counter it. Authenticity is achieved through the involvement of actors from the setting who have both lived and researched the situation to be portrayed in the film, and who seamlessly can transform their combined experience into story and improvisational script. *A Hard Way Out* illustrates this process well.

PAR has been shown to be transformational at both individual and social levels, but it is the actions through educating policymakers, community organizing, and advocacy that are likely to result in social change. Social change efforts continue to require face-to-face dialogue and mobilization. Now youth and others use social media to express their opinions, mount advocacy efforts, and mobilize on-the-ground campaigns. The placement of brief films on Facebook, YouTube, and websites for public audiences, with accompanying material created by youth, has sustainable spatial and temporal reach and influence far beyond site-specific advocacy. ICR youth films are posted on these sites, where they can be viewed as a part of larger campaign efforts. Newer technologies—smartphones, tablets, and still/video cameras—are available worldwide. Blending research, representation through film, and organizing on the ground and through Internet platforms will form the contemporary infrastructure for YPAR campaigns for social change and social justice locally and globally.

REFERENCES

Bandura, A. (1994). Self Efficacy. In *Encyclopedia of Human Behavior*, edited by V. S. Ramachaudran (Vol. 4): 71–81. New York: Academic Press.

Berg, Marlene, Emil Coman, and Jean J. Schensul. 2009. Youth Action Research for Prevention: A Multi-Level Intervention Designed to Increase Efficacy and Empowerment among Urban Youth. *American Journal of Community Psychology* 43(3–4): 345–359.

Boal, Augusto. 1992. *Games for Actors and Non-Actors*. London: Routledge.

Cammarota, Julio, and Michelle Fine. 2010. *Revolutionizing Education: Youth Participatory Action Research in Motion*. London: Routledge.

Cohen, Cathy J., Joseph Kahne, Benjamin Bowyer, Ellen Middaugh, and Jon Rogowski. 2013. *Participatory Politics: New Media and Youth Political Action*. Oakland, CA: MacArthur Research Network on Youth & Participatory Politics. http://ypp.dmlcentral.net/sites/default/files/publications/Participatory_Politics_Report.pdf

Chowdhury, Ataharul Huq, Helen Hambly Odame, and Michael Hauser. 2010. With or Without a Script? Comparing Two Styles of Participatory Video on Enhancing Local Seed Innovation System in Bangladesh. *Journal of Agricultural Education and Extension* 16(4): 355–371.

Christens, Brian D., and Tom Dolan. 2011. Interweaving Youth Development, Community Development, and Social Change through Youth Organizing. *Youth & Society* 43(2): 528–548.

Darder, Antonia, Marta Baltodano, and Rodolfo D. Torres (eds.). 2003. *The Critical Pedagogy Reader.* London: Psychology Press.

Denzin, Norman K. 2003. *Performance Ethnography: Critical Pedagogy and the Politics of Culture.* Thousand Oaks, CA: Sage.

Escobar, Arturo. 2008. *Territories of Difference: Place, Movements, Life, Redes.* Baltimore, MD: John Hopkins Franklin Center.

Freire, Paulo. 1970. *Cultural Action for Freedom.* Cambridge, MA: Harvard Educational Review and Center for the Study of Development and Social Change.

———. 2008. Teachers as Cultural Workers. In *Handbook of Research on Teacher Education: Enduring Questions in Changing Contexts*, edited by Marilyn Cochran-Smith, Sharon Feiman-Nemser, D. John McIntyre, and Kelly E. Demers (p. 208). London: Routledge.

Gardner, Howard. 1999. *Intelligence Reframed: Multiple Intelligences for the 21st Century.* New York: Basic Books.

Giroux, Henry A. 1989. *Schooling for Democracy: Critical Pedagogy in the Modern Age.* London: Routledge.

Howard, Leigh Anne. 2004. Speaking Theatre/Doing Pedagogy: Revisiting Theatre of the Oppressed. *Communication Education* 53(3): 217–233.

Mosher, Heather. 2012. Creating Participatory Ethnographic Videos. In *Specialized Ethnographic Methods: A Mixed Methods Approach,* edited by J. J. Schensul and M. D. LeCompte, 363–410. Lanham, MD: AltaMira Press.

Radcliffe, David. 1998. *Charter Oak Terrace: Life, Death and Rebirth of a Public Housing Project.* Hartford, CT.: Southside Media.

Rothschild, Jacob Edward. 2014. Race, Gender, and Deliberative Democracy: Overcoming Oppression through the Theatre of the Oppressed. University of Southern Mississippi, Hattiesburg. *Master's Theses.* Paper 24. http://aquila.usm.edu/masters_theses/24.

Schensul, J. J. (1998). Community-Based Risk Prevention with Urban Youth. *School Psychology Review* 27(2): 233–245.

Schensul, Jean J. 2011. Building an Applied Educational Anthropology beyond the Academy. In *A Companion to the Anthropology of Education,* edited by B. A. U. Levinson and M. Pollock, 112–134. Oxford, UK: Wiley-Blackwell.

———. 2012. Youth Participatory Action Research. In *Encyclopedia of Action Research,* edited by D. Coghlan and M. Brydon-Miller (Vol. 2), 831–834. Thousand Oaks, CA: Sage Publications.

Schensul, Jean J., and Marlene Berg. 2004. Youth Participatory Action Research: A Transformative Approach to Service-Learning. *Michigan Journal of Community Service Learning* 10(3): 767–780.

Schensul, Jean J., Marlene Berg, Daniel Schensul and Sandra Sydlo. 2004. Core Elements of Participatory Action Research for Educational Empowerment and Risk Prevention with Urban Youth. *Practicing Anthropology* 26(2): 5–9.

Watts, Roderick J., Matthew A. Diemer, and Adam M. Voight. 2011. Critical Consciousness: Current Status and Future Directions. *New Directions for Child and Adolescent Development* 134, 43–57.

Weiss, Judith A. 1989. Teyocoyani and the Nicaraguan Theatre. *Latin American Theatre Review* 23(1): 71–78.

Participatory Mapping and GIS

Counter-Mapping as Situated Knowledge: Integrating Lay Expertise in Participatory Geographic Research

Nicholas A. Rattray

In 2007, a group of students and university staff members sat around a table covered with brightly colored aerial maps of the University of Arizona (UA). The group puzzled over information gleaned from "map interviews" they conducted a few weeks earlier addressing issues of accessibility and disability. Many of those present self-identified as a person with a disability, ranging from those with sensory impairments to wheelchair users to one student with an anxiety disorder. Now in the latter stages of their mapping project, they had come to recognize the value of the embodied expertise that stemmed from their personal experience navigating through campus barriers. One student explained how their findings differed from the "official accessibility map" of the campus.[1] Most universities in the United States have created maps that delineate the location of accessible parking spaces and elevators, populated by the ubiquitous blue wheelchair user symbol that identifies accessible entrances and inaccessible buildings. One student argued that the official map offered a skewed representation of the accessibility. Not only does the map cater to a subset of issues faced by the broader disabled community, she explained, such maps offer a static snapshot of features susceptible to misuse or malfunction. When such maps are presented as evidence of an accessible campus, they elide issues of stigma and inadequacy that often accompany architectural features. Another student summarized barriers that often go unnoticed: backdoor entrances for wheelchair users; a lack of attention to cognitive and other hidden disabilities; nonfunctioning wheelchair lifts; and the lack of Braille for students with visual impairments. Inaccessibility consisted of barriers hidden in plain sight.

Nicholas A. Rattray, "Counter-Mapping as Situated Knowledge: Integrating Lay Expertise in Participatory Geographic Research" in *Participatory Visual and Digital Research in Action,* Aline Gubrium, Krista Harper, and Marty Otañez, eds., pp. 131-146. © 2015 Left Coast Press, Inc. All rights reserved.

The students debating the accessibility of the UA campus were involved in a participatory mapping project that offered an alternative perspective to the top-down, technocratic view of the campus accessibility map. Drawing from the findings of this case study, in this chapter I explore issues of situated knowledge, lay expertise, and spatial literacy in participatory geographic research. The research presented here arose in the context of broader debates among critical geographers around issues of situated knowledge and the politics of geospatial data. I begin with my experience with Neighborhood Knowledge Los Angeles (NKLA), a web-based mapping project that leveraged local knowledge of neighborhood conditions into social justice mobilizations in California. The projects I discuss combine both the technological capacity of geographic information system (GIS) software and participatory research methods.

Social scientists have appropriated geospatial techniques into participatory GIS (PGIS) projects, which generally refer to community or neighborhood participation in formal GIS, cartography, or other map-making projects (Corbett and Keller 2005). Building on the "counter-mapping" tradition (Kwan 2002; Peluso 1995), I show how lay experts engaged in PGIS destabilize dominant representations of their community. I conclude by linking the politics of the PGIS project to the cultural significance of the exponential growth in "volunteered geographic information" (Goodchild 2007), or geospatial data collected through smartphones and other personal devices. Reflecting on this case study of disability and space offers important lessons for researchers interested in participatory mapping, such as considerations of multiple modes of learning, expertise, and combining qualitative and spatial research methods.

Cartographic Representation as Situated Knowledge

First emerging in the late 1960s, GIS began to be used for intensive data analysis in the 1980s. Geographers later began to challenge the technocratic orientation of geospatial technologies, building on scholarship that problematized cartographic representation (Harley 1989; Pickles 1995) in part by framing GIS as an information and communication technology comprising contested social practices imbued with distinct histories (Elwood and Ghose 2001). Geographers debated whether GIS technologies perpetuate the "God-trick," Donna Haraway's (1988, 584) label for scientific perspectives of the

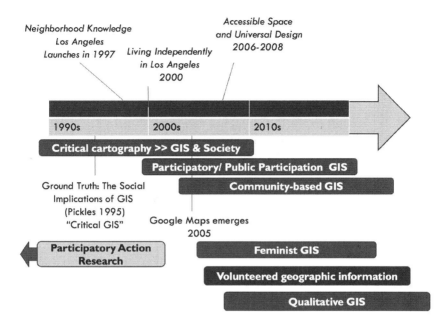

FIGURE 8.1: Timeline of participatory GIS: case studies and conceptual fields

world that take a "view from nowhere." In an attempt to reimagine GIS, Mei-Po Kwan (2002) has called for "counter-mapping"[2] as an alternative capable of discerning "subjugated knowledges" (Foucault and Gordon 1980, 82). As a form of feminist visualization, counter-mapping projects are grounded in locally situated forms of spatial knowledge created by embodied actors. Many PGIS projects attempt to unearth knowledge often marginalized by dominant representations of local communities (Elwood 2008). Figure 8.1 depicts several developments in critical and participatory GIS.[3] Like geographers, anthropologists have long been attuned to power differentials over cartographic representation. While archaeologists use geovisualization in fieldwork, cultural and applied anthropologists have often contested official maps of indigenous territories (Herlihy and Knapp 2003). As anthropologists have devised ways to incorporate qualitative data into community mapping projects, spatial patterns often emerge that might not be apparent if strict official boundaries are respected (McMahan and Burke 2007).

The Utopian Potential of Participatory Mapping

"Neighborhood improvement and recovery is not just for the experts!" This motto expressed the ethos of a community-based mapping project that arose in the late 1990s. Based at the University of California, Los Angeles (UCLA), the Neighborhood Knowledge Los Angeles (NKLA) project assembled property tax information that could ultimately serve as an "early warning system" for neighborhood deterioration (Krouk et al. 2000). NKLA aspired to democratize access to information technology tools that could detect spatial patterns of tax delinquency and building code complaints. Tenant rights groups, community development organizations, and city residents had access to housing data commonly reserved for urban planners via interfaces available in English and Spanish.

While the first iteration of NKLA offered residents the opportunity to play a "watchdog" role in their communities, emphasizing patterns of code complaints and violations also painted a negative picture of neighborhoods. Influenced by the asset-based community development model (Kretzmann and McKnight 1993), we developed a spin-off program called Interactive Mapping in Los Angeles (IAMLA). We collaborated with youth groups, elders, and disabled residents to elicit local knowledge embedded in the social memory of specific neighborhoods (Pitkin and Rattray 2002). Combining workshops on spatial literacy with community organizing, we aimed to build local understanding of neighborhood conditions. Composed of mostly African-American elders and Latino youth, community research teams sought to counter negative depictions of their neighborhoods. At city council meetings, they attempted to reframe local perceptions of distressed neighborhoods by highlighting economic and cultural assets through maps and digital photos from NKLA. We later expanded into a California-wide version of the community mapping platform that included free tools for uploading user-specific geographic data (Rattray 2006).

Yet, while some have suggested that NKLA helped unleash the "utopian potential" of GIS (Graham 2005; Warren 2004), such depictions should be taken with caution. We were often reminded that geographic literacy or the ability to interpret maps should not be assumed. Drawing from his personal experience with NKLA, Pitkin (2007) recommends that community researchers remain cognizant of the ethics of the expert/non-expert divide while considering the unintended consequences of their work.

As I discuss next, the challenges we faced in sustaining PGIS projects at UCLA relate to issues raised by critical geographers regarding the history and politics of geospatial knowledge: issues we faced as we studied accessible space and universal design.

Participatory Research on Accessible Space and Universal Design

Scholars studying accessibility and physical disability have argued that urban environments have been constructed in ways that privilege "able-bodied" users. People with atypical embodiments, including wheelchair users but also others with sensory impairments or age-related chronic illnesses, find themselves facing barriers on a daily basis (Gleeson 1999; Imrie 2001). Steps and curbs are obvious non-neutral methods of directing pedestrian traffic that communicate ideological messages through architecture (Rodman and Cooper 1995). If built environments inscribe cultural assumptions about how spaces are governed (McDermott and Varenne 1995; Rattray 2013), participatory counter-mapping offers one method for visualizing delineating the non-neutrality of urban environments.

Since the 1970s, activists with disabilities have formed what is popularly known as the Independently Living movement. Rejecting models of residential institutionalization that had predominated since the nineteenth century, disabled citizens sought to assert their right to decide where they lived and worked (Brisenden 1986; Shapiro 1993). These citizen-activists influenced the adoption of the Americans with Disabilities Act (ADA), as well as the proliferation of "independent living centers" that supported autonomy for people with disabilities (Fleischer and Zames 2001). Borrowing from the empowerment paradigm implicit in the disability rights movement, our UCLA team developed a project that built on NKLA's approach to mapping local knowledge. Known as Living Independently in Los Angeles (LILA), the project aimed to empower disabled residents to integrate into their communities (Toy and Richman 2004). LILA's locally trained lay experts used a mediated platform to elicit grassroots knowledge about resources relevant to people with a variety of physical, mental, and sensory impairments.

TABLE 8.1: Two models for creating accessible educational environments

Accommodation Model	Universal Design Model
Access to course material is a problem for individual students and should be addressed by the student and Disability Services	Access issues stem from an inaccessible curriculum and can be addressed by instructor in the design of the course
Access is achieved through accommodations and retrofitting existing requirements	The course is designed, to the greatest extent possible, to be usable by all students
Access is retroactive	Access is proactive
Access is often provided in a separate location or through special treatment	Access is inclusive
Access must be reconsidered for each new student in each course	Access is sustainable

I had LILA in mind when I approached the UA Disability Resource Center (DRC) in 2006 about investigating accessibility of the campus for students with disabilities. We developed a project guided by the idea that people who work, live, and attend class at universities cannot be assumed to have healthy, "normal" bodies free of illness, anomaly, or disability (Kitchin 2001). Rather than assuming a universal, disembodied subject, we sought to explore how campus users—nondisabled and disabled alike—navigated the university campus. A corollary goal entailed encouraging students with disabilities to get involved in undergraduate research opportunities in science, GIS, applied anthropology, and disability studies.[4]

We structured the project around two semester-long phases consisting of seminars, methods training (including human subjects training), and field research. The participants included staff and students with hearing and visual impairments, wheelchair users, and able-bodied students. The first six weeks of the project offered lectures and discussion on models of disability, the politics of public space, GIS, and architectural barriers. In conceptualizing barriers, the participants used the DRC's vocabulary; whereas older conceptual models of accessibility emphasize individual accommodations, more recent approaches incorporate principles of "universal design" (Scott et al. 2003; Story 1998), as depicted in Table 8.1.

FIGURE 8.2: Sample aerial map interview instrument

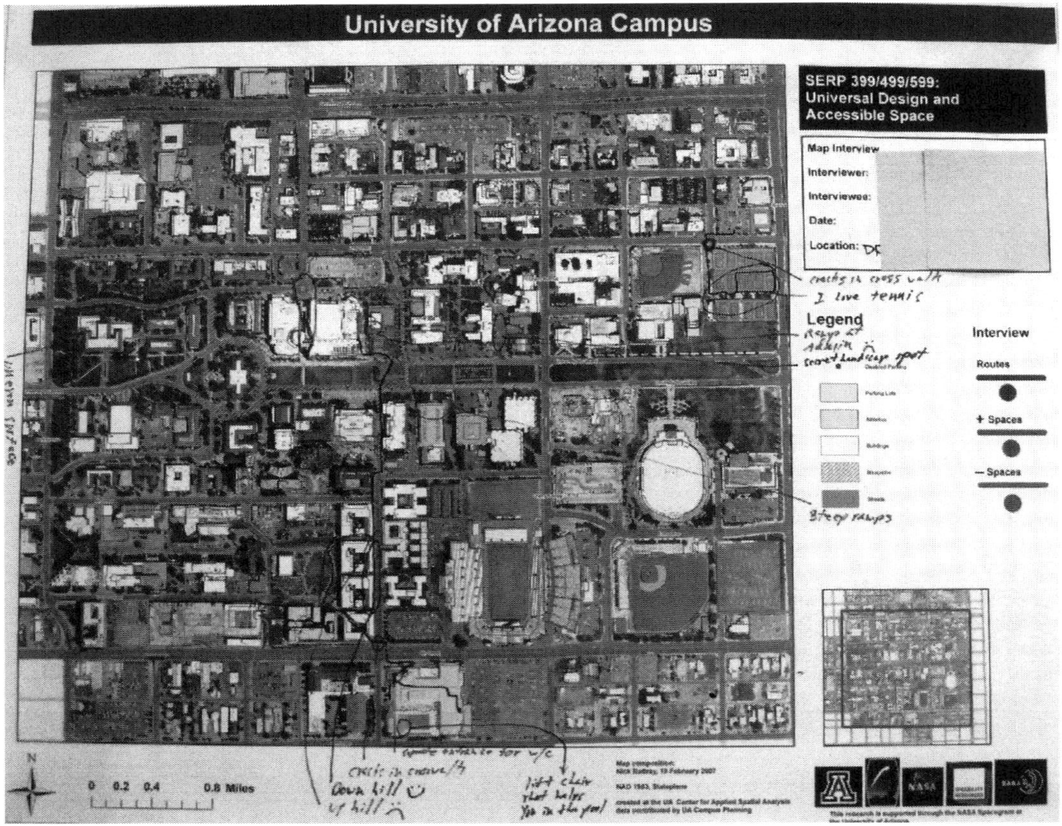

137

In terms of data collection, participants engaged in "map interviews," or semistructured sessions that assessed participant experience by marking a poster-sized aerial map of the university campus (see also Rattray 2007). Each participant conducted three map interviews: two with people who identified as disabled,[5] and one who identified as nondisabled. Collectively, we had decided that while an inductive approach was most appropriate, it was nonetheless important to formally compare patterns of travel between disabled and nondisabled campus users. The map interviews lasted between 15 and 60 minutes. In each interview, informants used different colored markers to indicate how they typically moved through campus, drawing directly on printed maps.

Blue marks indicate typical routes used for daily travel. Red marks represent areas, locations, or regions where barriers exist: they could be physical (e.g., potholes), social (restricted access), or attitudinal (due to negative perceptions). Green marks signify locations that represent positive areas; these could result from the presence of friendly people, accessible building design, or useful resources. Interviews also covered questions about past experiences, perceptions about disability, and future expectations about campus accessibility. Once the interviews were complete, I "digitized" the spatial data from the paper-based maps using ArcGIS. The resulting lines and polygons were given 20-foot buffers and amalgamated into composite layers. A series of maps displayed patterns of typical routes and positive and negative areas that were compared with qualitative findings.

Proponents of participatory research approaches argue that community members or non-experts who conduct data collection must also be involved in interpretation and dissemination of findings (Park 1999). We hoped that the involvement of students and staff in public discussion about accessibility would eventually open opportunities for more inclusive models of architecture (Kitchin 2001). Student-researchers volunteered to present their results in a public forum, highlighting the tensions existing between meeting the legal requirements of the ADA and pushing toward universal design. Our research revealed widely divergent interpretations of the built environment, such as how particular buildings expressed attitudes about disability, equity, and charity. An important example of positively received architecture was the recently constructed entrance to the Arizona State Museum. Guided by principles of universal design, the zero-grade entrance prominently led into the front doors. In contrast, a newly built administration building had been constructed with a steep, awkwardly placed wheelchair ramp that included a plaque suggesting the construction company donated the ramp. While none of the nondisabled interviewees noticed the plaque, one wheelchair user called it a "demeaning slap in the face." Members of UA's disabled community lamented that the ramp symbolized a "charity" approach to disability, as well as a missed opportunity to integrate aspects of universal design into a prominent building.

During the second phase of the project in the fall of 2007, I collaborated with two students on a paper reflecting on the involvement of undergraduates in disability studies research (Rattray et al. 2008). By analyzing reflective essays from students involved in the second phase of the research, we linked the heterogeneity of the disabled community on campus to "hidden" barriers, such as how the needs of visually impaired students could be quite diametrically opposed to those of wheelchair users. Many students contrasted their experience on campus with previous time spent in inhospitable towns or high schools. Taken together, the data collected through interviews demonstrated a wide range of tactics used by people with disabilities to circumvent architectural barriers.

Probing Hidden Discourses of Bodily Difference

While participatory research aspires to address everyday concerns faced in community settings, working toward solutions can lead to deeper inquiries into underlying premises. Borrowing from Friere's (1993) ideas about critical pedagogy, Park (1999) distinguishes between *problematizing* rather than *direct problem solving* in participatory research. In our research on accessibility, student researchers found themselves questioning broader campus policies on building construction, transportation, and learning environments. Along with the advisors who contributed to planning the project, I sought to equip students with interpretative frameworks that could broaden their perspective on accessibility. We were optimistic that rather than simply offer solutions to problems they discovered, students would formulate analytical questions about deeper social dynamics on campus. We encouraged students to confront the ethical dimensions of representation, questions about digital technologies, and challenges in collaboration.

We found that destabilizing the expert/non-expert divide in interpreting geographic information as well as establishing who has the authority to speak about accessibility issues proved effective. For instance, we focused on developing the capacity of students and staff to devise research questions, interpret qualitative and spatial data, and publicly present their findings.

Another strategy involved engaging with guest speakers training in research methods or urban planning. The students particularly enjoyed an open discussion with a staff member from the university planning office. While the planner gained an important perspective on the requirements of disabled users of the campus, the students also appreciated difficult tradeoffs between creating accessible environments and issues of sewage. For example, the heavy precipitation that occurs in monsoon season in Tucson meant that diverting rainfall was an important safety and ecological concern. The intermixing of undergraduate and graduate students, DRC staff, and people with a variety of impairments helped the group appreciate diverse types of expertise. Even the director of the DRC, who technically was the instructor of record and a sponsor of the projects, engaged in interviews and data analysis. We cultivated the notion that disabled members of the community offered an embodied form of expertise that was most often missing from typical discussions of campus planning.

We faced both ethical and practical constraints. Throughout the project, our use of GIS and digital technologies evolved; some of our initial ideas proved to be inappropriate. For instance, students viewed the suggestion from one of the faculty advisors to "simply attach global positioning [system] (GPS) devices to wheelchair users" as ethically problematic. In addition to being overly invasive, GPS monitoring would generate quantities of data that would be challenging to analyze. Time constraints impeded my original goal of training a few students in formal GIS analysis, so the map interview emerged as a technique for encouraging spatial literacy among participants through a nuanced appreciation for a "bird's eye" view of campus. While cognizant of the dangers of purely technocratic cartographic representation, students felt that the use of aerial maps helped create a common framework. Data on positive and negative areas of the university offered phenomenological perceptions of space, supplemented with digital photos. The combination of interview transcripts, digital photos, amalgamated route GIS maps, and hardcopy aerial maps offered an intriguing array of data. Interpreting the map interviews yielded fascinating insights, such as barriers faced by people with a diagnosis of multiple chemical sensitivities or anxiety disorders. Some students identified the trade-offs between developing accessible paths or ramps for wheelchairs that then created barriers for blind people using canes. The students insisted on the power of the printed maps as artifacts demonstrating not just barriers to accessibility, but also as representing areas that facilitated a sense of belonging for students with disabilities.

Participants also explored issues of power related to conducting research. In the first few weeks, the disabled students discussed stories about spatial exclusion or unintended discrimination they faced in cities or schools where they lived in the past. Personal experiences of entering public buildings from the back or coping with stigma perhaps made them receptive to "emancipatory" disability research that aims to include people with disabilities in all phases of academic research (Mercer 2002; Oliver 1992). Students drew from their "situated knowledge" to conceptualize how disability is based not solely on one's individual impairment but rather in the interaction of people with their physical and cultural environments.

As a group, we also debated the ethics of conducting disability simulations, which refer to activities where mostly nondisabled people attempt to mimic the experience of living with an impairment by temporarily wearing a blindfold or using a wheelchair. After reading arguments in favor and against such simulations (e.g., Burgstahler and Doe 2004), the group reached consensus on eschewing simulations in favor of a more open-ended "walking assessment." Our walking tour of campus led to a valuable encounter near the campus cafeteria. After we exited the cafeteria, one of the wheelchair users with us attempted to hold the door open for two nondisabled patrons. In nearly all cases, people refused to walk through a door held open by students in wheelchairs, demonstrating the power of thinking about stigma. As much as messages about architectural barriers, this scene suggested the power of discourses of tragedy around disability. These able-bodied students appeared to be unable to accept that wheelchair users could exercise the courtesy of holding open a door. Walking through a door held open by someone with a mobility impairment dangerously inverted notions of dominance and subordination.

Like many participatory research projects, we were forced to improvise according to emergent methodological and contextual challenges. In retrospect, it was clear that training students in qualitative research, GIS, and disability studies was overly ambitious. Students were unable to participate in the formal GIS analysis. We underestimated the degree to which the students and staff needed to work through the background scholarly material to establish a common framework that could serve as the basis for cooperative research, possibly due to an erroneous assumption that disabled students and staff members who work on disability issues would share a common conceptual framework. We also faced the specter of raised expectations, as students hoped that their project would alter the way the campus addressed accessibility barriers. Instead, our successes were more individual than collective. While students were involved as coauthors and benefited from the project in terms of developing their own capacity in research, they were also frustrated with the lack of accountability from the campus administration or the potential for change. The students' proposal for maintaining a blog that would track construction areas that create accessibility barriers found little support during their public presentation. Participatory research often entails navigating tensions between identifying local problems and antagonizing powerful stakeholders.

Participatory GIS in an Era of Volunteered Geographic Information

If "GIS is a new way to unsettle other people's knowledge" (Warren 2004, 14), its utopian appeal stems from the plasticity of representation it enables. These case studies of PGIS projects demonstrate how lay expertise can challenge dominant discourses about marginalized communities. In Los Angeles, community advocates used the spatial patterns of housing conditions shown through NKLA to argue for affordable housing and community development. At UA, our fine-grained approach positioned students and staff with disabilities as community experts with unique knowledge of campus accessibility. GIS maps offered a common analytical framework for comparing nondisabled users and people with widely varying bodily differences. Digital photos, map interviews, and the resulting spatial analysis of routes and areas of concern on campus offered a rich set of artifacts for interpretation. Although hampered by the limited scope of the projects, the researchers found opportunities to capture successes and challenges faced by other disabled students.

Taken together, these PGIS projects offer important lessons. One unintended outcome of successful PGIS projects occurs when they get subsumed into broader systems or appropriated in new contexts. For example, NKLA evolved into serving as the information system for the city of Los Angeles for tracking residential properties, code complaints, and building permits. NKLA launched a statewide version that included tools for users to upload their own community data, as well as the LILA project created by and for people with disabilities across Los Angeles County. In the UA project on accessible space, the issue of universal design has received increased attention in broader discussions of planning and construction on campus. Discussions about the GIS maps of accessibility barriers have problematized the assumed neutrality of campus architecture.

The PGIS projects presented incorporate formal GIS data together with narratives about accessibility in the built environment. Informed by the theoretical lens of disability studies, we examined how disabled and able-bodied users experience their local environment. Yet other topics may lend themselves a more general approach that combines qualitative data with participatory geospatial methods, such as themes of food security, water sustainability, or mass transit, to name a few. Community researchers interested in fostering new collaborations or considering how to incorporate geographic data into their projects may apply discussions of counter-mapping to their own research agendas. For anthropologists and other social scientists interested in participatory research, PGIS offers intriguing methods for combining qualitative methods with emerging geographic technologies. Key concerns that have emerged in the last two decades in participatory mapping projects—such as spatial literacy, ethical matters, and power—have become paramount with the arrival of "wiki-maps" and the ubiquity of geospatial data. Geographers place PGIS projects in the broader context of location data that we voluntarily tag, submit, and verify through any number of social media via our smartphones, digital cameras, apps, exercise monitors, etc.: "New forms of digital spatial data are created through a growing proportion of our daily activities, such as using electronic payment cards to board a bus whose location is tracked by the public transit agency, or using GPS-enabled cell phones that trace our location" (Elwood 2008, 133). Yet our ability to sort out the ethical and cultural implications of voluntary surveillance has not kept pace with the sheer volume of geographic data. In an era when we have begun to produce and consume massive amounts of geodata, the challenge for anthropologists is to ensure that locally situated forms of knowledge are incorporated into public policy and governance. As in these PGIS projects focused on housing and disability issues, anthropologists can play an important role in unearthing undervalued perspectives while foregrounding issues of literacy and expertise.

Acknowledgments

This research is based on the valuable contributions of the participants of the Universal Design and Accessible Space project: Kyle Mutz, Jackie Cimino, Aaron Foster, Meghan Sooy, Jean Dill, Zack Fogle, Jean Paul Jorquera, Paul Brooks, Bryan Barten, Bunny Sumner, Jordan Glovsky, Ryan Buchholtz, Hunter Fattaleh, Chris Woods, Alberto Guzman, Sarah Raskin, and Dara

Sherafat. Thanks also to the Cariñoso Foundation of Tucson for funding to support project interns, and to Wendy Vogt and Krista Harper for their thoughtful feedback.

REFERENCES

Brisenden, Simon. 1986. Independent Living and the Medical Model of Disability. *Disability, Handicap & Society* 1(2): 173–178.

Burgstahler, S., and T. Doe. 2004. Disability-related Simulations: If, When, and How to Use Them in Professional Development. *Review of Disability Studies: An International Journal* 1(2): 4–17.

Corbett, Jon M., and C. Peter Keller. 2005. An Analytical Framework to Examine Empowerment Associated with Participatory Geographic Information Systems (PGIS). *Cartographica* 40(4): 91–102.

Elwood, Sarah. 2008. Volunteered Geographic Information: Future Research Directions Motivated by Critical, Participatory, and Feminist GIS. *GeoJournal* 72(3–4): 173–183.

Elwood, Sarah, and Rhina Ghose. 2001. PPGIS in Community Development Planning: Framing the Organizational Context. *Cartographica: The International Journal for Geographic Information and Geovisualization* 38(3/4): 19–33.

Fleischer, Doris Zames, and Frieda Zames. 2001. *The Disability Rights Movement: From Charity to Confrontation*. Philadelphia: Temple University Press.

Foucault, Michel, and Colin Gordon. 1980. *Power/Knowledge: Selected Interviews and Other Writings, 1972–1977*. New York: Pantheon Books.

Freire, Paulo. 1993. *Pedagogy of the Oppressed*. New York: Continuum.

Gleeson, Brendan. 1999. *Geographies of Disability*. London: Routledge.

Goodchild, Michael. 2007. Citizens as Sensors: The World of Volunteered Geography. *GeoJournal* 69(4): 211–221.

Graham, Stephen D. N. 2005. Software-Sorted Geographies. *Progress in Human Geography* 29(5): 562–580.

Gubrium, Aline, and Krista Harper. 2013. *Participatory Visual and Digital Methods*. Walnut Creek, CA: Left Coast Press.

Haraway, Donna. 1988. Situated Knowledges: The Science Question in Feminism and the Privilege of Partial Perspective. *Feminist Studies* 14(3): 575–599.

Harley, J. B. 1989. Deconstructing the Map. *Cartographica: The International Journal for Geographic Information and Geovisualization* 26(2): 1–20.

Herlihy, Peter H., and Gregory Knapp. 2003. Maps of, by, and for the People of Latin America. 62(4): 303–314.

Imrie, Rob. 2001. Barriered and Bounded Places and the Spatialities of Disability. *Urban Studies* 38(2): 231–237.

Kitchin, Rob. 2001. Using Participatory Action Research Approaches in Geographical Studies of Disability: Some Reflections. *Disability Studies Quarterly* 21(4):61–69.

Kretzmann, J. P., and J. L. McKnight. 1993. *Building Communities from the Inside Out*. Evanston, IL: Asset-Based Community Development Institute, Northwestern University.

Krouk, Danny, Bill Pitkin, and Neal Richman. 2000. Internet-Based Neighborhood Information Systems: A Comparative Analysis. In *Community Informatics: Enabling Community Uses of Information Technology*, edited by Michael Gurstein, 275–297. Hershey, PA: Idea Group Publishing.

Kwan, Mei-Po. 2002. Feminist Visualization: Re-envisioning GIS as a Method in Feminist Geographic Research. *Annals of the Association of American Geographers* 92(4): 645–661.

McDermott, Ray, and Herve Varenne. 1995. Culture "as" Disability. *Anthropology & Education Quarterly* 26(3): 324-348.

McMahan, Ben, and Brian Burke. 2007. Participatory Mapping for Community Health Assessment on the US-Mexico Border. *Practicing Anthropology* 29(4): 34–38.

Mercer, Geof. 2002. Emancipatory Disability Research. In *Disability Studies Today*, edited by Colin Barnes, Mike Oliver and Len Barton, 228-249. Cambridge, UK: Polity Press.

Oliver, Michael. 1992. Changing the Social Relations of Research Production. *Disability, Handicap & Society* 7(2): 101–114.

Park, Peter. 1999. People, Knowledge, and Change in Participatory Research. *Management Learning* 30(2): 141–157.

Peluso, Nancy Lee. 1995. Whose Woods Are These? Counter-Mapping Forest Territories in Kalimantan, Indonesia. *Antipode* 27(4): 383–406.

Pickles, John. 1995. *Ground Truth: The Social Implications of Geographic Information Systems*. New York: Guilford.

Pitkin, Bill. 2007. Community Informatics for Community Development: The "Hope or Hype" Issue Revisited. In *Networked Neighborhoods; The Connected Community in Context*, edited by Patrick Purcell, 77–89. London: Springer.

Pitkin, Bill, and Nick Rattray. 2002. Community Mapping for Neighborhood Knowledge in Los Angeles. *Community Technology Review* Winter-Spring, 15–17.

Rattray, Nicholas A. 2006. A User-Centered Model for Community-Based Web-GIS. *Urban and Regional Information Systems Association Journal* 18(2): 25–34.

———. 2007. Evaluating Universal Design: Low and High-Tech Methods for Mapping Accessible Space. *Practicing Anthropology* 29(4): 24–28.

———. 2013. Contesting Urban Space and Disability in Highland Ecuador. *City & Society* 25(1):25–46.

Rattray, Nicholas A., Sarah Raskin, and Jackie Cimino. 2008. Participatory Research on Universal Design and Accessible Space at the University of Arizona. *Disability Studies Quarterly* 28(4). http://www.dsq-sds.org/article/view/159/159.

Rodman, M., and M. Cooper. 1995. Accessibility as a Discourse of Space in Canadian Housing Cooperatives. *American Ethnologist* 22(3): 589–601.

Scott, Sally S., Joan M. McGuire, and Stan F. Shaw. 2003. Universal Design for Instruction: A New Paradigm for Adult Instruction in Postsecondary Education. *Remedial and Special Education* 24(6): 369–379.

Shapiro, Joseph. 1993. *No Pity: People with Disabilities Forging a New Civil Rights Movement.* New York: Times Books, Random House.

Story, M. F. 1998. Maximizing Usability: The Principles of Universal Design. *Assistive Technology* 10(1): 4–12.

Toy, Alan, and Neal Richman. 2004. *Lessons From Establishing a Community Information System Built for and by People with Disabilities.* Los Angeles: UCLA Advanced Policy Institute.

Warren, Stacy. 2004. The Utopian Potential of GIS. *Cartographica: The International Journal for Geographic Information and Geovisualization* 39(1): 5–12.

NOTES

1 As universities have attempted to meet the guidelines of the Americans with Disabilities Act (ADA), web-based "accessibility maps" have proliferated. First passed in 1990 and amended in 2008, the ADA is intended to prohibit discrimination on the basis of disability in part by requiring equal access to public facilities.

2 The term "counter-mapping" is often attributed to Nancy Peluso's (1995) research on alterative boundary making and contestation over forest conservation in Indonesia.

3 Participatory GIS shares common issues with other approaches used by anthropologists concerned with the active participation of the community members being studied. See Gubrium and Harper (2013) for a review of links between PGIS, participatory action research (PAR), and community-based participatory research (CBPR); each of these approaches typically conceptualizes participation as a continuum rather than a strictly enforced methodology.

4 With support from the UA Center for Spatial Analysis, the DRC, and the Bureau of Applied Research in Anthropology, I received funding for two years from the National Aeronautics and Space Administration (NASA) Space Grant Graduate Fellowship. The Space Grant program awards fellowships to graduate students at land-grant universities for spatial science outreach projects that benefit the wider community or underserved groups.

5 For the purposes of our project, disabilities included mobility/motor, sensory (e.g., sight or hearing), learning, or emotional/psychological.

Beyond Words: The Transformative Practice (and Politics) of Digital Spatial and Visual Ethnography in a Rural Shale Gas Boomtown

Simona L. Perry

They speak of changes approaching
As quickly as a thief's sleight-of-hand,
As slowly as the final minutes
By a loved one's death-bed.[1]

Bradford County, Pennsylvania, is a rural place. In 2008 the U.S. Census reported that the county had a little more than 61,000 inhabitants spread across its 1,147 square miles of valleys and hills and concentrated within six townships. The leading source of revenue for the county was agriculture, namely dairy and veal, and the majority of employment opportunities were in manufacturing plants operated by large corporations such as Craftmaster, DuPont, Global Tungsten Powders, and Cargill, and in education, health, and social services. In July 2009, the month and year I began ethnographic fieldwork in the county, 76 Marcellus Shale or unconventional gas wells had already been drilled, and the anticipation of a "Shale Gas Boom" in jobs, family income, and county revenue was the topic of most interest to the landowners and local officials I met.

During those initial trips to plan for the development of a community-integrated geographic information system (GIS) of local meanings of place and environmental change, I visually observed changes to the local landscape and population, including the clearing of large tracts of forests, the destruction of local roadways, and the increasing population of young men between the

Simona L. Perry, "Beyond Words: The Transformative Practice (and Politics) of Digital Spatial and Visual Ethnography in a Rural Shale Gas Boomtown" in *Participatory Visual and Digital Research in Action,* Aline Gubrium, Krista Harper, and Marty Otañez, eds., pp. 147-161. © 2015 Left Coast Press, Inc. All rights reserved.

ages of 19 and 29. And, as an important place-based marker of the pace of change in this new rural boomtown, an economic survey conducted by Pennsylvania State University reported that on average between 2007 and 2010, there was an 18.7% decline in the number of dairy cows by county when the number of Marcellus Shale gas wells exceeded 150 (Kelsey 2011). By July 2012, the number of Marcellus Shale or unconventional gas wells drilled in Bradford County had reached 785 (Pennsylvania Department of Environmental Protection [PA DEP] n.d.).

Rethinking Environmental Decision-Making and Social Science Practice

The oil and gas industry has acknowledged that the top-down decision-making and public relations strategies typically used in promoting shale energy and other unconventional oil and gas developments may be a contributing factor in the growth of local and global public opposition and conflicts over what has popularly been referred to as "fracking" (Control Risks 2012). What began as local grassroots initiatives against fracking are now regional, continent-wide, and global social and political action movements typified by groups such as the Americans against Fracking coalition (based in New York), Bold Nebraska (the Nebraska-led opposition group to the Keystone XL Pipeline), the indigenous movement Idle No More, and many others. One of the common elements among these groups is a demand that local rural people have a seat at the table and a voice in environmental decision-making processes and institutions. It is within this growing demand for greater diversity and local public participation in our collective decisions about energy production that this case study in visual, digital participatory research is situated.

Top-down and elite planning processes and management strategies operate within a highly technical politic-economic context that does not always recognize culturally appropriate, equitable and just, or sustainable decision-making. Top-down processes rarely include room for proactive public participation and open communication about the full range of local visions for the present and future that may more accurately capture people's everyday lives and experiences. When working in rural areas, planning for and facilitating meaningful stakeholder involvement from a diversity of local people is a necessity when seeking to reduce later conflict. A lack of this type of local involvement might threaten the ecological and economic sustainability of rural places (Pepperdine 2000). In addition, the reliance on top-down or expert-driven environmental management processes contributes to an erosion of public trust in environmental management institutions (Renn et al. 1995).

Saying Hello to Participatory Mapping and Photovoice

As an environmental regulator and social science practitioner I have worked in the development and implementation of public participation programs. In this consulting role, "public participation" is defined as activities undertaken by members of the public to influence the decisions made by government officials (Warner 1971). The public, instead of sharing information or agenda setting alongside decision-makers, gains access to the decision-making process only when problems arise or when their interests are not being met. Thus, those with more access to power have a disproportionate input on final decisions, and those with less access have little to no input. In different cases from the Arctic to inner-city Boston, I have seen firsthand how this paradigm of public participation quickly becomes the setting for entrenched mistrust and alienation. The conflicts over the promotion of shale energy and fracking across the globe are no exception.

The two-year project I led in a rural north-central Pennsylvania county sought to turn this paradigm on its head through the use of critical and interpretive methods of participatory inquiry and community-integrated GIS mapping (Harris and Weiner 1998; Kwan 2002; Matthews et al. 2005; McLafferty 2002; Mohan 2000; Palin 2004; Pavlovskaya 2002). Using this approach, the project set out to partner directly with local people to capture "everyday life" by scaling down to individual, household, and neighborhood levels through ethnographic fieldwork methods (Fox et al. 2003). I envisioned that the participatory process of creating these snapshots of everyday life would allow local people who might not otherwise participate in environmental decision-making a way to share their local knowledge and concerns about local changes brought about by the shale gas boom.

It became clear after initial observations and interviews in the county that the idea of deploying digital GIS technologies in the ways in which I had imagined might not be logistically feasible or even immediately useful to participants. Access to digital geographic datasets and high-speed Internet was lacking in most homes. There was also a relatively low level of computer literacy among many of the landowners who were interested in participating. In general, when it came to methodology, the key challenge was to develop a less computer-dependent means of collecting geographic and visual data while still generating the expected digital outputs in GIS and other formats. This involved careful attention to the design of a participatory digital research process that honored both the expectations of local participants and the visions and needs of researchers and funders. It also became clear that my initial focus on how change affects place and natural resources would need some rethinking.

A Rural Case Study in Landscape Change and Emotional Wellbeing

At first, the project was designed to focus on identifying and geographically documenting local landowners' senses of place and the meanings of land and water resources in the face of change. But when landowners began sharing their experiences and expectations about changes related to shale gas developments, they also shared important facets of their rapidly changing emotional lives. Beyond an exploration of place and environmental meanings, this project had the potential to serve as a way for landowners to articulate their personal and collective feelings, experiences, concerns, and uncertainties about how shale gas developments were affecting their emotional wellbeing (Perry 2012a). This presented a unique opportunity to facilitate both a visual and affective exploration of the everyday lives and experiences of rural landowners during a period of rapid environmental and social change.

One of the consistent qualities of the early interviews I conducted were the intense emotions that came to the surface—sadness, excitement, anger, greed, jealousy—when participants spoke about shale gas developments. However, it was not until I received a phone call from one of the female dairy farmers who had agreed to participate in the focus group that I recognized the role this project could play in documenting local landowners' emotional wellbeing and psychological lives.

> …they were afraid that if they signed the new lease, with the non-disclosure clause, and participated [in the focus group] they would be violating the lease and could lose the lease deal, or worse, their farm. She said the money wasn't that important to her, but the farm and her

work was what she lived for. Through her tears, she continued by saying "We are just so stupid," "We'll do anything for money," and "We're just all a bunch of dumb farmers up here." I hung up the telephone feeling shaken and helpless and realizing that this was a turning point in how I was going to conduct this project (Bradford County digital field notes, February 18, 2010).

The way in which locals spoke about the development of the Marcellus Shale and how change was unfolding was revealing perceptions and feelings about self, family, occupation, money, natural resources, neighbors, outsiders, and community. Other researchers and community organizers had turned these highly charged emotional periods of change into transformative and positive experiences. Most important, I embraced the concept of ethnography as a "therapeutic praxis" in which individual and community emotions that may be painful or traumatic can be shared—with a voice, a picture, a map, a poem, a story—and in that sharing be released and even transformed (Ainslie and Brabeck 2003). I began to see my fieldwork as not only collecting ethnographic, spatial, public planning, and natural resource data for creating GIS maps and geographically explicit images that represent the relationships between a place and people at a particular time of environmental and social change, but even more urgently as facilitating a process that allowed people to articulate and share their emotional relationships to change.

Methods: Focus Groups, Participatory Mapping, and Photovoice

Recruitment of focus group participants took six months. This lengthy process was due to my own learning curve and status as an "outsider" in such a remote and rural part of Pennsylvania and the need to overcome mistrust and fear. In the end I was able to recruit and maintain a total of seven landowners. I divided them based on the primary use of their lands: one group of crop and livestock farmers, one group of forest and timber owners. In addition to focus groups, we conducted close to 100 individual ethnographic and oral history interviews with landowners, town residents, and local officials.

All focus group sessions lasted between two and four hours. There were three to four separate sessions and one joint session. Sessions were audio- and videotaped. To the first sessions we brought large laminated maps of participants' properties and the county. This allowed participants to draw on the maps when questions were asked. Examples of questions included: *Where are the groundwater and surface water features on your property? What geographic locations in the county have special meaning to you?* We used ArcMap to digitize the results of participants' initial map drawings, printed and laminated the revised GIS maps, and in later sessions gave them to participants for their refinement and final approval.

During the second session, disposable cameras and notecards were given to participants along with ideas about photographing what was meaningful to them about their land, natural resources, or other qualities of the place they lived. During the last two sessions, participants shared these photographs and writings (Pierce 2008; Wang et al. 2004). During these Photovoice sessions participants were prompted with questions for discussion such as: *How do the images relate to your views on change? What words would you use to collectively describe these images as they relate to the people and places of Bradford County?* Participants were encouraged to converse freely about their photographs and writings, particularly with regard to memories, everyday lived experiences, and their perceptions of developments specifically related to Marcellus Shale gas and the future. They were asked to select photographs and words that best captured their individual senses of place as well as their collective sense of what Bradford County meant to them.

In the final session, both focus groups met for the first time. I presented a draft of the final maps and slideshow of the Photovoice process. Following the presentation I asked each group to share their experiences with participants from the other focus group. This was followed by wider group dialogue and feedback about the project, including a critique of my role as researcher and facilitator and a discussion about the future of the project.

Audio, video, GIS, and Photovoice data were analyzed separately after each session, and then together and more comprehensively from October 2010 to July 2011. In these iterative analysis stages we identified the groups' shared concerns about the rapid acceleration of shale gas development and its impact on quality of life, generated maps of "special places" and landowner-generated water resources (Figure 9.1), identified and documented threats to water and land resources, and began to describe how landowner attachments to places and resources may relate to their experiences with the natural gas industry in Bradford County (Perry 2012a).

Out of the analysis of the Photovoice sessions, a PowerPoint slideshow was developed that captured each groups' individual and collective images and words. A geospatial database using ArcCatalog was used to organize all

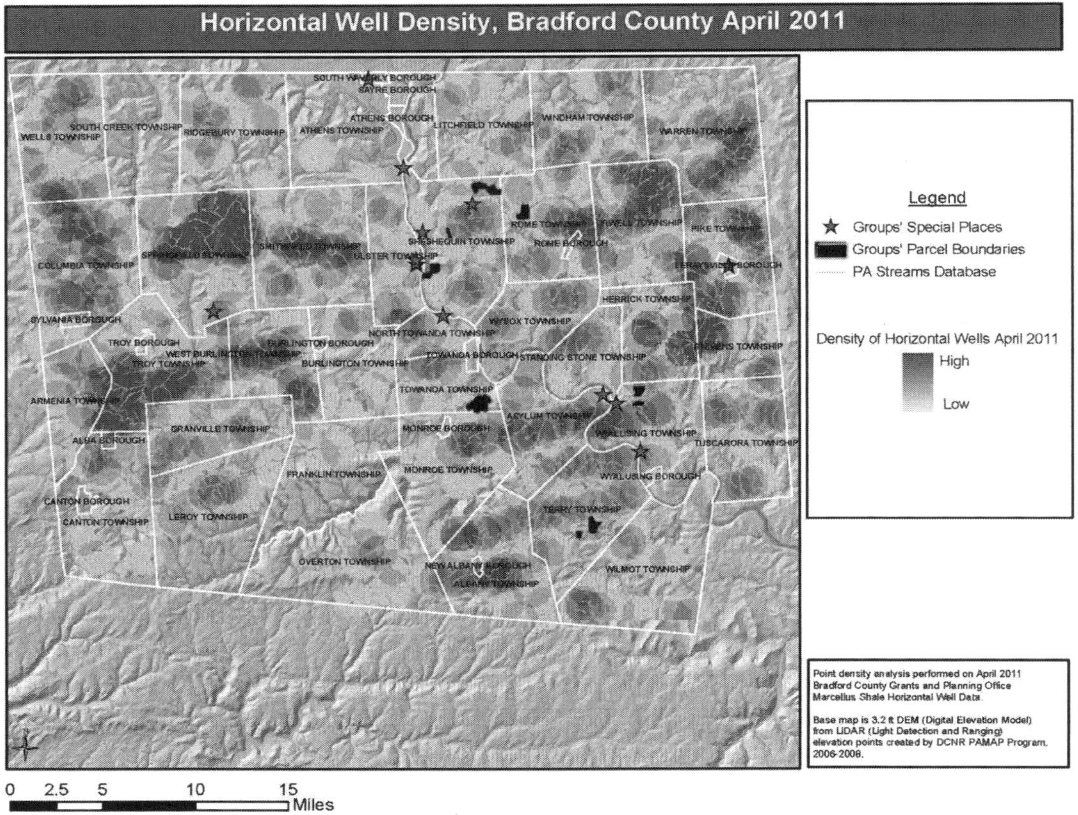

FIGURE 9.1: GIS map of landowner-identified special places, water resources, and shale gas developments (density of shale gas wells)

Horizontal Well Density, Bradford County April 2011

Legend

★ Groups' Special Places

▬ Groups' Parcel Boundaries

⎯ PA Streams Database

Density of Horizontal Wells April 2011

High

Low

Point density analysis performed on April 2011 Bradford County Grants and Planning Office Marcellus Shale Horizontal Well Data.

Base map is 3.2 ft DEM (Digital Elevation Model) from LiDAR (Light Detection and Ranging) elevation points created by DCNR PAMAP Program, 2006-2008.

0 2.5 5 10 15 Miles

spatial data and to facilitate the production of participant maps. But, most important, what emerged from the analysis was a way of geographically and culturally describing agricultural landowners' perceptions and experiences about the development of Marcellus Shale gas in their lives and communities. In addition, the results of this analysis served as a framework for conducting longer-term studies into community impacts related to rapid social, economic, and environmental changes taking place as a result of shale gas developments in Bradford County and elsewhere (Perry 2012b, 2013).

Challenges of Ethnographic Fieldwork and Participatory Visual Methods in a Rural Shale Gas Boomtown

Undertaking an ethnographic fieldwork project in a small rural community on a politically charged topic like Marcellus Shale gas development was fraught with logistical, ethical, and political challenges. With the addition of digital and visual methods, those challenges mounted. In general, four types of logistical challenges were encountered: gender barriers to participation, legal barriers to participation, technological access and limitations, and preservation of participant confidentiality in the presentation of spatial data. Among the various ethical and political challenges, two are worth noting: sensitivity to the power differentials within the community and among participants, and defining, separating, and maintaining roles as ethnographer, scientist, facilitator, and advocate.

Logistical Challenges

From the outset of fieldwork I encountered gender differences in local landowners' willingness to participate, especially in the focus group aspects of the project. Gaining and maintaining the trust of local people in a small rural county was an overall challenge, but male landowners and particularly male dairy farmers were the greatest challenge. Most would not agree to participate after hearing about the focus group process; however, in many cases they would recommend I ask their wives or daughters to participate. When I asked both female and male landowners why they believed men did not want to participate, they said that it was primarily because men, particularly those working on farms, did not feel like they had time to sit around and talk for hours about the environment. In addition, female landowners told me that they suspected it was difficult for me to get men to participate simply because I was a woman. Such comments made me aware of strong gender stereotypes and the specific gender roles played within farm families, and offered my first insights into social expectations based on gender at the county level.

Perceived legal barriers to participation, while encountered less frequently than gender barriers, changed the nature of how I recruited participants, conducted my fieldwork, and chose to present the results. There were several instances in which non-disclosure clauses in oil and gas leases or in other legal agreements between landowners and oil and gas companies prevented people from sharing their experiences publicly, and thus precluded certain landowners from participating in focus groups. For those who could not participate in the groups because of these legal constraints, I still offered to interview them individually, although without audio or video recording and without reference to specific relationships to their lands and homes. This handwritten data, while not location specific, was still very useful for analyzing local psychological, economic, and social consequences of shale gas developments.

Lack of access to computer technology was evident upon my first visit to the county. Most people not living in one of the larger towns, if they had a computer in their homes, only had dial-up Internet access, with limited access to high-speed Internet outside of the towns. In addition, there was great variability in participants' computer literacy. I soon realized that computer "assisted" mapping was not possible in this rural place where people do not have access to high-speed Internet in their homes and there is low computer literacy. These technological limitations meant revising how the GIS would be created. Instead of placing participants in front of computer terminals where they could digitally manipulate data and maps, we produced laminated maps from county and national datasets and brought them to focus group sessions. Participants could draw on, place photographs on, and annotate these maps in whatever way necessary to capture the questions asked and conversations that emerged from each group session. The laminated maps annotated by participants were taken back to the geospatial lab at Dickinson College, where they were digitized using ArcMap. These new, digitized maps were printed and brought back to the next group sessions for review and revision. This iterative process would continue until the participants were satisfied with the results. This ended up being a much more time-consuming process, and in some ways it perpetuated the "expert-driven" research paradigm that I was intending to overturn. How we undertook the project did work to generate a type of community-integrated GIS, but it left me wondering how different and perhaps more useful the GIS would have been if participants had been able to more directly participate in locating, creating, and manipulating the datasets behind the maps. I suspect that if they had had the technological access and know-how, the project's resulting "static" GIS would instead have become a much more dynamic and living system.

Another key logistical consideration was how to present individual landowner property data and maps in a way that protected participant privacy as much as possible. The geospatial database was designed and created with this in mind; thus, each landowner layer was identified by a code not associated with the name of the landowner, and the database itself was password protected. Each landowner who participated in the focus groups received a PDF or hardcopy "Participant Map Package" that contained both their individual maps and related data and the maps and data from their focus group. These Participant Map Packages are not publicly available. On the other hand, GIS maps and geospatial information shared on websites, in professional journals, or at professional conferences contain no names or other identifying information to protect the identities and locations of participants.

Ethical and Political Challenges

As a digital spatial and visual ethnographic project rooted in critical and interpretive methods of participatory inquiry, this study not only explored rural senses of place and experiences with landscape change and emotional wellbeing, it also documented the spatial nature of injustice and unmasked social power differentials among individuals, communities, and organizations. In this way, it was a political project from the outset. The participatory nature in particular laid the groundwork for giving voice to the less powerful for the purpose of finding more just solutions to environmental conflicts, promoting greater public participation in environmental decision-making, and building a sustainable community based on trust.

This approach was not easily understood or welcomed in Bradford County, and I had to become attuned to local suspicion as I told potential new participants or interviewees, local political officials, and oil and gas industry staff about the project. Despite my care in describing the work as participant driven and in the service of the community itself, rumors flew about myself and the project. According to one story, I was working public relations for the oil and gas industry to find out more about local landowners; according to another story, I was working for the U.S. Environmental Protection Agency to develop stricter oil and gas regulations. I suspect that one of the reasons for these suspicions was because my entry into the field coincided with the recent arrival of the oil and gas industry. As I was knocking on doors and sitting in township meetings to conduct initial interviews and participant observations, the oil and gas industry representatives were also showing up at people's kitchen doors and community meetings. I also suspect the political nature of the project may have raised concerns among those who traditionally held power in the county—namely, elected officials—and individuals who anticipated financial gain from the development of the Marcellus Shale.

Many of the first landowners who became part of the project were dairy farmers and small landowners who had never been involved in environmental decision-making or, if they had been involved in environmental decisions, they believed these were always rigged to favor "environmental activists," "tree huggers," and "special interests." Most knew little to nothing about the regulations or the process for how decisions regarding land use, natural resource allocation, and fossil fuel extraction were made at the county, state, or federal levels. So, in return for their participation in the project, I began providing them with information about the county, state, and federal government's regulations, policies, and decision-making processes regarding water and land resources and the new shale gas developments. I placed large amounts of new information in front of them, or provided them with resources for getting that information, and some of them used it to make their voices heard. Some of these landowners began attending county commissioner meetings for the first time, going to public hearings held by different government agencies and elected officials, requesting records from the Pennsylvania Department of Environmental Protection, writing letters to the editor, and even starting landowner groups for educating neighbors.

The political underpinnings of the project made me ask important questions about the ethics of participatory community research. These questions mainly revolved around clearly defining and separating several different roles I found myself either playing intentionally or being asked to play by participants. As an ethnographer, my primary ethical concern was managing participant expectations during what could be emotionally charged interviews and group meetings. As a social scientist and environmental researcher, I was ethically concerned with finding a way to widely present the results of the project without compromising the safety, confidentiality, and trust of participants. As a group facilitator, my primary ethical goal was to ensure that everyone had an equal chance to voice their opinions; share their stories, maps, photographs, and written words; and, when appropriate, provide feedback to myself or others in a constructive manner. And, as a community advocate (a role I did not set out to play), my ethical consideration was how to provide an opportunity for those who have had their power removed, or who feel powerless, to choose for themselves how they want their voices to be heard and seen regardless of how I or others believed their voices should sound or appear. In the end, I discovered that the overall ethical considerations for conducting participatory spatial and visual ethnography in a rural shale gas boomtown are really the same ones that should be considered when conducting community research and ethnography anywhere: a commitment to honesty, reflexivity, awareness, humbleness, and openness to creativity, change, and other ways of knowing.

Saying Goodbye: Participatory Spatial and Visual Ethnography as a Path to Rural Community Transformation and Researcher Awareness

In conclusion, this participatory visual ethnographic project became a transformative experience for local participants. Through mapping and Photovoice exercises, participants articulated the meaning of their personal relationships to their land, water resources, neighbors, and special places in the county. They also were able to not only give voice to their concerns about how development of the Marcellus Shale may alter those place-based relationships in the future, but also were able to *show* their concern through Photovoice and eventually a traveling exhibit of their photos, poems, and maps. At the same time, in my various roles as ethnographic fieldworker, meeting facilitator, advocate, and friend, I was led into unexpected methodological, political, and ethical terrain. There were times when the local political quicksand made me question every word I said, association I made, and action I took. As an ethnographer and social scientist, using visual materials and not just written or spoken words allowed me to expand my openness to other ways of seeing and doing and allowed a new flexibility to present information in different and sometimes unexpected ways; however, it also came with some unexpected professional consequences.

I discovered that asking local people to be participants alongside me in a primarily spatial and visual ethnographic process about their personal lives also carried various ethical and political burdens for them. It is important to recognize that asking others for ethnographic openness and flexibility may be completely foreign and even a little frightening to those new to ethnographic practice. Working with photographs taken by participants as well as other personal visual materials, such as old maps and family photographs, can evoke strong emotional responses that are beyond words and have the possibility of leading to psychological and cognitive transformation. Fear and concern that widespread and rapid shale gas developments could forever alter the rural landscape of Bradford County meant that each photograph of a favorite creek, tree, pond, church, roadway, or forest clearing felt to them like looking into an old family photo album in which most of their loved ones are dead or dying. As I began to grasp the enormous emotional weight these images had in describing participants' relationships and attachments to places, I slowly began to say goodbye to my preconceived notions of what I was doing in Bradford County and the type of outcomes that I expected the project would yield. In the end, letting go of my research expectations for what I thought the project should give back to the community and how I should facilitate the outcomes was a difficult, but necessary, step. Standing back and listening and watching as community participants took the lead in presenting their own voices became the greatest lesson of all, and also the greatest reward.

Acknowledgments

Financial support for this project (2009–2011) was provided by a GIS postdoctoral fellowship from the Mellon Foundation and Dickinson College.

REFERENCES

Ainslie, Ricardo C., and Kalina Brabeck. 2003. Race, Murder and Community Trauma: Psychoanalysis and Ethnography in Exploring the Impact of the Killing of James Byrd in Jasper, Texas. *Journal for the Psychoanalysis of Culture and Society* 8(1): 42–50.

Control Risks. 2012. *The Global Anti-Fracking Movement: What It Wants, How It Operates and What's Next.* London: Control Risks Group Ltd.

Fox, J., Ronald, R. Rindfuss, Stephen J. Walsh, and V. Mishra. 2003. *People and the Environment: Approaches For Linking Household and Community Surveys To Remote Sensing and GIS.* Boston: Kluwer Academic Publishers.

Harris, T., and D. Weiner. 1998. Empowerment, Marginalization and "Community-Integrated" GIS. *Cartography and Geographic Information Systems* 25: 67–76.

Kelsey, Timothy W. 2011. Economic Assessments of Marcellus Shale Development: An Agricultural Perspective from Pennsylvania. Presented at the Agribusiness Economic Outlook Conference, Cornell University, Ithaca, NY, December 13. http://dyson.cornell.edu/outreach/outlook/2011/Kelsey_Outlook_Dec2011.pdf, accessed February 2012.

Kwan, M. P. 2002. Feminist Visualization: Re-Envisioning GIS as a Method in Feminist Geographic Research. *Annals of the Association of American Geographers* 92(4): 645–661.

Matthews, S. A., J. E. Detwiler, and L. M. Burton. 2005. Geo-ethnography: Coupling Geographic Information Analysis Techniques with Ethnographic Methods in Urban Research. *Cartographica* 40(4): 75–90.

McLafferty, S. L. 2002. Mapping Women's Worlds: Knowledge, Power and the Bounds of GIS. *Gender, Place and Culture* 9(3): 263–269.

Mohan, J. 2000. Geographies of Welfare and Social Exclusion. *Progress in Human Geography* 24(2): 291–300.

Palin, Rachel. 2004. Social Geography: Participatory Research. *Progress in Human Geography* 28(5): 652–663.

Pavlovskaya, M. E. 2002. Mapping Urban Change and Changing GIS: Other Views of Economic Restructuring. *Gender, Place and Culture* 9(3): 281–289.

Pennsylvania Department of Environmental Protection (PA DEP). n.d. Program, Oil and Gas Reports. Oil and Gas Management PA DEP. http://www.portal.state.pa.us/portal/server.pt/community/oil_and_gas_reports/20297, accessed July 28, 2014.

Pepperdine, Sharon. 2000. Social Indicators of Rural Community Sustainability: An Example from the Woady Yaloak Catchment. Paper presented at the First National Conference on the Future of Australia's Country Towns, June 28–30, 2000, Bendigo, Australia. http://web.archive.org/web/20070830054205/http://www.regional.org.au/au/countrytowns/strategies/pepperdine.htm#TopOfPage, accessed July 6, 2014.

Perry, Simona L. 2012a. Development, Land Use, and Collective Trauma: The Marcellus Shale Gas Boom in Rural Pennsylvania. *Culture, Agriculture, Food and Environment* 34(1): 81–92.

———. 2012b. Addressing the Societal Costs of Unconventional Oil and Gas Exploration and Production: A Framework for Evaluating Short-Term, Future, and Cumulative Risks and Uncertainties of Hydrofracking. *Environmental Practice* 14: 352–365.

————. 2013. Using Ethnography to Monitor the Community Health Implications of Onshore Unconventional Oil and Gas Developments: Examples from Pennsylvania's Marcellus Shale. *New Solutions* 23(1): 33–53.

Pierce, J. 2008. On Community Capitals as We See Them Through Photovoice: Cowell Oyster Industry in South Australia. *Australasian Journal of Environmental Management* 15(3): 159–168.

Renn, O., T. Webler, and P. Wiedemann. 1995. *Fairness and Competence in Citizen Participation*. Dordrecht, Netherlands: Kluwer Academic Publishers.

Wang, C. C., S. Morrel-Samuels, P. M. Hutchison, L. Bell, and R. M. Pestronk. 2004. Flint Photovoice: Community Building among Youths, Adults, and Policy Makers. *American Journal of Public Health* 94(6): 911–913.

Warner, K. P. 1971. *Public Participation in Water Resource Planning*. Arlington, VA: National Water Commission.

NOTE

1   S. L. Perry, unpublished poem in field notes, "Like Saying Goodbye: Sheshequin Focus Group, Towanda, Pennsylvania, May 2010."

Resurrecting Rosewood: New Heritage as Applied Visual Anthropology

Edward González-Tennant

Introduction

In this chapter I explore how new heritage intersects painful pasts. Scholars of difficult heritage and sites "representing painful and/or shameful episodes in a national or local community's history" (Logan and Reeves 2009, 1) continue to seek new methods for producing meaningful engagements while simultaneously supporting the goals of social justice. *New heritage* refers to the use of new media to document, analyze, and interpret cultural heritage (Kalay et al., 2008) by drawing upon the study of new media, or the "translation of all existing media into numerical data accessible through computers" (Manovich 2001, 20). This includes the translation of analog materials into digital formats as well as the creation of fully digital artifacts like 3D models. This chapter's case study is drawn from nearly a decade of ongoing research into the tragic history of Rosewood, Florida, a primarily African American town destroyed during a weeklong episode of violence commonly referred to as the 1923 Rosewood Race Riot.

My journey to embracing new heritage grew out a mix of concerns and experiences. I have been a long-time user of geographic information systems (GIS), and experiences with GIS and archaeology (González-Tennant 2009, 2011) encouraged me to think about the various ways researchers could represent the spatial aspects of heritage. In addition, my dissertation committee at the University of Florida alerted me to ways scholars can participate in positive social transformation. Peter Schmidt's

Edward González-Tennant, "Resurrecting Rosewood: New Heritage as Applied Visual Anthropology" in *Participatory Visual and Digital Research in Action,* Aline Gubrium, Krista Harper, and Marty Otañez, eds., pp. 163-177.

work among the Buhaya in Tanzania (2006, 2010) linked representation, cultural memory, and community empowerment, while James Davidson's work questioned the uncritical ways historical archaeologists interpret the lives of others (2004, 2007, 2008). Faye Harrison (1997, 1998, 2005, 2008) pushed me to recognize my own positionality as a transformative step towards decolonizing anthropology, while marilyn thomas-houston (2005) supported my exploration of creative, visual methods for sharing scholarship and Paul Ortiz (2005) challenged me to question the public intellectual potentials of my research. As a PhD student at the University of Florida, the methodological focus of my earlier training supported a growing engagement with social justice. As an assistant professor, I endeavor to use new heritage and engaged pedagogy (Freire 1970, 2002; hooks 1994, 2003, 2010) to impart a similar experience to each of my students.

New Heritage and the Contemporary Past

There is relatively little use of new heritage for researching, interpreting, and representing the recent past (Harrison and Schofield 2010, 249–281). The majority of previous work, typically referred to as *virtual archaeology* (Reilly 1990), examines the use of virtual technologies to represent archaeological contexts (Forte 1997). A small group of archaeologists recently have been exploring the interactive potentials of virtual world environments, calling this approach *cyber-archaeology* (Forte 2010, 10). Cyber-archaeologists believe online worlds have "the potential to provide insights into the ways in which the notions of heritage are transforming in the early twenty-first century" (Harrison 2009, 16). These scholars focus on the ways people use such technologies to explore historical topics. For instance, Morgan (2009) used the online world of Second Life to create digital reconstructions of archaeological work at Çatalhöyük, a Neolithic site in modern-day Turkey. These online worlds allow visitors to experience archaeological work undertaken by the University of California, Berkeley. Unfortunately, this project was discontinued in 2011 because of budgetary constraints associated with maintaining a presence in Second Life. New heritage embraces these approaches, and yet it remains a distinctive practice by combining perspectives and methodologies from a range of disciplines (e.g., historical archaeology, oral history, visual anthropology). This approach also supports the use of digital technologies to further the goals of collaboration and social justice (González-Tennant 2013). While most virtual archaeology focuses on monumental and prehistoric contexts, exciting examples of the use of these technologies for reconstructing and exploring the recent past do exist. This includes the virtual reconstruction of a mid-twentieth-century African-American neighborhood in West Oakland, California, and a video game allowing users to interact with non-player characters (NPCs) to explore the site's local history (Kalay and Grabowicz 2007). A similar project explores serious gaming to reconstruct the urban environment associated with the 1976 displacement of a black community in Soweto, South Africa (Nieves 2009). These projects harness new heritage to investigate difficult pasts while supporting sensitive engagements with multiple publics. My work in Rosewood, Florida, similarly uses new heritage to investigate the history of African-American disenfranchisement by translating academic research into publicly accessible knowledge.

Case Study: The Rosewood Heritage Project

In this section I provide a brief overview of the 1923 Rosewood Race Riot and my methods for researching and sharing the town's history. The primary reason I embrace this approach is that it allows me to share heritage research with a wide audience. These formats include virtual world environments, online worlds like Second Life, and digital storytelling videos. These various formats are likely to engage a broad range of society. For instance, younger visitors are more likely to explore the virtual world environment, while older audiences may engage with the research through more traditional formats such as video. My research combines these formats to share the history of Rosewood with as large an audience as possible.

Development and Demise of Rosewood

The former site of Rosewood is nine miles from the Gulf of Mexico in Levy County, Florida (Figure 10.1). Rosewood was settled in the mid-nineteenth century by a diverse group of people. By the early twentieth century, Rosewood was majority black and Sumner was a company town with a mix of black and white workers. Then, on New Year's Day 1923, a white woman in Sumner fabricated a black assailant to hide her extramarital affair with a white man. A white mob quickly formed and headed for Rosewood. They first encountered

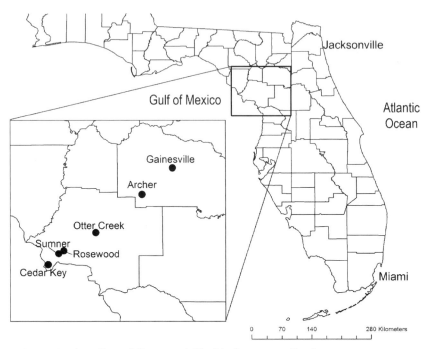

FIGURE 10.1: Location of Rosewood, Florida (source: author)

the home of Sam Carter, a long-time black resident of Rosewood, and proceeded to interrogate him by hanging him from a tree by the neck; then, when it seemed the mob might release him, a man leveled his gun at Carter's face, and New Year's Day ended with the sound of a shotgun blast.

At first, it seemed that the violence would end with Carter's murder. However, more than two days later, whites in Sumner heard that the black assailant had returned to Rosewood with local resident Sylvester Carrier. Before the night was out, at least two whites lay dead on his doorstep after attempting to set his house on fire, with his family still inside. Rumor and hatred spread quickly through rural Florida, eventually reaching the Klu Klux Klan in Gainesville, only 40 miles away. Residents of Rosewood knew the response for killing whites would be swift and violent; black men armed themselves and headed into the woods, and women and children hid with one of Rosewood's only white residents, John Wright, to wait out the violence. However, by January 6, three other blacks had been brutally murdered and the white mob, now numbering in the hundreds, began the systematic burning of Rosewood. During this time a train was brought through town at four in the morning to pick up the women and children, who had moved to the swamps and spent the previous couple of nights hiding after John Wright was unable to guarantee their safety. The train took dozens of families to towns such as Otter Creek, Archer, and Gainesville's black district, where descendants live to this day. On Sunday January 7, 1923 the mob returned to Rosewood and burned every remaining African American building.

Residents of Rosewood—those who survived long enough—would have to wait for more than seven decades to receive any trace of justice. Though a grand jury convened in January 1923, no convictions were made, and the jury's records have since been lost. Rosewood lingered at the edges of collective memory for decades. Then, in a 1994 landmark decision, the State of Florida decided to pay compensation to survivors and descendants (D'Orso 1996; Jones et al. 1993).

New Heritage in Rosewood

My work in Rosewood centers on the use of three technologies. The first involves the use of GIS to reconstruct historic property boundaries because no historic maps or city directories exist for the town. I meticulously analyzed and reconstructed the metes and bounds information from hundreds of historic property deeds to reconstruct historic parcels using ESRI's ArcGIS software. The resulting Historic Properties GIS (HP-GIS) shows property ownership and transfers between Rosewood residents for 50 years (1870–1930). I added U.S. Census data to determine additional aspects of each property owner's identity. In addition to supporting a deeper contextualization of Rosewood's community, this GIS work provides a spatial template of Rosewood as it existed prior to the events of 1923. Archaeological research has been undertaken at several properties to successfully verify the HP-GIS's ability to accurately predict the location of past structures on the landscape.

The second technology used in my research draws on this spatial template to reconstruct a virtual world environment of Rosewood. Virtual world environments allow users to interactively explore virtual content. The first step in creating a virtual Rosewood begins with the creation of several dozen 3D models representing historic structures. The appearance of these structures is based on oral history accounts, property descriptions, and the documentation of extant historic structures. These individual structures were initially created with Autodesk's 3DS Max, which is freely available to educators and students. These 3D models are then placed in a virtual world environment created with the Unity3D game engine. The public can access the virtual world environment (Figure 10.2) at the Rosewood Heritage Project website (www.rosewood-heritage.net), which I maintain on a private server.

I also explored the use of Second Life (www.secondlife.com), an online world created by users but maintained by a private corporation. I initially used Second Life to create a Virtual Rosewood Museum. The virtual museum allows visitors to experience the site in a number of ways. The museum itself takes the form of a repurposed home where visitors can explore the history of Rosewood. In a second, modern-looking building visitors can view a 25-minute digital documentary about Rosewood. A smaller structure represents the home of an African American family next to a timeline of the 1923 riot itself. Unfortunately, the cost of maintaining a presence in Second Life is prohibitive. The Virtual Rosewood Museum was discontinued in 2014 after more than four years of operation. At present, a replacement virtual museum is being created using Unity3D. A complete discussion of my use of Second Life is available elsewhere (González-Tennant 2013, 68–77).

The third technology used to share the history of Rosewood with a wider audience is digital storytelling. The use of digital technologies to share personal histories traces its roots to a series of workshops held in Los Angeles during the early 1990s. These workshops proved so successful that the Center for Digital Storytelling soon launched a series of national workshops exploring the topic (Lambert 2009, 1–10). While the majority of digital stories last around 10 minutes or less, my use of digital storytelling resulted in a 26-minute digital documentary created in consultation with Rosewood's descendant community. A significant portion of the documentary provides a glimpse into the lives of survivors. A particularly touching moment in the documentary occurs when Robie Mortin, who was eight years old in 1923, describes meeting her father for the first time several months after the riot. Mortin's father recognized early on how the early attacks on Rosewood residents might turn into large-scale violence, and sent Robie to nearby Williston with her sister. After hearing about the destruction of Rosewood, and not being able to meet their father, the girls found work as migrant farmworkers and made their way to Riviera Beach, Florida. Mortin shares what happened one morning when she went to a newly constructed church months after moving to Riviera Beach:

> There was a ditch that separated Riviera Beach from Kelsey City, there
> was a long ditch there. There had a bridge across it, and of course all
> the milk houses were there, and the Hearst Chapel AME Church there.

FIGURE 10.2: View of Rosewood Virtual World Environment available via the Rosewood Heritage Project website (source: author)

They had built that church right on that side of the ditch. So, we went to church, and would you believe our daddy was there, and we didn't know where he was, we didn't know where he was, hadn't seen him in months. We walked into the church that Sunday, and there was our father (Robie Mortin, video of interview with author, 2009).

The ability of digital storytelling to share emotionally touching moments like these with a wide audience represents an important point for heritage workers interested in creating collaborative and engaging projects. The viewer feels Robie Mortin's words—delivered in her soft, 94-year-old voice—in an unmistakable, visceral way. The emotional impact of her brief story demonstrates the trials and happy surprises that make a life scarred by trauma bearable.

Difficult Heritage, Collaboration, and Visual Technologies

The history of Rosewood and the traumatic experiences of its African-American community is one example illustrating the darker elements of modernity. Like the Holocaust and Apartheid, the American system of racial inequality forces us to question "key tenets of the project of modernity such as progress, rationality, science, technology, industrialization and liberal democracy" (Lennon and Foley 2000, 21). These sites and histories often inspire intense discomfort. Grappling with this "dissonant heritage" (Tunbridge and Asworth 1996) is becoming increasingly central to heritage and tourism studies. The growth of "dark tourism" (Seaton 2002; Sharpley 2005; Stone 2006; Tarlow 2005) forces us to question the growing attraction of concentration camps, shantytowns, and other locations of racial violence as tourist destinations. Sites like Rosewood can contribute to broad conversations about the nature of intolerance and hatred. This requires the recovery of hidden histories, what Sharon Macdonald refers to as "memory interventions" designed to "challenge forgetting in the public sphere" (2009, 94). The Holocaust and South African Apartheid are internationally recognized events, but more local histories are often neglected through various amnesiac practices. Macdonald's work specifically addresses public forgetting in regards to local sites related to the Holocaust (Macdonald 2008). Similar memory interventions are needed in America. As a nation, we easily misrepresent racial intolerance as a thing of the past and view racism in the present as a self-correcting practice. It is not, of course.

Finding sites that successfully confront past trauma while encouraging critical reflection produces mixed results. Lennon and Foley (2000:21) believe the Simon Wiesenthal Center's Museum of Tolerance (MOT) successfully supports critical reflection by combining survivor testimonies and visual displays with a rigid tour schedule designed to impart a sense of the rational planning at the heart of the Holocaust. Wendy Brown's (2006) ethnographic engagement with the MOT provides a powerful counterpoint. Her analysis better represents the museum's imposing architecture, overly structured tours, and the deep ambivalence produced by a stupefying array of media. The MOT's "extensive trafficking in stereotypes and clichés" (Brown 2006, 120) depoliticizes its pro-Zionist agenda, naturalizes history, and collapses complex categories of identity (e.g., race, religion, nationality) into a struggle between good and evil. Dark tourism sites must strive to balance the legacy of social inequality with eliciting strong feelings of anxiety. If successful, these sites encourage thoughtful tourists to confront the legacy of modernity. New heritage provides a powerful suite of tools for exactly this type of work.

My exploration of new heritage is not designed to subject visitors to "sensory and emotional overload" while simultaneously delivering "an intense moral-political didactism" (Brown 2006, 125). The Rosewood Heritage Project creates a personal engagement with the history of the town as a meaningful place with a long and complex history. The virtual world environment promotes individual exploration, and the virtual museum is available for group exploration. The digital documentary avoids stereotyping Rosewood as simply a site of death and tragedy by collapsing the town's history into a single event. This is a complaint descendants have of John Singleton's film *Rosewood*. My use of new media deviates in many ways from locations where multimedia exhibitions engulf the visitor's mind, where "power and history make little or no appearance in representations or accounts of ethnicized hostility or conflict" (Brown 2006, 109). The Rosewood Heritage Project combines various forms of new media to explore the complex history of minority disenfranchisement with a thorough contextualization of Rosewood's history, as both a location and a community, past and present.

Research into Rosewood's past has benefited from the use of new heritage in numerous ways. In addition to providing new information regarding the town's development and the lives of descendants, these technologies create new opportunities for collaboration with descendants and current property owners. After the events of 1923, no African Americans returned to the area, and the property passed through various hands until the approximately few dozen current landowners came to own the properties. Most of these property owners purchased their properties within the last generation or so, and few have deep roots in Levy County or family ties to the events of 1923. I reached out to numerous property owners in various ways (e.g., letters, word-of-mouth, phone calls) in the five years prior to the launch of the Rosewood Heritage Project website. Few responded to these traditional attempts at communication. Some were not interested in having Rosewood commemorated, while others chose to remain silent because of previously negative experiences with other researchers. This latter group included the current owner of Rosewood's African-American cemetery, which is no longer in use. This landowner saw a feature story on the project in the *St. Petersburg Times* in 2011. He visited the project's website, explored the (then-preliminary) virtual world environment, and viewed the digital documentary. Afterwards, he reached out to me and, citing the website's honest depiction of the project's goals, invited me to assist him in preserving the cemetery (Figure 10.3).

Gaining access to this property was important for the future of my research. From a scholarly standpoint, cemeteries act as central locations anchoring memory to place. In addition, this particular landowner is much respected by his neighbors. The 2012 cemetery documentation supports the next stage of research. I am working closely with this landowner to find a steward for the

FIGURE 10.3: Documenting Rosewood's African American Cemetery in 2012 (source: author)

cemetery. We are contacting heritage preservation agencies and groups to purchase and care for the site. The friendly engagement with this landowner is expanding my network of collaborators to include additional landowners and previously unknown descendants. This in turn supports the creation of an active oral history program and collection of additional historical documents (e.g., photographs) from family archives in Levy County and elsewhere.

New heritage represents a suite of technologies useful for engaged heritage work. Collaborative work in Rosewood faces unique challenges because of the range of experiences associated with the site's history and ongoing commemoration. Scholars interested in working with non-academic groups typically find themselves challenged to explore new theoretical and methodological terrain. Applied visual approaches (Pink 2006) often require a period of experimentation on the part of the researcher. I am continually excited and renewed by this aspect of new heritage. However, this type of work does not easily map onto traditional modes of scholarship, which focus upon concentrating expertise in academic hands and then distributing research through tightly controlled hierarchical networks of knowledge production (e.g., university classrooms, peer-reviewed publications).

The decision to embrace participatory visual research directly speaks to issues of power and ethics. For instance, a major benefit of digital storytelling over traditional film/documentary making is cost. Modern media, such as filmmaking, follows an industrial logic (i.e., large-scale production studies, expensive equipment costs, necessity of labors), whereas new media provides a postindustrial method that is not regulated by mass standardization (Manovich 2001, 29–30). This aspect of new media means its potential as an emancipatory form is literally hardwired into its very structure. Approximately half of the digital documentary created for this project is composed of interviews with two survivors. The focus on personal narrative central to digital storytelling allows me to focus the narrative and research on the experiences of survivors, and specifically on the ways survivors coped with the destruction of their town in the intervening decades between 1923 and the early twenty-first century. My decision to embrace new heritage was motivated by the descendants. When I began this research in 2005 I expected to develop a traditional archaeological project, complete with large-scale excavations. However, my growing network of collaborators felt this would add little to their understanding of Rosewood. This is a common sentiment among African-American communities "because they have never seen themselves reflected in the makeup of the practitioners or in those being served by the outcome of the research agendas" common to archaeology (Battle-Baptiste 2011, 70). I reexamined my own research agenda and dedicated time to learning and applying the various digital technologies at the heart of new heritage. This approach has revealed new information about Rosewood's past, expanded my network of collaborators, provided unexpected research opportunities, and promoted a growing public dialogue on Rosewood in Levy County, Florida, and beyond.

Conclusion

This chapter discusses the use of new heritage for investigating racial violence in twentieth-century America. New heritage represents a mixed-methods approach combining various digital technologies. A central tenet of heritage is the idea that the past and present are mutually constitutive, and that we need to investigate the complex ways the present uses the past (Lowenthal 1985). Rosewood remained at the edges of public memory for decades, until reporters and scholars began to retrieve this history in the 1980s and

1990s. New heritage offers a way for researchers to communicate their results with a broader public. The memory interventions (Macdonald 2008, 2009) this supports represent an act of translation. In using these technologies I seek to translate academic research into enriched public knowledge. This centers on promoting an honest engagement with Rosewood. The Rosewood Heritage Project includes a complete virtual world environment, details on accessing the Virtual Museum (currently being moved to the Rosewood Heritage website as part of a National Endowment of the Humanities–funded grant), the digital documentary, and a data warehouse containing some of the same information I used for my study (e.g., census records, oral history transcriptions). The Internet allows me to provide access to my data for use by the public and other researchers alike.

New heritage is not a panacea. Simply constructing a virtual world environment or hosting a virtual museum in Second Life is not enough to contribute to the goals of social justice. An ethnographic engagement is required to realize the full potentials of these technologies. I return to Levy County and the area around Rosewood once or twice a year. This is necessary to renew my network of collaborators. I am currently working closely with libraries and historical societies in Levy County—especially the Cedar Key Library and Cedar Key Historical Society—to maintain an active oral history program. The history of Rosewood is painful and continues to elicit discomfort from many residents of Levy County and the rest of Florida. My approach to new heritage, combined with an ongoing ethnographic engagement making use of oral history, helps convince residents that my intentions are not to denigrate one ethnically/racially defined group. As one recent attendee to my public talk at the Cedar Key library remarked, I am "not interested in pointing fingers at whites."

In addition to the need for an ongoing ethnographic engagement, new heritage technologies are constantly evolving. This includes new versions of programs to construct 3D models and new ways of representing the past. As such, for scholars to make effective use of these technologies, the period of experimentation is not going to end. I am currently remodeling the 3D assets (e.g., historic structures) with open source software such as Blender (www .blender.org). These programs allow me to create assets in nonproprietary formats and explore more cost-effective techniques for new heritage. Ultimately, it does not matter which technology is used to bring the past to life. If the goal is to engage the public in meaningful and ethical reflection, then an engaged, ethnographic focus must remain an integrated part of any new heritage project.

REFERENCES

Battle-Baptiste, Whitney. 2011. *Black Feminist Archaeology*. Walnut Creek, CA: Left Coast Press.

Brown, Wendy. 2006. *Regulating Aversion: Tolerance in the Age of Identity and Empire*. Princeton, NJ: Princeton University Press.

Davidson, James M. 2004. "Living Symbols of the Lifelong Struggles": In Search of the Home and Household in the Heart of Freedman's Town, Dallas, Texas. In *Household Chores and Household Choices: Theorizing the Domestic Sphere in Historical Archaeology*, edited by Kerri S. Barile and Jamie C. Brandon, 75–108. Tuscaloosa, AL: University of Alabama Press.

———. 2007. "Resurrection Men" in Dallas: The Illegal Use of Black Bodies as Medical Cadavers (1900–1907). *International Journal of Historical Archaeology* 11(3): 193–220.

———. 2008. Identity and Violent Death: Contextualizing Lethal Gun Violence within the African-American Community of Dallas, TX (1900–1907). *Journal of Social Archaeology* 8(3): 321–356.

D'Orso, Michael. 1996. *Like Judgment Day: The Ruin and Redemption of a Town Called Rosewood*. New York: G.P. Putnam's Sons.

Forte, Maurizio. 1997. *Virtual Archaeology: Great Discoveries Brought to Life Through Virtual Reality*. London: Thames & Hudson.

———, ed. 2010. *Cyber-Archaeology*. London: Archaeopress.

Freire, Paulo. 1970. *Pedagogy of the Oppressed*. New York: Continuum.

———. 2002. *Pedagogy of Hope: Reliving Pedagogy of the Oppressed*. New York: Continuum.

González-Tennant, Edward. 2009. Using Geodatabases to Generate "Living Documents" for Archaeology: A Case Study from the Otago Goldfields, New Zealand. *Historical Archaeology* 43(3): 20–37.

———. 2011. Creating a Diasporic Archaeology of Chinese Migration: Tentative Steps Across Four Continents. *International Journal of Historical Archaeology* 15(3): 509–532.

———. 2013. New Heritage and Dark Tourism: A Mixed Methods Approach to Social Justice in Rosewood, Florida. *Heritage & Society* 6(1): 62–88.

Harrison, Faye V. 1997. *Decolonizing Anthropology: Moving Further Toward an Anthropology for Liberation*. Washington, D.C.: American Anthropological Association.

———. 1998. Introduction: Expanding the Discourse on "Race." *American Anthropologist* 100(3): 609–631.

———. 2005. *Resisting Racism and Xenophobia: Global Perspectives on Race, Gender, and Human Rights*. Walnut Creek, CA: AltaMira Press.

———. 2008. *Outsider Within: Reworking Anthropology in the Global Age*. Urbana, IL: University of Illinois Press.

Harrison, Rodney. 2009. Excavating Second Life: Cyber-Archaeologies, Heritage and Virtual Communities. *Journal of Material Culture* 14(1): 75–106.

Harrison, Rodney, and John Schofield. 2010. *After Modernity: Archaeological Approaches to the Contemporary Past*. New York: Oxford University Press.

hooks, bell. 1994. *Teaching to Transgress: Education as the Practice of Freedom*. New York: Routledge.

———. 2003. *Teaching Community: A Pedagogy of Hope*. New York: Routledge.

———. 2010. *Teaching Critical Thinking: Practical Wisdom*. New York: Routledge.

Jones, Maxine D., Larry E. Rivers, David R. Colburn, R. Thomas Dye, and William R. Rogers. 1993. *A Documented History of the Incident Which Occurred at Rosewood, Florida, in January 1923: Submitted to the Florida Board of Regents 22 December 1993*. Tallahassee, FL: Board of Regents.

Kalay, Yehuda E., and P. Grabowicz. 2007. Oakland Blues: Virtual Preservation of Seventh Street's 1950s Jazz Scene. *The Proceedings of DACH* 2007: 205–227.

Kalay, Yehuda E., Thomas Kvan, and Janice Affleck, eds. 2008. *New Heritage: New Media and Cultural Heritage*. London. Routledge.

Lambert, Joe. 2009. *Digital Storytelling: Capturing Lives, Creating Community*. 2nd ed. Berkeley, CA.: Digital Diner Press.

Lennon, John, and Malcolm Foley. 2000. *Dark Tourism: The Attraction of Death and Disaster*. London: Continuum.

Logan, William, and Keir Reeves. 2009. Introduction: Remembering Places of Pain and Shame. In *Places of Pain and Shame: Dealing With Difficult Heritage,* edited by William Logan and Kei Reeves, 1–14. London: Routledge.

Lowenthal, David. 1985. *The Past Is a Foreign Country*. New York: Cambridge University Press.

Macdonald, Sharon. 2008. *Difficult Heritage: Negotiating the Nazi Past in Nuremberg and Beyond*. New York: Routledge.

———. 2009. Unsettling Memories: Intervention and Controversy over Difficult Public Heritage. In *Engagement and Demission in the Contemporary World*, edited by Marta Anico and Elsa Peralta, 93–105. New York: Routledge.

Manovich, Lev. 2001. *The Language of New Media*. Cambridge, MA: MIT Press.

Morgan, Colleen L. 2009. (Re)Building Çatalhöyük: Changing Virtual Reality in Archaeology. *Archaeologies: Journal of World Archaeological Congress* 5(3): 488–568.

Nieves, Angel David. 2009. Places of Pain as Tools for Social Justice in the "New" South Africa: Black Heritage Preservation in the "Rainbow" Nation's Townships. *In Places of Pain and Shame: Dealing With Difficult Heritage*, edited by William Logan and Keir Reeves, 198–214. London: Routledge.

Ortiz, Paul. 2005. *Emancipation Betrayed: The Hidden History of Black Organizing and White Violence in Florida from Reconstruction to the Bloody Election of 1920*. American Crossroads. Berkeley, CA: University of California Press.

Pink, Sarah. 2006. *The Future of Visual Anthropology: Engaging the Senses*. London, New York: Routledge.

Reilly, Paul. 1990. Towards a Virtual Archaeology. *In Computer Applications in Archaeology*, edited by K. Lockyear and S. Rahtz, 133–139. Oxford, UK: British Archaeological Reports.

Schmidt, Peter R. 2006. *Historical Archaeology in Africa: Representation, Social Memory, and Oral Traditions*. The African Archaeology Series. Lanham, MD: AltaMira Press.

———. 2010. Social Memory and Trauma in Northwestern Tanzania. *Journal of Social Archaeology* 10(2): 255–279.

Seaton, A. V. 2002. Thanatourism's Final Frontiers? Visits to Cemeteries, Churchyards and Funerary Sites as Sacred and Secular Pilgrimage. *Tourism Recreation Research* 27(2): 73–82.

Sharpley, Richard. 2005. Travels to the Edge of Darkness: Towards a Typology of Dark Tourism. *In Taking Tourism to the Limits: Issues, Concepts and Managerial Perspectives*, edited by Chris Ryan, Stephen Page, and Michelle Aicken, 215–226. London: Elsevier.

Stone, Philip R. 2006. A Dark Tourism Spectrum: Towards a Typology of Death and Macabre Related Tourist Sites, Attractions and Exhibitions. *Tourism* 54(2): 145–160.

Tarlow, Peter E. 2005. Dark Tourism: The Appealing "Dark" Site of Tourism and More. *In Niche Tourism: Contemporary Issues, Trends and Cases*, edited by Marina Novelli and Elsevier Butterworth-Heinemann, 47–58. Oxford, UK: Elsevier.

thomas-houston, marilyn. 2005. *"Stony the Road" to Change: Black Mississippians and the Culture of Social Relations*. New York: Cambridge University Press.

Tunbridge, J. E., and G. J. Asworth. 1996. *Dissonant Heritage: The Management of the Past as a Resource in Conflict*. London: Belhaven Books.

PART

5

Participatory Digital Archives and Museums

Ethnography of an Ethnographic Somali Photography Archive in Maine

Catherine Besteman

During 1987 and 1988, I lived in Banta, Somalia, with my photographer husband, Jorge Acero, to carry out ethnographic fieldwork for my dissertation. During our stay we created a collection of about a thousand photographs that captured quotidian village activities: nomadic pastoralists migrating in the bush outside the village with their large herds, ritual life, landscapes, and more than a hundred formal portraits requested by friends and neighbors.

When we left Somalia in 1988 with suitcases filled with negatives, prints, and slides, we promised to return within a few years to resume our studies and maintain friendships. But shortly after our departure, the government collapsed under the pressure of oppositional militias and reduced foreign aid. When the militias, who began fighting against each other after the government collapsed, reached Banta, their violence forced most villagers to flee for their lives across the border into Kenya, where they spent a decade and a half in refugee camps.[1] Somali Bantus, as ethnic minorities with a history of discrimination, had no allies among the Somali militias vying for control, who instead targeted Somali Bantu villages for looting, rape, kidnapping, and murder. In the upheaval of the war I lost touch with everyone I knew, but learned in 2001 about a plan to bring Somali Bantus from Kenyan refugee camps to the United States under a special resettlement program for "persecuted minorities." Somali Bantu refugees began arriving in the United States from 2004 to 2006, where many were initially resettled in large cities. Feeling unsafe and unable to manage the high cost of living, some

Catherine Besteman, "Ethnography of an Ethnographic Somali Photography Archive in Maine" in *Participatory Visual and Digital Research in Action*, Aline Gubrium, Krista Harper, and Marty Otañez, eds., pp. 181-195. © 2015 Left Coast Press, Inc. All rights reserved.

began relocating to more affordable cities, including Lewiston, Maine, a city of 35,000 with abundant low-cost housing, a low crime rate, and a low cost of living, just an hour from where I live.

After years of inquiries with refugee resettlement agencies, I had lost hope that I would find anyone from Banta in the United States, but when Lewiston's new immigrants and I met for the first time in January 2006, I learned that, astonishingly, many were from Banta. Our surprising and wonderful reunion resulted in several collaborative advocacy and educational outreach projects, including some that made use of our archive of photographs of prewar life in southern Somalia. Our archive thus gained a second life as its subjects regained possession of their portraits and could show their children photographs of their deceased extended family members and lost family farms. In this chapter I recount how our photography archive became the basis of a series of collaborative educational projects that included a website, two museum exhibitions, and an ELL (English Language Learner) book, 20 years and 6,000 miles away from its original creation. The following sections juxtapose a description of each project with ethnographic observations that reveal important dimensions of collaborative work, summarized in the concluding section. Through such juxtapositions, I hope to illustrate several facets of these collaborative projects as a form of engaged ethnography that includes encounters between Somali Bantu immigrants, other Mainers, college students in civic engagement classes, and myself.

A Second Life

After our unexpected reunion, Banta's former residents were eager to arrange a slideshow in Lewiston to see photographs of the life they left behind. Jorge and I assembled hundreds of slides and poster boards covered with photographs to display, but were anxious that the photographs of deceased loved ones and a lifestyle destroyed by war would be traumatic for a community that had lost so much. Our Banta friends insisted that everyone was eager to see the photographs and remember their lives before the war. The first form of engagement with the photography archive was thus simply about enabling personal and intimate (re)connections through viewing and sharing the photographs (Figures 11.1, 11.2).

> 1/2006. As people arrived for the event we found mutual recognition in each other's aged faces. The son of our neighbor and dear friend Cabdulle Cabdi was one of the first through the door. Iman was just

a baby when we lived in Banta and has no memory of his parents, who died when he was a toddler. Nor does he remember his dead grandfather, caught in a stately pose by Jorge's camera. Iman examined their photos in the poster display, searching for his likeness in their faces. Axmed Jabiq caught my eye over the crowd: he had been married to Binti, one of my first friends in Banta. Our poster display included a photograph of Binti and their son; both are now dead. Daliya's daughter arrived and burst into tears upon discovering our portrait of her dead mother sifting corn. Everyone started naming those captured in the poster display: Ganuun is dead. Although Caliyow Isaaq is dead, his only surviving wife Jimcoy is moving to Maine with some of their surviving children. One of his other wives, Amina, is dead, but their daughter Binti, caught on camera as a delightfully happy baby, now lives in Texas.

When the slide show began the audience quieted, engrossed, as they struggled to make sense of the photographs and the faces, frozen as they were 18 years before. After people got used to what they were seeing, they asked to repeat the entire show a second time, this time calling out names to identify those appearing on the screen. The photograph of Abshirow, elegantly dressed in his velvet jacket, standing with his wife Muslimo and baby son, evoked shrieks: "Look how dressed up he looks, standing in front of his *mundul* [round house made of mud and grass]," someone yelled out. Abshirow and his family were resettled in Texas, but, like many other survivors from Banta, later moved to Lewiston. A photograph of Axmed Jabiq provoked cries of delight. In the photograph he appears young and very strong, wearing shorts and a large wrap on his head while working with a group of men to construct a frame for the room of a new *mundul*. Axmed Jabiq himself was far more excited about a photograph of one of his farms, calling out the name of the farm location. Several women exclaimed with satisfaction at the beauty of the nicely tilled farms that appear in several photographs. The photographs of young children guarding fields of sesame against the trepidations of birds and monkeys elicited lots of comments, as did images of hoes, machetes, and other long-lost farm tools.

After listening three times to tapes of music that we recorded in Banta, everyone wanted to watch the entire slideshow again, identifying still more people. The third time through the slideshow people recognized the images of religious and ritual activities, commenting in excitement on their old festivals.

As the festivities wound down, everyone asked for copies of photos. Over the course of the following year I went from house to house in Lewiston, reconnecting with people from Banta and distributing photographs from that long-ago life. When I gave 17-year-old Iman the photograph of him as a baby in his mother's arms, his friends gathered around to stare as one exclaimed, "You are the only one of us who has a baby picture for the [high school] yearbook!" Looking at the likeness of his grandfather for the first time, Ambiya's son Daoud gently ran his hand over his forehead, ears, eyebrows, nose, lips, and chin, comparing every feature with the man in the photograph. Abdulkadir's eight children gathered around to see photographs of their father as a young unmarried man, posing with his niece and deceased nephew. Bashir asked for a new portrait of him standing next to his car to display alongside the old photograph of him in the unsteady village canoe: a visual commentary on his life trajectory. Jimcoy wanted a new photograph of herself in which she copies her pose from her portrait taken 20 years ago, only this time she wants to hold the baby of the daughter that she is holding in the earlier photograph (Besteman in press).

FIGURE 11.1: Binti and her son, Banta, Somalia, 1988 (photograph by Jorge Acero)

FIGURE 11.2: Iman's grandfather, Banta, Somalia, 1988 (photograph by Jorge Acero)

During that year, Somali Bantu refugee community leaders identified their desire to teach people in Lewiston about their history, culture, and experiences as a top priority, and I received many requests for copies of photographs from Banta's refugees living in other parts of the United States and even the Kenyan refugee camps. To meet these requests, we conceived the idea of creating an open access website featuring the photography archive (and new photographs of Banta people in Lewiston) that could be accessed by people all over the world and used as a teaching tool in Lewiston and elsewhere. Creating *The Somali Bantu Experience: From East Africa to Maine* (www.web.colby.edu/somalibantu/) was our first collaborative photo-archive project, followed by a museum exhibition of the same name at the Colby College Museum of Art, which in turn became the center of an expanded exhibition at the Museum L/A in Lewiston, called *Rivers of Immigration: Peoples of the Androscoggin.* In addition, we used the photographs to develop the first ELL book published in English, Somali, and Maay-Maay.

The Collaborative Projects

The Somali Bantu Experience Website

The Somali Bantu community leaders and I envisioned the website as a source of historical and contemporary information about Somali Bantu refugees living in the United States that would be useful and accessible for teachers and advocates, for Somali Bantus living throughout the world to access photographs of their villages and possibly relatives, and for refugees and advocates searching for information about refugee rights and assistance. After digitizing the slides and photographs in our archive as well as all my tape-recorded interviews, I offered a civic engagement course through my college to create the website.

We began with several weeks of ethnographic background study, visits to Lewiston, and visits to the college of members of the Somali Bantu refugee community. Then the class divided into six groups, each with responsibility for a specific part of the project. One group built the website template; two groups did fieldwork in Lewiston, where they worked with Somali Bantu teenagers to interview refugee community members about life in Lewiston and take contemporary photographs to complement the archive photographs. A fourth group worked with schoolteachers in Lewiston to develop age-appropriate curricular materials to be used in conjunction with the website; another group worked on developing historical materials and resources for advocates and refugees; and a final group developed an educational outreach and public relations plan for marketing the website. Each group had responsibility for developing the textual, visual, and technological components of their portion of the website, and we workshopped each section of the website with other class members and members of the Somali Bantu community. I maintained editorial oversight and fact-checking responsibilities, and the Somali Bantu community leaders reviewed the entire website before it went public.

March 2008. Somali Bantu elders are visiting the class this week, after our first fieldtrip to Lewiston last week. I knew the hour-long travel time would be difficult for elders who are busy with work, English classes, caring for young children, or managing illnesses, but we all thought it was important to try to organize reciprocal visits to start the project. Mohamed Farah, the president of the Somali Bantu community association, offers to bring whoever is free on the appointed day. Axmed Jabiq has a medical appointment. Abshirow cannot sit in a car for such a long trip because of his physical problems. Asha, Jimcoy, and Ali agree to come, but get the dates confused and are delayed getting ready. Our meeting is scheduled from 1 to 3 p.m. We talk on the phone at 11:30, at noon, at 12:30, and at 1. They still are getting organized. At 2 we talk again, and they are lost in Waterville. Everyone is laughing: Asha is saying in the background that she had no idea I was so far away! Even though Mohamed has been here several times before, my instructions don't work this time and they end up touring the entirety of Waterville before finding our classroom, a half-hour before the end of our meeting time. The visitors need a restroom stop, and then file into the class, where they introduce themselves with great formality and brevity. Asha and Jimcoy have dressed carefully and beautifully, with golden earrings, necklaces, bracelets, and rings, their colorful clothing covered in sequins: gold for Asha, silver for Jimcoy.

I have set up my computer to screen photos from Banta as we talk, and as the slideshow plays Asha and Jimcoy cannot take their eyes off it. Mohamed and Ali field most of the questions, but my students seem shy, or maybe confused by Asha and Jimcoy's lack of interest in them. Watching the photographs flashing on the screen, Asha and Jimcoy comment to each other about those they recognize in the photos, ignoring the class discussion going on around them. But they do not recognize the photos of themselves. Mohamed says, "Asha does not know herself!" We have to point out, "Asha, this is you!" Mohamed chuckles at Asha and Jimcoy's fascination with the photographs.

The students ask tentative questions that are hard to translate and even harder to answer. "What do you want in the exhibit?" "We are fine with the exhibit!" they proclaim, emphatically. "You can have whatever you want in the exhibit." The students ask, "What jobs do you do?" Mohamed lists all the jobs he has held: forklift operator, cleaner, cashier, translator. Ali removes his shoe and sock and lifts his leg over the table to show why he can't work. He was shot during the war, leaving his left leg disfigured and crippled. His right eye is gone. Although he receives disability, he wishes to work. Another student asks, "Are you afraid of losing your culture?" They answer, simply, "No." Another question, "Will you forget what happened to you"? Again, "No. Never. We will never forget." The students are subdued, unsure how to ask their questions.

Class ends and the students troop out. I sit with my guests as they eat the meal we ordered hours ago for lunch. We discuss the project: they are much more animated and excited about it now that the formality of the class meeting is gone. Mohamed is enamored of the idea of presenting a "Then and Now" vision of their lives; Ali adds that when it goes online, everyone in Somalia will see their lives here and want to come. We watch the slideshow loop one more time before they head home, seeing images of Asha's dead husband and daughter, her kidnapped daughter, her two children still living in the refugee camp, her dead sister, images of Jimcoy's dead husband, dead co-wife, all those lost in the war.

The website, which took three months to create, includes sections (many with clickable links) on Somali political history and the history of refugee resettlement from Somalia to the United States, life in Lewiston (including sections on Community and Environment, Family and Food, Making a Living, Medicine and Health, Religion and Community Life), Family Stories (including the "Then and Now" section), Resources and Information (including downloadable ELL books, maps, and resource links for refugees and advocates), and links to the digital archive of photographs and tape-recorded interviews from 1987 and 1988. Moving past the subdued formality of the initial group meetings, students worked in pairs with teenage Somali Bantu collaborators to develop material for the website. The teenagers organized visits with people in their homes, on the playground, at weddings, and at the local shops, and they in turn visited their collaborators at Colby. The project's collaborative methodology thus matched particular students with community members to deepen their interpersonal connections, vet photographs, record interviews, identify appropriate subjects to include, and gather relevant resources, as well as with teachers to develop pedagogical materials and the college's information technology staff on the technological components of the site. When the website went public, teachers in local schools and ELL adult education classes began using it, and Somali Bantu friends recommended it to family members throughout the United States and in Kenya who searched the photo archive for images of their villages and family members.

The Somali Bantu Experience *Exhibition*

The website became the basis for two subsequent museum exhibitions. The first exhibition at the Colby College Museum of Art carried the same name as the website, but was developed by a new class with a new group of students working with the same Somali Bantu collaborators. As with the website class, the museum exhibition class divided up responsibilities for crafting the exhibition, tasking students with creating a set of digitized, projected wall maps to demonstrate the journey from southern Somalia to different refugee camps in Kenya to Maine; writing the wall text; developing an audiovisual component to feature Somali Bantu music, poetry, and interviews with community members; curating, researching, and writing text about Somali Bantu material culture objects selected for the exhibition; producing an exhibition brochure; and managing publicity for the exhibition. The exhibition included about 30 photographs, a dozen material culture objects, a video installation of music, poetry, and interviews, the projected wall maps, and explanatory text. Again, students worked with Somali Bantu collaborators on the video and the explanatory wall text, and Somali Bantus vetted the selected photographs and material culture objects.

For the opening, we arranged bus transportation for Somali Bantu community members from Lewiston, who spoke during the ceremony about their involvement in the project. Following the opening, the Museum provided transport for about 2,000 school children throughout Maine to visit the exhibition, including hundreds from Lewiston. Students from my course acted as guides for the exhibit and offered public outreach presentations to the campus and docents. We also hosted panel discussions with Somali Bantu elders on campus.

> November 2008. Seventy Somali and Somali Bantu kids from Lewiston's middle-school ELL classes visit the exhibit. The college students who acted as museum guides for the exhibition reported that the kids were so eager to view and listen and touch everything that the allotted half hour in the gallery was not enough time. They also reported being taken aback by racist comments from some visiting teachers and adult chaperones. While a group looked at a mounted photograph of a Somali Bantu parent at work in L.L. Bean, a student guide explained that the refugees are hardworking and work at a wide variety of jobs in the United States. The teacher accompanying the group said, "Yeah, and they take jobs away from hardworking Americans." Another teacher talked

on her cell phone during the entire tour, demonstrating no interest at all in the material on display.

The next day the Lewiston High School ELL kids came, accompanied by six teachers. The visiting students recognized many people in the photographs, which clearly thrilled them. The teachers spoke about their use of the website in their classes, one even remarking on the difference it made in the attitude of some of the Somali Bantu students, who seemed validated and proud to be part of a community featured in this way. Speaking about one student in particular, a teacher told me that the website was a "healing process" for him, noting how the student had "gained motivation and self-confidence" from participating in its development. And yet, high school friends from the refugee community tell me later of their disappointment that the school had sent only the ELL students and not the entire school to visit the exhibit, which made them feel singled out and isolated rather than celebrated and recognized. They would have liked to share the exhibit with their non-Somali classmates as well, but this was not a school priority.

"A Somalia Album" ELL Booklet

Another priority the Somali Bantu leaders identified was English language acquisition and literacy. The lack of schools in their Somali villages meant that hardly any adults in the refugee community ever learned to read, and only a few spoke English. Given the paucity of culturally appropriate ELL materials, we agreed to create an ELL booklet in English, Somali, and Maay-Maay (the two official languages of Somalia) using the photography archive to draft text based on the images of life in Somalia. A non-Somali ELL teacher, three literate English-speaking Somali Bantus, and I selected the photographs and drafted and translated the text. A generous graphic designer at Colby designed the book for free. A grant from the Maine Humanities Council covered the publication costs and free distribution of the booklets in Maine, and a national Somali Bantu advocacy organization covered the cost of providing copies to all the Somali Bantu communities in the United States (Maine Humanities Council n.d.).

Lewiston schools and adult ELL classes began using the book immediately, as did language and literacy programs elsewhere in the country. The images primarily depict rural life, showing village scenes as well as people migrating with their animals. Most of the women in the photographs are wearing the

FIGURE 11.3: Quran School in Banta, Somalia, 1988 (photograph by Jorge Acero)

traditional one-shouldered dress that was universal in rural areas in the 1980s, but that has since been replaced with loose-flowing dresses and scarves that cover the arms and shoulders. The images of rural prewar life provoked an unexpected range of reactions (Figure 11.3):

> February 2009. An afterschool program for Somali Bantu youth in Syracuse introduced the book in a daylong literacy workshop during which the young students wrote an essay about the book. The Somali Bantu teacher reported the overwhelming response was, "We were really poor!" The kids were amazed to see how their parents lived, writing things like, "We never want to go there! We want to work really hard to get our relatives out of there [for those who are still in Africa]! We never want our parents to be that poor again! Here is SO much better."

When a local Lewiston newspaper asked to publish an article about the project, one of the women whose photograph appeared in the book expressed concern about publishing an image in the local newspaper of her wearing the one-shouldered dress because of the perception that the people in the book's photographs look so poor. Her son told me that Somali refugees who are not from rural Somalia are upset that the apparent material deprivation depicted in the photographs contradicts their efforts to cultivate a professional, educated, urban, cosmopolitan image, although he insists that he is not embarrassed by the poverty that others read in the photographs: "This is where I was born and I'm proud of it. We worked hard, we did everything for ourselves, and I am proud of it."

> November 2009. I visit a high school ELL class that contains both Somali and Somali Bantu students, and when the teacher brings out the ELL book one of the Somali girls sits back, saying "I don't want that book. I don't know those people." The teacher tells her she is being rude. Eventually they all take a book, but the Somali girls are emphatic that their families come from a place in Somalia with roads, cars, electricity, "real" houses, TV sets. They are clearly hostile to the images in the book and do not want to be associated with those images. I gently talk about how the images show a community that was very strong, dignified, and self-sufficient. The students gradually get pulled into a discussion about the book, eventually discussing with excitement their Quran school experiences in response to the images of Quran schools and a teacher reading his Quran. One girl asks what I wore when I was there, and I said the one-shouldered dress in the image on the cover because all women dressed like that, prompting the Somali girls to object that their mothers never dressed like that! Two Somali Bantu boys call out that their mothers had indeed dressed like that. I try to calm the escalating argument by explaining that some women in the cities wore long, loose dresses made by a tailor rather than the one-shouldered dress, which seemed to placate everyone. The students ask what I liked best about living in Somalia, and I describe how families spent their time talking and sharing poetry in the evenings because there was no TV. The girls immediately object, "Our families had TVs!" I acknowledge that yes, some families in the cities had TVs, but most Somalis did not, and where I lived there were none, so I had enjoyed how families spent their time in the evenings telling stories. The girls, placated again, agree that evening storytelling sounded nice.

Rivers of Immigration Exhibition

In 2009, the Museum L/A, dedicated to the story of work and community in Lewiston, agreed to mount a collaboratively curated exhibit based on the 2008 exhibition at the Colby College Museum of Art. Members of the Museum L/A staff, the local ELL adult education director, Somali Bantu community representatives, and other local community members met monthly to plan the exhibition, which expanded the scope to include a timeline of immigration to Lewiston and stories about contemporary and past immigrants from other origins. The museum director explained her preference for the title *Rivers of Immigration* because local people would react negatively to an exhibition title that included the word Somalia, imitating their reaction: "Hmph. I'm not going to see that. I don't want to see that." Somali Bantu leaders were also supportive of expanding the scope of the exhibition to include other immigrant populations, having experienced a backlash to the success of the website, the Colby exhibition, and the ELL booklet from some fellow Somali refugees who were upset about the attention Somali Bantu ethnic minorities were receiving, asking, "Why are your pictures everywhere? Why are you getting so much attention? Why are you so important?" We all agreed that the exhibition should seek to build bridges by ensuring that the new exhibition is broadly inclusive of all immigrant groups in the region.

> June 2010. At the close of the yearlong show, the museum director expressed her feeling that the exhibit had successfully challenged the prevalent local myth that Somalis, as refugees, had an easy and direct trip to the United States, where everything was arranged for their care. "Those who have gone through the exhibit have learned from it. I gave a tour to a group who said, 'Wow, we didn't realize they'd been through so much.' They don't know. No one's ever explained it to them…. [Our museum visitors] didn't have any idea they spent time in refugee camps and how horrible it was. They didn't know about the war, about the loss, the horror…. Viewers never realized how hard they had it in their country and why they had to leave. Genocide was never on their radar. Rape was never on their radar." Her staff assistant interjected, "All the stories about walking for hundreds of miles. They thought they just got on a plane and came straight here! Having to stay in refugee camps for years, people didn't know that. That was a big learning curve." While the museum staff acknowledges that local residents continue to make racist comments about Somalis, they believe the exhibition altered the anti-Somali hostility that some viewers may have carried into the exhibition.

The exhibition won two awards: a 2011 Leadership in History Award of Merit from the American Association for State and Local History, and a 2010 Leaders in Innovation Award from the New England Museum Association.

Conclusion

The collaborative projects produced successful outcomes that have been heavily used locally and that have reached national and—in the case of the website—international audiences. For many Somali Bantu refugees, the photography archive has contributed to a personal and community validation of history and identity in a time of loss and provided publicly available historical information that offsets popular perceptions of refugees as people stripped of history and culture by violent displacement. I conclude by summarizing a few of the issues that emerged in ethnographic moments during the collaborative research process.

1. Collaborative research between college students and community members can begin with awkward initial encounters as each group figures out how to talk to each other and how to meet each other's expectations. Placing Somali Bantu teenagers in charge of organizing interviews between students and refugee elders allowed them to take a leading role in guiding the collaboration.

2. The projects provoked feelings of resentment or jealousy on the part of some other immigrants, who felt overlooked or slighted by the focus on Somali Bantus. Although the initial projects were limited to the population featured in the photography archive, we tried to address this complaint by expanding the group of collaborators for the Museum L/A exhibition to ensure a more inclusive treatment of immigration.

3. The photographs from the archive carried different meanings for different refugee groups from Somalia. Some Somali immigrants read the photographs as representing poverty and deprivation rather than a dignified agrarian life, a tension that opened challenging conversations within the refugee population in Lewiston about self-representation and whose history should be promoted in public venues.

4. The photographs also offered different meanings for different viewers in Lewiston and elsewhere, and some museum visitors simply affirmed their own xenophobic views rather than expanding their understanding of their new neighbors. Some teachers and school administrators used the photographs to illustrate the impoverished background of new refugee immigrants in ways other teachers found demeaning. And because the photographs were publicly available through the website, some were incorporated into projects in other cities without the permission of the photographers or the subjects for purposes quite different than those envisioned by the project collaborators. Open access enables public engagements and uses of all kinds.

In sum, these collaborative projects demonstrated that longer-term engagements between project directors, college students, and community members can help ameliorate initial awkwardness, and that joint ownership and leadership of collaborative projects is essential because outcomes can be unpredictable. When the results of collaborative projects are made publicly available—in the form of museum exhibitions, websites, and so forth—project members cannot always control how the material is interpreted, used, understood, or appropriated for other purposes. Because unanticipated problems or challenges *will* most likely arise in any complex engaged community project, success will be dependent upon the sort of trust and open communication that long-term collaboration fosters.

REFERENCES

Besteman, Catherine. 1999. *Unraveling Somalia: Race, Violence, and the Legacy of Slavery.* Philadelphia: University of Pennsylvania Press.

———. In press. *Making Refuge: Somali Bantu Refugees and Lewiston, Maine.* Durham, NC: Duke University Press.

Maine Humanities Council. n.d. *A Somalia Album.* Portland, ME: Maine Humanities Council.

NOTE

1   See Besteman (1999) for an analysis of the war.

Showcasing Heritage: Engaging Local Communities through Museum Practice

Madeleine Tudor and Alaka Wali

Introduction: Visualizing Participation in a Museum Context

At the 2014 Field Museum Members' Night in Chicago (an annual event that allows museum members to go "behind the scenes" and interact with staff), we displayed a newly accessioned selection of objects collected from the Calumet region of southeastern Chicago and northwestern Indiana. We were excited to show these new collections to our members, in part to make them aware that our collections program was a way in which the museum was addressing contemporary, relevant concerns by documenting the urban lifeways that are taking place within the milieu in which the museum itself is embedded. However, this demonstration of relevance was lost on some of the members. Since this was a special event and not an exhibit, the objects were laid out on a table, without the usual label copy, graphic design, or photographic accompaniment that provide the interpretive exhibition experience. Also, these objects were different from what our members normally encounter at the museum: they appeared to be too "ordinary" to be in the Natural History Museum's collections. Even so, many visitors were drawn to the objects, and they elicited responses. When viewing a steelworker's green uniform and hard hat, for example, members said: "Wow, those are just like your uncle's!" or "I know what those are…" or "I had a hat just like that."

Madeleine Tudor and Alaka Wali, "Showcasing Heritage: Engaging Local Communities through Museum Practice" in *Participatory Visual and Digital Research in Action,* Aline Gubrium, Krista Harper, and Marty Otañez, eds., pp. 197-212. © 2015 Left Coast Press, Inc. All rights reserved.

This attempt to engage the museum's audience with our collections reminded us both of the power and the problematic of incorporating visual (including material culture) approaches in participatory action research. In our work, we use the term "participatory action research" to refer to a *collective* commitment among museum researchers, partner organizations, and community members to engage with each step in the collection process (McIntyre 2008, 1). The participatory nature of our work emerges from the intersection between our engagement with contemporary urban collections and with a regional effort to conserve the natural landscape and create a National Heritage Area. Although we mainly address our collections work in this chapter, it is its existence alongside our other projects in the community that makes our research participatory (compare with Austin 2003; Ostergaard and Wali 2006). We have been using a variety of such approaches for close to two decades now. The use of visual techniques is "natural" in a museum setting, where mixed media are the core for presenting research to broader publics. In transferring museum-based representational strategies to our action research efforts, we find that we can more effectively build collaborations and communicate findings in ways that make them more useful.

In this chapter, we discuss how museums, as mediating institutions, can play a key role in telling local stories to broad audiences: specifically, how we as museum anthropologists use visual and ethnographic research methods to form the basis of artifact collection, documentation, interpretation, and display to help make visible the social and cultural practices that undergird the ways community residents create and conceive heritage in the Calumet region of northeastern Illinois and northwestern Indiana. After presenting the methods and relationship between research, visual strategies, and action, we discuss some of the dilemmas of power, positionality, and ethics that we have encountered during this project, including our relationship with ArcelorMittal, a major steel manufacturer in the region who has funded a part of our work.

Calumet is a complex and paradoxical landscape of vast, heavily industrialized and postindustrial areas juxtaposed with expanses of biologically significant ecosystems and diverse communities, old and new. The steel mills and other manufacturing industries have played a central role in the shaping of both the natural landscape and the social terrain. Today, the steel industry is greatly diminished in size and presence, and residents' struggles center on how best to forge a dignified livelihood that also sustains the remnants of rare wetlands, forest savannahs, and prairies. Our objective is to use participatory visual research strategies to participate in the creation of the National Heritage Area together with a loose coalition of local organizations. We start with a description of the relevance of our approach to museum anthropology by providing contextual information on its development.

The Unfolding of Visual Participatory Research at The Field Museum

In the early 1990s, The Field Museum created a new department, the Center for Cultural Understanding and Change, with a mission of expanding the public engagement role of the museum to make closer connections with the urban communities and neighborhoods that lay outside of its doors. This "call to action" was part of the museum's struggle with what it meant to "remain relevant (Anderson 2004, 9; see also Cameron 1971). The center's staff of cultural anthropologists worked on exhibitions and developed programs that leveraged an interdisciplinary approach to "focus on critical environmental and cultural issues…relevant to the public's daily lives and civic responsibilities," as Robert Janes describes in his book *Museums in a Troubled World* (2009, 125). Janes cites the center's work as a model for museum-based "activism," and he remarks that "social action" and the "commitment to sound anthropological research in combination with pressing socio-environmental issues" are "not incompatible but are necessary allies" (2009, 125).

One of the center's formative early projects was the development of an exhibition called *Living Together: Common Concerns, Different Responses*, which presented anthropology's perspective on the factors that shape cultural diversity. It used cross-cultural comparison to suggest that social groups' different responses to common human concerns are caused by the interaction between their environments, their histories, and human creativity (see Wali and Tudor, in press). To create the Chicago components of the exhibit, the center's staff together with exhibit developers brought in objects from city residents: shoes, clothes, home décor, and the like (Figure 12.1).

Three facets of this work had a lasting influence on subsequent projects. First, we learned about effectively deploying non-text-based media to communicate relatively complex ideas. Neither of us had ever worked on a museum exhibit before and had to shift from two-dimensional academic modes of discourse to the three-dimensional forms of representation that museums use. The shift entailed not just choosing a different communication

FIGURE 12.1: Shoes as a medium through which a comparison of cultural similarities and differences were presented to the public (Living Together: Common Concerns, Different Responses exhibition, The Field Museum. Photo © The Field Museum, GN88517_29c, Photographer John Weinstein)

technique, but also a shift in perspective about *what* information was important to convey. We found the incorporation of multimedia into our work to be exhilarating, not just for communicating research, but for engaging people in more participatory processes.

Second, we also developed a model of local partner engagement, beginning with the relationships we formed with the community partners who gave us objects for the exhibit, such as the Filipino American Historical Society of Chicago, the Polish Museum of America, and a range of community social service organizations. This model changed over the years and from project to project, but it centered on building long-term relationships with grassroots organizations of different sizes and types. In some instances, we conducted applied research without significant participation by community members. In other instances, community organizations were deeply involved in crafting the project. For instance, an exhibit we created for the museum on urban gardens entailed collaborative work with the gardeners and their organizations to craft the message and select the visual representation of their efforts. Another exhibit we developed based on collaborative research, *Urban*

Expressions, was almost entirely created by youth participants in a video/ media program and was the first time that the museum had showcased urban youth perspectives.

Third, we gained an abiding interest in understanding the role of heritage in shaping place and place attachment in urban contexts. In conversations with diverse collaborators we discovered that despite significant demographic and economic changes, "neighborhood" remained a salient category; people resisted the erasure of the distinctive qualities of their home-places in the face of accelerating gentrification. This place-based strategy requires "visual representations informed by anthropological theory, analysis of visual aspects of culture, and the use of visual ethnographic research methods" (Pink 2007, 3).

The results of our approach are best illustrated through our continuing work in the Calumet region. We began working in this region about 15 years ago, through a two-year, team-based ethnographic research project documenting perceptions of residents' relationships to nature in their home-place. The visual methods we used included participatory photography and photo elicitation, which, as Wolowic (2011, 223) explains, engage participants in the research process, provide content and context, and act as "a powerful mechanism for revealing future research themes as well as establishing the trusting relationships needed for future research" (see also Gubrium 2009; Harper 2009). We then created a multilayered website called "Journey through Calumet" (http://archive.fieldmuseum.org/calumet) of photos, video, text, and social asset-maps to make the research findings accessible to local residents, government agencies, and other stakeholders involved in economic and environmental revitalization efforts (Field Museum 2011; Wali and Tudor, in press). Since then, with varying degrees of intensity, we have continued to conduct both applied and participatory action research in the region. In the next section, we discuss our most recent endeavor to demonstrate the unique combination of visual media that a museum can deploy in both ethnographic research and heritage management efforts.

Heritage Management in the Calumet Region

The Calumet region is a bi-state (Illinois and Indiana) region that spans four counties, containing multiple municipalities and one national park (Indiana Dunes National Lakeshore). It has seen many changes in the last 150 years. From the earliest years of the establishment of Chicago as an urban metropolis (see Cronon 1991), the Calumet region was an important site for fueling the city's economic growth. It was most well known as the location of the steel mills, owned by major corporations such as Republic Steel, U.S. Steel, and Wisconsin Steel, and associated manufacturing industries. By the early 1990s, when the steel industry had shut down the vast majority of its manufacturing in the United States, Calumet residents experienced the consequences of deindustrialization (Walley 2013). As the region deindustrialized, various schemes emerged for its revitalization. In one instance, the local governments (the City of Chicago, principally) proposed a new economic development project: the creation of a third major airport, which would have wiped out entire neighborhoods and destroyed critical ecological habitats. Environmental organizations fought the airport plan, citing evidence that the region was a globally significant site for rare biological diversity found in fragments of prairie and wetland habitats that dotted the landscape amid the manufacturing sites and residential neighborhoods of diverse ethnic heritage (Bouman 2001).

Environmentalists proposed instead the protection of the natural areas and use of them for recreation and ecotourism. A grassroots effort arose, working on two fronts: 1) protection of the natural areas and 2) environmental justice demanding remediation from the effects of toxic air and soil pollution. Local activists, allied with regional conservation organizations, were successful against the airport and also subsequent economic schemes, such as the expansion of waste storage sites and landfills. After the City recognized the environmental value of the region, these activists created a network in the late 1990s—the Calumet Stewardship Initiative (CSI)—to promote environmental stewardship and education. The CSI is affiliated with a wider regional environmental conservation effort, Chicago Wilderness—now a strong coalition comprising more than 250 organizations protecting natural areas throughout the region (Heneghan et al. 2012). A similar network—the Calumet Heritage Partnership (CHP)—formed in 1999, brought together cultural heritage, historical, and environmental organizations to "identify, preserve, protect, and reclaim the natural, historical, cultural, and recreational heritage of the Calumet region of Illinois and Indiana for the purposes of educating and inspiring the public, restoring regional pride, and revitalizing our communities and their interconnectedness" (Calumet Heritage Partnership 2013), thus putting the region's environmental activism into a more integrative context.

The Field Museum has been a major stakeholder in these efforts, and our ongoing research and programmatic work has played a strong role in shaping the direction of the strategy for the Calumet region. The most recent focus of our efforts is centered on the creation of a National Heritage Area for the bi-state Calumet region. National Heritage Areas (NHAs) is a program connected to the National Park Service. Members of the CHP chose the NHA designation because it provides flexibility in managing both natural areas and cultural resources. The NHA program as it is currently constructed is based on an active concept of heritage: "using the past as a resource for the present" (Graham et al. 2000, 11).

An NHA is like a massive exhibition, including associated educational and community programs, that takes place on the landscape instead of within the confines of a museum. Using signage, themed trials, and a range of programs, NHAs showcase local grassroots perspectives on the landscape. Through public-private partnerships, NHA entities support historic preservation, natural resource conservation, recreation, arts, heritage tourism, and educational projects. Local residents, communities, and leaders develop NHAs in collaboration with governmental agencies, nonprofit institutions, and private partners (National Park Service 2003). The process of designation is complicated and requires an act of Congress. Cultural institutions such as The Field Museum are good partners to lead and facilitate local efforts in pursuit of NHA designation. Our division, the Science Action Center of The Field Museum, is working with the Calumet Heritage Partnership to move the application process forward. The first step is to undertake a feasibility study that documents the natural, industrial, historical, and recreational assets of a region and sets out interpretive themes under which regional "stories" can be organized and represented.

As anthropologists, we have been contributing to the effort through both ethnographic research and the building of a museum-quality collection that documents the nature of heritage in the region. In building the collection, our hope is that local residents will come to see themselves represented in the museum. As with other natural history museums, The Field Museum's exhibits and collections are overwhelmingly dedicated to non-Western cultures. Only very recently have efforts been made to include Chicago examples, and deliberate efforts made to provide research access to the collections to local communities. An NHA expert who is consulting on the feasibility study stressed the importance of rooting overarching themes in ethnography to "recognize and give shape to all of the intangible elements that make up our heritage" (A. Carlino, personal communication, March 18, 2014). Although we had conducted ethnographic research before, as mentioned above, the new focus on heritage required a different approach. In addition, in 2012, we realized that we could leverage collection-building to more effectively engage local residents in the identification of themes that would support the NHA designation and programs. We have been able to more thoroughly incorporate participatory visual and digital media strategies into the action research agenda. Here, we describe preliminary research findings and the techniques we have been using; in the next section we analyze their impact on collaboration and also discuss some of the problematic aspects.

Our work has identified three themes that can be used to support the NHA narrative: 1) transformation as manifest in multiple dimensions, including labor, that transforms raw material into finished product; 2) the significance of Calumet's natural areas for place attachment and heritage construction; and 3) the role of art making in making heritage visible. These themes arose through the use of participatory visual media techniques that weave together the collection of specific objects, the use of photography to initiate conversations of remembrances about place and social process, and storytelling captured during public events, structured focus groups, and interviews.

The theme of transformation surfaces through the participatory visual research. It appears in stories from residents who work or used to work in the steel mills, in their accounts of the material culture associated with steel production, and in the accounts of environmental and community activists as they describe the natural and built environments of their home-place. For example, a retired steelworker during an ethnographic interview in 2012 described her feeling about her work in the mills:

> ...to think that you're just starting with scrap and limestone and coal, just these rocks from the ground and then it's making our cars, our bridges, our skyscrapers. You're starting from scratch and you're building something.

We have collected uniforms, hard hats, and protective gear worn by the workers (Figure 12.2). In most cases, the steelworkers themselves, who wanted to participate in the documentation of their heritage, donated this material. One former steelworker donated his hard hat, work boots, green uniform, gloves, and ear plugs; all "transform" him into a steelworker, ready to face the heat and noise of the factory floor. Visible on a hard hat donated from another steelworker is evidence of his transformation of the object from generic helmet to a marker of his personal and social identity: his nickname and stickers with his union affiliation. On the back of his hat is an Earth Day sticker from the early 1970s. His espousal of environmental concerns belies

FIGURE 12.2: Standard-issue hard hats often displayed the owner's affiliations. This one worn by a steel worker in the 1970s symbolized ties to industry and environment through an Earth Day symbol on the back of the hat (photo © The Field Museum, M. Mazhar 2012)

the popular notion of tension between heavy industry and environmental stewardship. We also "collected" stories of steelworkers' sense of pride about their labor in transforming raw material into manufactured steel.

When those who had donated or sold material objects to the museum visited the collections, they were able to reinterpret their possessions within the wider global heritage represented in the museum's collections. As they walked with us through the aisles replete with objects from North American Indians (among which the contemporary North American collection is housed), they commented on the pride they felt in having their material included. The transformation from object to museum-worthy artifact added value to the reflection of heritage.

The second theme of the significance of nature for place attachment and heritage construction has emerged through ethnographic photo-documentation of the natural and built environments (and the intertwining of the two) (Figure 12.3). The photo collection of more than 3,000 images

FIGURE 12.3: Photographs such as this one of the lakefront in Portage, Indiana, capture the juxtaposition of elements in the Calumet landscape (photo © The Field Museum, H. A. Graver 2012)

has been used in presentations to local and regional environmental and heritage organizations in the region and in the form of brochures, event flyers, reports, and other documents to advance heritage management and natural area protection.

The third theme that has emerged from the research is the expansive presence of art-making in the Calumet region. There has been an expansion of "art districts," art galleries, and valuation of local artists. For example, an old, local hardware store in Indiana has now evolved into a partial art gallery and artisan jewelry store, and it has an open-mic night. Here, woven baskets, pottery, and paintings hang from the shelving along the west wall. The store's owner said that the wooden slats sat in the paint-mixing area of the hardware store for years. He saw their value as art, and framed them (Figure 12.4).

Local artists tell us stories about how they came to make art and how they draw on local heritage and the nature around them. Some artists use

FIGURE 12.4: Public art evoking the region's heritage helped to reframe this former substation-turned-art gallery (photo © The Field Museum, C. Griskavich 2013)

"found objects," such as scraps and remnants from steelmaking; others are inventing new techniques. For example, one local artist uses an encaustic technique involving pigmented hot wax to evoke the plumes of smoke produced by heavy industry that he sees from his window, reflecting the region's industrial, social, and environmental heritage. Inspired by his work as former director of a municipal waterway, it is a meditation on the processes by which place is made and transformed by the interactions between people and environment. He is also active in environmental efforts and is collaborating on the NHA initiative. We conducted more than 10 hours of interviews with him over the course of a year about his art and his activism, and decided to purchase the painting for the Museum's collection. The painting's presence in the collection provides value to the artistic endeavors of local activists and residents, who otherwise might not be recognized.

Discussion: Museum-Based Participatory Action Research

The case study described here demonstrates how a museum can use its unique combination of visual and digital media resources to do both research and programmatic action that advances the social and environmental objectives of a region and its residents. The integrated use of collection-building, photography, and storytelling provide a powerful suite of methods that can deepen collaboration, not just between the museum and community organizations, but also among community organizations themselves. We, as representatives of a large cultural institution, and as a result of our long-term collaborative work with partner organizations, can convene organizations that may not have otherwise worked together (in this case, for example, labor organizations, environmental organizations, and environmental justice organizations). This project has thus pushed the boundaries of the relationship between research and action for us. We find ourselves to be not just "researchers" collaborating with "actors," but actors ourselves. Furthermore, it is the first time that we have positioned collection-building as an "act" to foster collaboration. When we began making the Calumet heritage collection, we were aware that collecting urban material culture for a natural history museum would be problematic from a number of perspectives. We wanted to avoid the types of collection practices that stereotype such museums (see Rotenberg and Wali 2014): curator-driven acts of "salvage" for preservation of disappearing lifeways. We also wanted the collection to be appropriate for the anthropological mission of the museum and avoid redundancy with regional history museum collections. Finally, we had to be strategic in determining what, of the multitude of material objects, we could collect. The collaborative process of working with local organizations on the NHA effort facilitated the selection of objects and the accompanying photographic and digital material. Collaboration in the NHA effort has spurred us to also think about how the collection can be linked to other collections around the region, and how this might be useful to the heritage effort.

In effect, we have gradually in the course of this effort begun rethinking the relationship between heritage inside the museum and outside its walls. Therefore, in a sense, as much as our research has contributed to the collaborative effort, the collaboration has had a profound impact on our museum practice. The lived heritage we have uncovered, and its ongoing vital incorporation into the daily lives and activist struggles of the region's residents, can only be very partially captured in The Field Museum's collections. Yet, if the pieces we hold are perceived as anchors (once they enter the museum, they remain unchanged and become permanent) while the heritage outside— in the landscape and in people's memories—is continually transformed, the small selection takes on a significant value in the overall narrative that we are all constructing together.

The types of collaborations we have formed are at an organizational level. We have worked with local government agencies, national conservation organizations, and grassroots community organizations, among others. Although in this case, obviously the research component has remained "individualized," the collaborative elements are "collectivized." To a certain degree, this has helped balance the power between researcher and subject. The research is driven by the needs of the overall effort to build the heritage area. In this effort, The Field Museum, though it has a degree of prestige as a venerable civic institution, does not have more influence over the initiative than its partners.

Even so, we do confront power dilemmas. One concerns navigating the power dynamics within the organizations and communities with which we work. These dynamics are inflected by race and gender. Historically, the fault lines of race have affected activism in the Calumet region, as they have in society generally. The unions and environmental organizations were segregated or excluded African Americans and Latinos, especially in leadership positions. African Americans formed their own activist organizations to combat environmental injustices and racism (for example, People for Community Recovery, www.peopleforcommunityrecovery.org), which sometimes allied with largely white environmental organizations, but were not necessarily part of the same coalitions and networks. Although there have been strong female leaders of the environmental activist organizations, issues of gender inequality have not been emphasized as part of either labor or environmental struggles. We have paid attention to racial, ethnic, and gender intersections with both environmental and class issues, and uncovered both fault lines and avenues of collaboration across these divides. However, we have yet to fully engage with these concerns. In this sense, research, even using participatory techniques, reaches its limitations as a strategy for action. Research can illuminate tensions and divides between social sectors and organizations, but can it help to address these conflicts? How does our position, both as an ethnically diverse team of female and male ethnographers and as representatives of The Field Museum, affect conversations among the communities with whom we collaborate? Does awareness of exclusionary tendencies lead to action for inclusiveness? Do visual media provide more convincing evidence of areas of common ground between divided sectors than other ways of representing research findings? These are the questions that we need to explore as we advance further in the research and partnerships.

In addition to concerns related to power dynamics, we also must navigate an ethical borderline because our major source of funding is ArcelorMittal, the largest still active manufacturing corporation in the region. ArcelorMittal's social responsibility division has supported the NHA initiative and is partially funding The Field Museum's research and material culture collection effort. We are aware of the global corporations' (and the steel industry's overall) actions to quell action on climate change, and their record on environmental pollution and social justice and labor relations. We have discussed some of these concerns with collaborators, and have been transparent in all public meetings and informational literature about our funding. Although the labor–company issue is salient, most organization partners do not consider the local ArcelorMittal authorities to be inimical to their environmental and social goals. Indeed, there is a sharp contrast between the perception of ArcelorMittal and the perception of British Petroleum and its associated corporate partners in the region, whose actions have been the site of significant protests. It is beyond the scope of this chapter to delve into the complexities and nuances of corporate machinations, but we do struggle with how to navigate this terrain.

Conclusion

Our work on the Calumet National Heritage Area is a model of how an integrated, participatory approach that incorporates the core methodologies of museums can be effective in engaging local people and working toward heritage management that flows smoothly from the outside to the inside of the museum, and vice versa. The use of research to foster action, and the direct participation of researchers in the action arena, add significant value to grassroots efforts. Advocates of the Calumet NHA have garnered support from key political stakeholders (including members of Congress who represent the included districts in both Indiana and Illinois) and built amicable working relationships across state lines (not an easy feat because of historical tensions and issues of jurisdictional turf). Our commitment to the

NHA initiative is ongoing. As we write this, in the summer of 2014, we are engaged in organizing the annual local conference of the Calumet Heritage Partnership. The theme, in part based on our research, will focus on art and heritage in the Calumet region. We also are continuing to document local perceptions of the interwoven character of the region's natural and social heritage and building the collection, both at The Field Museum and at our collaborators' sites. As we move forward, we remain optimistic that the heritage management role of museums can make museums more accessible and more closely linked to the lives and concerns of their publics.

Acknowledgments

The authors would like to thank Hannah Eisler Burnett for her insightful contributions to this chapter.

REFERENCES

Anderson, Gail. 2004. The Role of the Museum: The Challenge to Remain Relevant. In *Reinventing the Museum: Historical and Contemporary Perspectives on the Paradigm Shift*, edited by Gail Anderson, 9–12. Lanham, MD: AltaMira Press.

Austin, Diane E. 2003. Community Based Collaborative Team Ethnography: A Community-University-Agency Partnership. *Human Organization* 62(2): 143–152.

Bouman, Mark. 2001. A Mirror Cracked: Ten Keys to the Landscape of the Calumet Region. *Journal of Geography* 100(3): 104–110.

Calumet Heritage Partnership. 2013. http://calumetheritage.org, accessed August 16, 2014.

Cameron, Duncan F. 1971. Museum, a Temple or the Forum. *Curator: The Museum Journal* 14: 11–24.

Cronon, William. 1991. *Nature's Metropolis: Chicago and the Great West.* New York: W. W. Norton.

Field Museum. 2011. Journey Through Calumet: Communities in Motion in Southeast Chicago and Northeast Indiana. http://archive.fieldmuseum.org/calumet/, accessed August 16, 2014.

Graham, Brian, Gregory J. Ashworth, and John E. Tunbridge. 2000. *A Geography of Heritage: Power, Culture, and Economy.* London: Oxford University Press.

Gubrium, Aline. 2009. Digital Storytelling as a Method for Engaged Scholarship in Anthropology. *Practicing Anthropology* 31(4): 5–10.

Harper, Krista. 2009. Using Photovoice to Investigate Environment and Health in a Hungarian Romani (Gypsy) Community. *Practicing Anthropology* 31(4): 10–14.

Heneghan, Liam, Christopher Mulvaney, Kristen Ross, Lauren Umek, Cristy Watkins, Lynne M. Westphal, and David H. Wise. 2012. Lessons Learned from Chicago Wilderness—Implementing and Sustaining Conservation Management in an Urban Setting. *Diversity* 4(1): 74–93.

Janes, Robert R. 2009. *Museums in a Troubled World: Renewal, Irrelevance or Collapse?* Hoboken, NJ: Taylor & Francis.

McIntyre, Alice. 2008. Participatory Action Research. *Qualitative Research Method Series* (52). Los Angeles, CA: Sage Publications.

National Park Service. 2003. *National Heritage Area Feasibility Study Guidelines Draft.* www.nps.gov/history/heritageareas/FSGUIDE/nhafeasguidelines.pdf, accessed August 16, 2014.

Ostergaard, Josh, and Alaka Wali. 2006. *Collaborative Research: A Practical Introduction to Participatory Action Research (PAR) for Communities and Scholars.* Chicago, IL: The Field Museum.

Pink, Sarah. 2007. *Visual Interventions: Applied Visual Anthropology.* New York: Berghahn Books.

Rotenberg, Robert, and Alaka Wali. 2014. Building A Collection Of Contemporary Urban Material Culture. *Museum Anthropology* 37(1): 1–5.

Wali, Alaka, and Madeleine Tudor. In press. Crossing the Line: Participatory Action Research in a Museum Setting. In *Public Anthropology in a Borderless World*, edited by Sam Beck and Carl Maida. New York: Berghahn Books.

Walley, Christine J. 2013. *Exit Zero: Family and Class in Postindustrial Chicago.* Chicago, IL: University of Chicago Press.

Wolowic, Jennifer. 2011. See What Happens When You Give Us The Camera. In *Collaborative Service Learning and Anthropology with Gitxaała Nation*, edited by Charles R. Menzies and Caroline F. Butler. *Collaborative Anthropologies* 4(1): 215–223.

PeruDigital: Ethnographic Storytelling through Iterative Design

Natalie M. Underberg-Goode

Introduction

In 2007, I teamed up with the late anthropologist and Andean studies scholar Elayne Zorn to develop the PeruDigital project (perudigital.org; Figure 13.1), a website designed to present and interpret Peruvian festivals and other folklore to English- and Spanish-speaking publics. On the site, the user is encouraged to adopt the perspective of the artist (performer of culture), ethnographer (researcher of culture), and/or sponsor (community-builder) within the digital environment.

The website introduces users first to a busy Lima, Peru, plaza where characters and objects indicate the perspectives found on the site. From there, users can visit the ethnographer's office and explore orienting information about Peruvian folklore, religion, and regions. These multimedia materials help users better understand and appreciate the interactive festival environment in Afro-Peruvian Piura. There, users can interact with festival performers such as a young girl preparing to perform in the *sarahuas* (a dance/drama about the historical conflict between the Christians and Moors in Spain), and objects such as the fieldwork videos are integrated into the ethnographer's virtual mobile player showing festival characters such as the *tamalera* (a playful representation of a local tamale-seller) in action. The goal is to introduce, via simulation, aspects of attending, performing in, and studying a festival (Underberg and Zorn 2013).

PeruDigital is based on archive materials from the Pontifical Catholic University of Peru—Lima's (PUCP) Institute of Ethnomusicology (IDE)

Natalie M. Underberg-Goode, "PeruDigital: Ethnographic Storytelling through Iterative Design" in *Participatory Visual and Digital Research in Action,* Aline Gubrium, Krista Harper, and Marty Otañez, eds., pp. 213-226.

as well as fieldwork conducted by the PeruDigital team. It represents a collaboration among individual faculty and students from the fields of anthropology, digital media, and modern languages (Spanish) at the University of Central Florida (UCF) and PUCP, as well as an international and interdisciplinary team of advisors.[1]

The PeruDigital Approach

In integrating these insights from reflexive and narrative ethnographies with digital humanities, the use of participatory design (PD) is essential, as the emphasis is as much on the design process as the product. This is done by bringing users and multidisciplinary scholars into the design process, analyzing their collaboration, and engaging in a methodology that moves from planning through iterative design cycles that produce prototypes for evaluation. The design team included project directors; an advisory board comprised of anthropologists and Andean, digital humanities, and Latin American studies scholars; a technical production group primarily of digital media students (including a graphic designer, interactive developer, video expert, and content manager); and a research and translation group.

PeruDigital began in 2007 and 2008 with trips to Peru to create the foundation for collaborations between UCF and PUCP. This included networking meetings and presentations, research trips to identify archive materials, and development and consultation with advisors. The second step involved prototype development, including weekly meetings with the production team, directed research and independent study classes with research assistants, and consultations with advisors. This permitted the team to develop a prototype of the interactive environment of Lima and Piura, Peru, including a limited number of characters, objects, and scenes, to allow us to present a pilot to advisors for evaluation. The team decided to focus on constructing two key areas: a busy Lima plaza, which includes access to characters such as a street musician as well as to the ethnographer's office; and Piura's Lord of Agony festival. The latter is a festival celebrated on the north coast of Peru that commemorates Christ's crucifixion.

In their evaluation, advisory board members praised the visual aspects and noted the broad opportunities for elaboration possible. The board asked repeatedly, however, for clarification on our intended audience. Several advisors noted that the site seemed aimed at children, but that the overall

FIGURE 13.1: PeruDigital homepage

project appeared targeted toward an older audience (such as university students and educated members of the public). Other comments included suggestions to specify more clearly which festivals the site will cover, the need to emphasize the IDE in the project, and the desire to see the Spanish revised. On the language issue we were able to consult with Norma Ledesma, a Spanish instructor at UCF, who polished the Spanish-language portions of the site. As the question of audience was the overarching issue raised by our advisory board, we focused much of the second phase of development on clarifying the intended audience. Perhaps because of the cartoon-looking style of the backgrounds and avatars, the site was interpreted as intended for children.

As part of the iterative design process, the issue of audience was initially addressed by integrating PeruDigital into two classes in the UCF digital media program: a graphic design and a digital cultures and narrative class. Through the projects in these classes, taught by PeruDigital art director Jo Anne Adams and myself, students devised alternative designs for the website and integrated research on Peru's culture into a storyline for the interactive environment.

Beth Hallman, a UCF graduate student, integrated the design recommendations of Adams's Digital Imagery students to create a more photorealistic website that improved the perceived level of sophistication and artistic skill. The redesign added more depth to the interactive environment, which emphasizes certain areas by creating a focal point. Cultural consultant Omar Vera suggested a further refinement to include a less region-specific image instead of the image from the Chimú culture from north Peru, and to integrate more red into the design instead of having a primarily green palette. We faced the challenge of communicating the site's intent to (eventually) cover multiple regions in Peru to show that the country is a multiethnic, multiregional place, a country that residents habitually explain is composed of three regions—the jungle, the desert, and the mountains—while finding a central organizing principle for the main page. After further consultation with cultural consultants and digital artists, the team decided on an Inca sun in the middle of the splash page combined with a background image that changed to cover different regions. Another revision made to improve navigation of the site was based on findings that when first-time users were asked to explore the site, they missed much of the content. Adding a revised navigation menu at the top with drop-down boxes helped make the site much more navigable, particularly for those more interested in information than narrative.

Students in the digital cultures and narratives class, on the other hand, took the basic guidelines and developed an interesting array of Peru-based interactive narrative experiences. Ideas from the proposed storylines were integrated into the curriculum developed for the website now available online. The objective of the curriculum is to allow people to learn about Peruvian festivals and folklore by adopting the role of an ethnographer, sponsor, or performer. To do this, the visitor must successfully answer questions learned by researching the PeruDigital website and then completing a series of tasks. The user experiences the PeruDigital interactive environment from the perspective of one of three characters: the PUCP student (ethnographer), the Lord of Agony *hermandad* or brotherhood member (sponsor), or the Lord of Agony *sarahua* performer (artist).

Choosing to experience PeruDigital as an ethnographer involves considering how Hector, a graduate student originally from Puno in the Peruvian highlands who is studying ethnomusicology in Peru, asks particular questions related to the meanings and functions of the festival in Piura. Questions include general ones such as, "Why do people all over the world seem to celebrate festivals?" to specific ones such as, "Where has the form of the *cumanana* (a form of verbal dueling) flourished?" Beyond this, users are asked to complete certain tasks that relate to ideas and themes explored in the site to the communities surrounding them, such as "Ask your friends and family if they can think of any other examples of stereotypes in festivals and other celebrations. Why do you think they exist?" To answer these questions requires a certain way of exploring that differs from the choice to experience PeruDigital as a sponsor. In this perspective, the user adopts the role of Xavier, a member of the local Piuran *hermandad* (brotherhood) responsible for festival organization. He wishes to do the best job possible undertaking his *mayordomo* (person in charge) duties, and in doing so needs to understand issues such as, "What does the *escribano* in a *hermandad* do?" and complete tasks that relate to the sponsor role, such as "Find out what dish(es) are traditionally served [at the celebratory meal after the festivity], and how to make them." Finally, in adopting the performer role, users are introduced to Ariana, a nine-year-old planning to perform in the *sarahuas* dance/drama in Piura. To understand the festival performer perspective, the user explores the website to understand questions such as "What is a *compadre*, for which the *serrano* character says he is looking?" and "To what does the term *palla* refer?" To carry out this role, the user completes tasks, including "find[ing] out more about the conflict that the *sarahuas* represent in dramatic form."

PeruDigital contributes to the development of digital anthropology by bringing together insights and methods from reflexive and narrative ethnography, digital humanities, and PD. The legacy of reflexive ethnography, inaugurated by Marcus and Fischer (1986), who introduced the idea of the "crisis of representation" (see also Del Rio and Álvarez 1999; Moral Santanella 2006; Vera Lugo and Jaramillo Marín 2007), encourages researchers to acknowledge and analyze the role of ethnographers in the research process. In addition to increasing attention to the researcher role, reflexive approaches involve understanding dynamics of researcher–research participant relationships, and considerations of how researchers actively construct knowledge (Finlay 2002; Pack 2006).

The narrative turn in ethnography, meanwhile, owes a large debt to Clifford and Marcus's (1986) work, which focused anthropologists' attention on the process of constructing ethnographic texts, and later work by Coover (2009). Ethnographers now clearly understand the overlap between narrative and ethnography (Gubrium and Holstein 1999), and pay increasing attention to writing conventions and storytelling tropes (Bishop 1992; Geertz

1988; van Maanen 1988). As Gubrium and Holstein (1999) point out, the overlap of narrative and ethnography "has relaxed concepts of standardized representation and produced intriguing experiments in representational practice" (1999, 563).

The field of digital humanities also offers useful insights for PeruDigital. Understanding the distinctive characteristics of digital environments provides ethnographers with ideas about how to effectively tell cultural stories using digital media. Digital humanities scholars identified features such as interactivity, a sense of navigable space, non- or multilinearity, and the blurring of author/audience boundaries (Bell and Kennedy 2007; Landow 2006; Murray 1997) as distinctive to digital media, and explored the new ways that narratives could be created and experienced.

This work also involves asking questions about what it means to tell stories about culture using multiple sources of data, and using archive data in potentially new ways. This can present ethical issues that anthropologists and other visual-based researchers and practitioners need to confront. One challenge faced during production was attributing who had collected the information and who had been interviewed or photographed. Since the archive recordings may date back 20 years, the original contributors may not be available to comment. Given this situation and the challenges that international collaborations can present, researchers on the team reached out to the Sechura community directly by contacting the local diocese where the festival is celebrated to gather information that could be incorporated into PeruDigital. This resulted in additional useful information that research assistant Susana Molina was able to include in her final research paper on the Lord of Agony festival (part of a directed research course), and which the website team was able to draw from in producing text for the website.

In addition, we based the characters' dialogue in the festival environment on fieldwork data, rather than having them say things they did not really say. The ethnographer was perhaps the character with whom we took the most creative liberties, giving him explanatory dialogue we wrote that was based on fieldwork and other research, but written by us. Because we had, so to speak, "put words into his mouth," the team decided the best choice for who to base the visual look of the character on was a member of the team, research assistant and cultural consultant Omar Vera, since he volunteered to be our "model" and was able to approve or suggest revisions to the words we attributed to him. The challenges posed by working with archive materials in this fashion was a main reason I returned to Peru to collect original ethnographic material and to have more open feedback sessions with actual interviewees as the team moved onto another stage of development.

Finally, PD provides useful ideas for carrying out digital media projects. Kim et al. (2009) define PD, which developed in the 1970s in northern Europe before becoming popular in Britain and the United States, as a type of user-centered design in which user needs are determined and concepts are validated through direct involvement of users into the design process at the assessment, design, and development stage. PD brings not only users but multidisciplinary scholars into the design, development, and evaluation process and examines how they collaborate (Kim and Underberg 2011). A characteristic of PD is a greater focus on the design process itself, with the goal of empowering users to be increasingly involved in the development effort (Kim et al. 2009). Watkins (2007) usefully characterizes the PD process as iterative, moving through planning periods and design cycles that repeat until the project has the desired performance. After the planning period, a prototype is produced that is evaluated to provide needed information for the next development cycle (Kim and Underberg 2011; Watkins 2007).

Designing Reflexivity and Perspective-Taking into PeruDigital

Insights from reflexive and narrative ethnography influenced the design and navigation of the website. Highlighting the role of the researcher, the dynamics of the researcher–researched relationship, and the question of how researchers construct knowledge provide the design rationale for an interactive environment that features multiple voices and identities. The user can view and adopt the role of the ethnographer-as-researcher, the artist-as-performer, and the sponsor-as-community builder within the virtual world of PeruDigital. This allows users to ask key questions such as how the ethnographer and research participants relate to one another and interpret culture in ways that are shared or different. This reflexive sensibility carries throughout the interactive environment. In the virtual Lima environment, users can interact with avatars from highland Puno, the north coast, and PUCP, and explore multimedia materials that introduce them to basic information about Peruvian culture that will help them better interpret and appreciate the festival environment of Afro-Peruvian Piura, where users can learn about the background, performance, and study of the Lord of Agony festival. Interaction with festival characters such as the *tamalera* (tamale-seller) and *serrano* (rural person from the highlands) introduce through aspects of role-play and simulation the experience of trying to understand and appreciate such complex cultural issues as ethnic identity and gender relations in the field.

Understanding the nature of ethnography-as-narrative also permits the design team to adapt storytelling tropes to a multimedia environment and thereby create new experiments in representational practice. The interactive environment provides a kind of story world in which insights about how such complex topics as history, economics, and gender and ethnic identities play out in the context of a festival, as well as how people navigate them. For example, users entering the Lord of Agony festival interactive environment set in Piura can see an image of the decorated statue of Christ and an ethnographer wearing a university sweatshirt and carrying fieldwork notes on the history and symbolism of and preparations made for the festival. Next, users can visit a street scene populated by festival participants, including the festival characters of the *serrano* and *tamalera*: in this case, a male dressed as a female tamale seller, a social role popularly associated with Afro-Peruvian women. The ethnographer also appears in the scene, holding a mobile video player in which Institute of Ethnomusicology (IDE) clips of the actual festival are included. By clicking on the characters, the ethnographer, and the mobile device in his hand, the user is introduced to issues surrounding history, aesthetics, and cultural identity.

The user might, for example, encounter the *serrano* character, who wears a mask topped with a straw hat and a poncho and asks, "Where is my *compadre* (ritual co-father)?" With a click, the user can see the fieldwork video of a *serrano* being interviewed, and note how he stays in character throughout the interaction. The user can choose to delve deeper into the history, development, and significance of this *serrano* character within the fieldwork notes and slideshows contained within the ethnographer's office. One lesson from the experience would be to gain a greater understanding of the way such festival figures may represent regional stereotypes. By enabling interaction with characters, objects, and multimedia texts, the user can gain a more experiential understanding of how culture is lived and how knowledge about culture is produced.

Applying these insights to a digital environment is made possible by exploiting the characteristics of new media that can be brought to bear on narrative ethnography: interactivity, a sense of navigable space, nonlinearity, and a blurring of author/audience boundaries. For example, the sense of immersion into a three-dimensional space and the possibility of nonlinear movement through it allows the user to imitate aspects of ethnographic and academic research, such as consulting ethnographic field notes, looking through a book, watching a slideshow presentation, viewing a video of a song or dance performance, and asking questions or making observations in the field. While navigating the virtual ethnographer's office in the virtual environment of downtown Lima, the user encounters a bookshelf that contains books about such topics as the country of Peru and the regions of Puno and Piura; a desktop computer loaded with slideshows about Peruvian folklore, religion, and festivals; a projector and screen that displays ethnographic videos; and a fieldwork notebook that contains notes about festival topics. The user can explore these items in any particular order, and then choose to visit the other interactive space where the festival takes place.

There, having perhaps already learned a little about the history and organization of the festival from looking through a slideshow in the ethnographer's office, or having read notes on the history of festival characters in that region such as the Afro-Peruvian tamale-seller, or some other combination of discoveries, the user can now navigate three spaces that relate to the festival in Piura. By exploring the small outdoor shrine to the festival's central figure and the objects around it, the user can learn about the history and meaning of the festival before moving onto interacting with festival characters, including the opportunity to "talk" with them by selecting questions to ask. Perhaps while doing so, the user desires more information on the history and cultural meaning of a character, so he or she might return to the ethnographic field notes to understand a bit more before proceeding. This process, an open but guided interaction of a narrative ethnographic environment, is enabled by digital media.

PeruDigital engages with such issues as participation and collaboration, the use of digital or visual technology, and issues of power/ethics. The main themes were developed in consultation with advisors from the fields of anthropology, ethnomusicology, Andean studies, Latin American studies, and the humanities. In so doing, the objective was to embody not only scholarly data but also scholarly methods through enabling role-playing and simulation of research scenarios and settings. As Hertz (1997) reminds us, "the reflexive ethnographer does not simply report 'facts' or 'truths' but actively constructs interpretations of his or her experiences in the field and then questions how those interpretations came about" (1997, viii). As an approach to including research participant voices in the production of ethnographic "texts," PeruDigital seeks to break down the boundaries between ethnographic descriptions and the accounts of participants. The juxtaposition of multiple voices, explorable through nonlinear or multilinear paths through information, can take us a step closer to doing this.

The goal is to bring users into the subjective experience of participating in a Peruvian festival using elements of storytelling and the potential for embodiment enabled by digital media. Through imitation, immersion, and interactivity, PeruDigital seeks to give users the sense of "being there" while inviting them to look deeper at the history and cultural context of the festival through exploration and interaction. Being reflexive, Hertz (1997) points out, involves talking about the experience while at the same time being present in that moment. Using digital technology to enable aspects of narrative ethnography can also be seen as an extension of a longer tradition in recent decades in which narrative genres are blurred and altered, and in which ethnographic insights are produced through diverse techniques and in diverse forms. Although PeruDigital makes use of new media to enable a narrative-based approach, exploring the site does require a significant time commitment. With the rise in popularity of digital tools such as Vine, which involves videos lasting seven seconds or less, we should consider how younger people in particular may develop and repurpose digital media tools to better reflect social media habits, and how this may affect their approach to learning about different cultures.

The approach undertaken in PeruDigital considers how to recreate reflexivity in an embodied digital medium by making explicit how ethnographers do their research and generate knowledge, and how one's perspective on a social event is influenced by one's social role. In being invited to consider how to ask questions about, look at, and interact with cultural spaces such as the Peruvian festival from multiple points of view, the goal is to help audiences realize the situated nature of knowledge and meaning-making. This represents a reaction against—or perhaps a corrective to—the long tradition of realist ethnography outlined by Marcus and Fischer (1986), which permits the ethnographer "to remain in unchallenged control over his account, delivering a distanced representation of cultural experience" (1986, 55). In contrast, our approach is one in which the ethnographer acknowledges the constructed nature of the ethnographic production. Like Bishop, we see our productions as "vivid subjective narratives" (1992, 150), albeit in a digital medium.

Conclusion

PeruDigital's approach attempts to integrate reflexivity on multiple levels—by including the researcher in a visceral, virtually embodied way in the representation of culture within the website; and in the spirit of participatory design—by being as transparent and explicit as possible about the construction of this online ethnographic "text." Digital heritage projects have the capacity to "wow" audiences with their enticing visuals and interactive characteristics; however, the approach outlined in this chapter makes clear that the process of designing, producing, and evaluating the digital media project is as central a goal as the outcome itself, and that the process is not always smooth. For example, one issue involved trying to incorporate advisory board and faculty member suggestions in a way that did not unduly tax the time, resources, or patience of the student digital media developers who were trained in a production pipeline model with clear preproduction and production stages. What a scholar or community member from a nontechnical background may not understand is that instructions to change a certain specific aspect of a website need to be received in a timely manner that corresponds with production timelines that have been agreed to by all, and that changing one minor element may require a much more complicated set of tasks than is immediately apparent. Asking for a character to have a different shirt, for example, after the graphic designer has created the asset and sent it to the interactive developer, is problematic in terms of maintaining a production schedule linked to available funding and student work schedules.

At the same time, another challenge is ensuring that the student production team understands and is sensitive to nuances in cultural representation that, while minor to an outsider, may be highly significant and even problematic. While from an artistic and perhaps common-sense standpoint a character represented as seated in an open plaza would be likely to have windblown hair, if this unintentionally conveys a message that the person is somehow unkempt in a way that is offensive to cultural consultants, revisions may be necessary to sacrifice some perceived realism for the sake of sensitivity. Communicating, translating, and negotiating these sometimes conflicting understandings among different team members is a major task of the project director, and one to which more study should be devoted.

While the goal of privileging process over product may resonate with an audience sympathetic to participatory research methods, the pragmatics of following this approach presents a potential downside when trying to manage the expectations of outsiders. Funding sources and faculty and administrative evaluators may privilege results over process. To secure the funding to build the project, something has to be built to show as a proof of concept. When I was evaluated at the university level for tenure (I was an assistant professor at the project's beginning), my research was judged primarily in terms of the peer-reviewed publications I produced, which could not be written until I had a robust-enough project about which to write. Some positive steps in this regard have been taken (see, for example, Modern Languages Association 2015; Ippolito 2009), but clearly more work needs to be done. Nonetheless, as more researchers undertake—and publish about—such participatory research methods and creative work projects, this situation may change, and indeed is changing, but not necessarily at the pace that best reflects the innovations taking place in the field.

PeruDigital continues, with plans to develop a new digital environment based on the Moche Route tourist corridor that unites communities on Peru's north coast. I recently returned to Peru to conduct ethnographic research on cultural heritage and tourism, and had the opportunity to teach a course on interactive media for social research at PUCP. To date, five digital stories have been produced based on the ethnographic fieldwork, with plans to integrate them into the projection screen within the virtual ethnographer's office. In the class, students learned to combine theory and practice in the design of interactive media for social research by combining the expressive potential of new media with the elements of story. In this way, the students collaborated in creating a design document and preliminary visual designs for an interactive environment in which the experiences of north coast Peruvian residents as they react to the reimagining of the historical past and cultural heritage of their region could be shared. In addition to its use in visual anthropology courses, the project can also enhance foreign language, digital storytelling, and Latin American studies courses.

This new project thus helped lay the foundation for another section of the website. We have formed an advisory board made up of experts from the north coast in the areas of culture, tourism, and community development to work with us in the design process. Our goal is to document the process of making design decisions, both visual and narrative, to create a culturally appropriate digital media representation of north Peruvian cultural heritage. Because this part of the project is largely based on ethnographic material and connections made by the project director rather than archival materials, it is our hope that future publications can focus in more detail on the complex conversations and negotiations that emerge in digital ethnographic storytelling.

REFERENCES

Bell, D., and B. Kennedy. 2007. *The Cybercultures Reader*. London: Routledge.

Bishop, W. 1992. I-Witnessing in Composition: Turning Ethnographic Data into Narratives. *Rhetoric Review* 11(1): 147–158.

Clifford, J., and G. Marcus, eds. 1986. *Writing Culture: The Poetics and Politics of Ethnography*. Berkeley: University of California.

Coover, R. 2009. On Vérité to Virtual: Conversations on the Frontier of Film and Anthropology. *Visual Studies* 24(3): 235–249.

Del Rio, P., and A. Álvarez. 1999. La puesta en escena de la realidad cultural. Una aproximación histórica cultural al problema de la etnografía audiovisual. *Revista de Antropología Social* 8: 121–136.

Finlay, L. 2002. "Outing" the Researcher: The Provenance, Process, and Practice of Reflexivity. *Qualitative Health Research* 12(4): 531–545.

Geertz, C. 1988. *Works and Lives: The Anthropologist as Author*. Stanford, CA: Stanford University Press.

Gubrium, J., and J. Holstein. 1999. At the Border of Narrative and Ethnography. *Journal of Contemporary Ethnography* 28(5): 561–573.

Hertz, R., ed. 1997. *Reflexivity and Voice*. Thousand Oaks, CA: Sage.

Ippolito, J. 2009. New Criteria for New Media. *Leonardo* 42(1): 71–75.

Kim, S.-J., T. Smith-Jackson, K. Carroll, M. Suh, and N. Mi. 2009. Implications of Participatory Design for Wearable Assistive Technology for Users with Severe Visual Impairments. *HCI International* 2009: 86–95.

Kim, S.-J., and N. Underberg. 2011. PeruDigital: Approaching Interactive Digital Storytelling and Collaborative Interactive Web Design through Digital Ethnography, HCI, and Digital Media. *HCI International* 2011: 20–28.

Landow, G. 2006. *Hypertext 3.0: Critical Theory and New Media in an Era of Globalization*. Baltimore, MD: John Hopkins University Press.

Marcus, G., and M. Fischer. 1986. *Anthropology as Cultural Critique: An Experimental Moment in the Social Sciences*. Chicago, IL: University of Chicago Press.

Modern Languages Association (MLA). 2013. *Guidelines for Evaluating Work in Digital Humanities and Digital Media*. mla.org/guidelines_evaluation_digital?ot=letterhead, accessed March 3, 2015.

Moral Santanella, C. 2006. Criterios de validez en la investigación cualitativa actual. *Revista de Investigación Educativa* 24(1): 147–164.

Murray, J. 1997. *Hamlet on the Holodeck: The Future of Narrative in Cyberspace*. New York: The Free Press.

Pack, S. 2006. How They See Me vs. How I See Them: The Ethnographic Self and the Personal Self. *Anthropological Quarterly* 79(1): 105–122.

Underberg, N., and E. Zorn. 2013. *Digital Ethnography: Anthropology, Narrative, and New Media*. Austin, TX: University of Texas Press.

van Maanen, J. 1988. *Tales of the Field: On Writing Ethnography*. Chicago, IL: University of Chicago Press.

Vera Lugo, J. P., and J. Jaramillo Marín. 2007. Teoria social, métodos cualitativos y etnografía: el problema de la representación y reflexividad en las ciencias sociales. *Universitas Humanística* 64: 237–255.

Watkins, J. 2007. Social Media, Participatory Design and Cultural Engagement. In *Proceedings of the 2007 Australasian Computer-Human Interaction Conference*, edited by Bruce Thomas, 161–166. Aldelaide, Australia: OZCHI.

NOTE

1 PeruDigital has been supported by internal funding and/or logistical support by the following UCF entities: School of Visual Arts and Design, Latin American Studies, Center for Humanities and Digital Research, CREATE, College of Arts and Humanities, Department of Anthropology, and Office of International Studies.

6

Participatory Design Ethnography

Participatory Design for the Common Good

Nancy Fried Foster

Introduction

I first became interested in participatory design for aesthetic reasons. When we do participatory design, we collect and interpret firsthand accounts of the practice of work using methods that are not just anthropological but also artistic. We use drawing, photography, and other arts to convey information, and many noncognitive and expressive approaches to understand it. As an artist and anthropologist, I find this appealing. The more I work in this field, the more I discover just how powerful it is for the individuals who engage in participatory design from their various perspectives and disciplines, and how well it works to produce design concepts and requirements.

Participatory design is not limited to producing pretty or enticing designs. It opens the possibility that through cooperative, egalitarian processes we can conceptualize and build the technologies, spaces, and services that are good for the many because they address needs that we identify ourselves. This contrasts with similar methods used in the design or "co-creation" of consumer and commercial goods, discussed later in the chapter, which share the creative work with the many but reserve ownership and profit for the few.

Participatory design as I practice it descends directly from projects such as DEMOS, an effort to help workers retain some control over their own tools during the introduction of computer systems into their workplaces (Ehn 1993). Ideally, in the participatory design approach, the people who stand to gain most from a well-designed tool or space initiate and facilitate

Nancy Fried Foster, "Participatory Design for the Common Good" in *Participatory Visual and Digital Research in Action*, Aline Gubrium, Krista Harper, and Marty Otañez, eds., pp. 229-242. © 2015 Left Coast Press, Inc. All rights reserved.

the design process in partnership with such traditional experts as architects and interior designers or software engineers, programmers, and graphic designers. Each participant contributes to the process according to his or her own expertise. Roughly speaking, the objective of those who are experts in the work that is to be done with the tool or in the space is to make sure that the architects and builders understand their work practices and needs. The objective of the architects and builders is to gain insight and achieve better designs by being well informed. A social scientist facilitates the process, playing a crucial role in the analysis and interpretation of the mass of information provided by work experts. That mass of information in its raw state is encoded in cultural symbols and local expressions. The social scientist helps the other kinds of experts on the team to recognize and understand the messages conveyed by work experts in drawings, photographs, and other data. In other words, the social scientist makes sure that the architects and designers receive understandable and actionable information from the work experts.

Although I was initially attracted to this field because it seemed like enjoyable work that combined art and anthropology, it is my belief that participatory design can benefit the people who participate as work experts in the participatory design process and, by extension, the larger group of workers they represent. This is what keeps me in the field and guides my development as a practitioner. In this chapter, I draw on examples of design work in academic libraries to explore how we work toward this ideal of participatory design for the common good.

The Need for Good Library Design

The rapid emergence and growing importance of electronic materials in instruction and research has affected all aspects of academic library use and planning, including resources, services, and facilities. In the case of library facilities, it is widely agreed that the spaces that supported research and learning with legacy materials are no longer sufficient to support new and emerging work practices. Moreover, as technology will continue to evolve rapidly in the foreseeable future, it is not yet possible to establish reliable design precedents. Older academic libraries, as beautiful as they may be, provide insufficient models for today's libraries. Even the best, most "modern" library built today may not provide an adequate model for meeting needs a few years from now.

Libraries need to change. However, in many academic libraries today, design decisions may look like reactions to technological and environmental changes, revealing a fear of looking out of date. Thus we see libraries everywhere installing outlets and every new kind of chair and tool. It is not that we should have retained the card catalog or limited ourselves to the old wooden tables and chairs, but in replacing them, we could have included researchers in planning for the transition to online catalogs, technology-assisted research practices, and global and local collaboration. The challenge is to design new academic libraries that support scholarship in a hyperconnected world that is ever more digital; that is, the challenge is to support the work of scholars.

The classic books on academic library design, written in the first half of the twentieth century, advised that the architect, university president, and trustees make all the important decisions. Inclusion of the library director, faculty, and students only appears in books from the latter part of the twentieth century (N. Foster 2013). Consultation with this broader base of stakeholders grew out of a need for more information about their research and learning practices in connection with the expanding resource demands of changing pedagogies and the emergence of new technologies, such as microforms. More and faster change has only increased the need for a better-informed design process. In the words of architect David Cronrath, "In unstable times a physical reprogramming can no longer depend on traditional, professional experts (architects and librarians), for whom precedent is now unreliable. We looked to our user community's expertise" (D. Conrath, personal communication, May 2012).

Indeed, the most promising path to better design is to place academic work in the conceptual center and array tools and resources around it, for they support the people doing the work. This conceptual arrangement mirrors the physical. As I write this chapter, I sit at the center with my questions and arguments surrounded by books and articles, reading and writing implements, and, of course, my colleagues, some of them very distant in time and space but linked to me through papers, screens, and communication devices. The digital tools are essential, but I want them on my terms. Academic workers want their tools and spaces to work for them and for others like them. They want the tools and spaces to support their work, connect them to colleagues, and help them share information with the greater community.

Participatory Design in Academic Libraries

Many academic librarians have found that participatory design helps them improve support for research, writing, and teaching by developing the capacity to collect information about the people who use the library for these and other purposes.[1] They may do this by training a team of librarians and library staff and having them conduct a large design project, such as creating a better software tool for finding and using library resources. Alternatively, they may have their team conduct smaller projects, such as monitoring the use of facilities and deciding how to update library spaces.

The toolkit for participatory design in libraries is extensive and includes a variety of visual methods, such as interviews that use photographs, maps, or drawings to develop and convey information; design workshops in which participants make drawings or mark plans or prototypes; and even observations, in which what is viewed is recorded on floor plans for later visual inspection and tabulation. In addition, many practitioners make video recordings of interviews and workshops so that team members can immerse themselves in the data, fill in blanks in their notes, or see the setting and the nonverbal information captured in the visual record.

Once learned and implemented, participatory design methods can be employed on an ongoing basis, and the information these activities yield can be used to guide strategic decision-making. The following case studies describe two large projects that incorporated design workshops and observations. In the first case, library faculty and staff of the University of Maryland's library system sought to understand current use of the main library building to inform a team of architecture students on work practices and work needs in a remodeled building. In the second case, library faculty and staff at Purdue University collected information in several existing science and technology libraries to inform the university's architects and planners on how to consolidate them into designated library spaces in a new combination classroom-library building. In both cases, information collected through visual and other ethnographic methods led to a better understanding of the community's needs and increased the likelihood that the resulting plans and decisions would take account of them.

Case 1: Reprogramming McKeldin Library

In 2011, Patricia A. Steele, dean of libraries for the University of Maryland, recognized a need to reprogram McKeldin Library, the main library on the College Park campus. The original 1958 library had been expanded in 1991 and further renovated in a series of projects that addressed one small area at a time. The result was a building with numerous infrastructure and navigation problems; even worse, its spaces were no longer fully usable for work done in new ways, whether by library employees or by faculty members, students, and other researchers. Although no funds had been allocated for a full renovation, the dean felt that she needed a unified, forward-looking plan to guide small-scale improvements or to make a successful case for funding a full-scale renovation.

Steele formed a partnership with the dean of architecture, David Cronrath, with a plan to have graduate architecture students assess space usage and develop a new quantitative program. Cronrath engaged a practicing architect, Sandra Parsons Vicchio, to do this work with the students in a studio class. At Vicchio's suggestion, Steele then extended the project to include a participatory design component, as had been done in the Gleason Library renovation at the University of Rochester, a project on which Vicchio and Foster had worked together (Gibbons and Foster 2007). Hearing about the project, a professor of anthropology, Michael Paolisso, decided that his graduate methods class would conduct an ethnographic study of the library. All of these activities— quantitative data gathering, library ethnography, and participatory design— yielded information on which a second group of architecture students, taking another studio class taught by Vicchio, based a set of designs for a completely reconceptualized building (Steele et al. 2015).

The participatory design activities comprised observation and gathering of focused data within the library, brief interviews with students at various campus locations, and a series of five design workshops in which undergraduates, graduate students, faculty members, and members of the library staff drew pictures of ideal library spaces (see examples in Figure 14.1). Teams of library faculty and staff received training from Foster and then facilitated all information gathering.

In the space design workshops, participants were encouraged to imagine a library or library space in which they and their friends and colleagues could do their work well. Once they had conjured a mental image of this space, they were presented with paper, markers, Post-it notes, and other supplies and asked to draw what they had imagined. Most participants set easily to work, although some found it difficult to draw despite reassurances that no one would judge the quality of the drawing. A few people wrote text but did not draw.

Respondents want the library to provide the basics, whether for solitary or group work. One said, "I need solitariness. Studying isn't a social thing," while another expressed a different desire: "I don't mind people talking. I actually like the idea that things are moving around me." Beyond just being a workable place, the library offers many a special ambience that inspires them

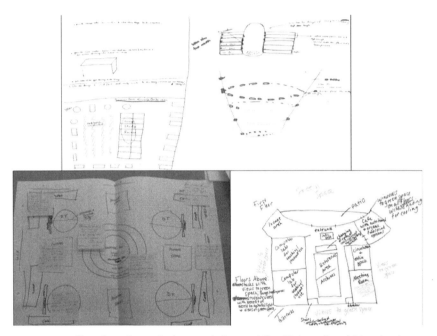

FIGURE 14.1: Drawings from design workshops at the University of Maryland and Purdue University

and makes them feel like doing good work: "There are people [in the library] but they aren't yelling or anything like that and I'm not tempted to turn on the TV. I sit down for five hours or whatever and just do everything that I need to do." Drawings by undergraduate students suggested that the library helps them do some of the work of maturation and self-invention that is so important during the college years (Strong et al. 2013). Faculty members cared much more about physical collections than students, and they and the graduate students suggested a strong role for the library in connecting scholars to their colleagues and disciplines. Library staff work daily in the library; it is a different sort of workplace for them. The concern they addressed was to engage easily with close colleagues and have ready access to necessary tools.

Students in the final studio course received reports and briefings on the participatory design activities, along with the quantitative program and the ethnography of the library. They distilled four themes from the

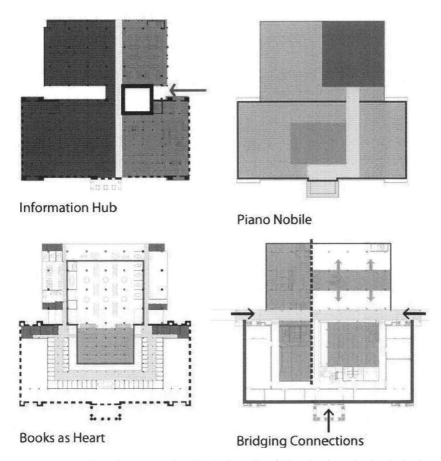

FIGURE 14.2: Four themes derived by University of Maryland graduate students in architecture from participatory design and ethnographic information

data: "Information Hub," "Piano Nobile," "Books as Heart," and "Bridging Connections" (see Figure 14.2). These themes addressed the higher purposes of the library as seen through the eyes of those who would work there, and served as a framework within which to address known issues in the building (such as heating and traffic flow) and provide for important activities (such as reading, studying, and use of new library technologies) while also connecting people and inspiring them.

Case 2: The Active Learning Center at Purdue University

Purdue University had begun a system-wide transition to flipped classrooms and other active learning strategies through their IMPACT program (Purdue University 2014). The program's growth coincided with pressure to contract Purdue's library system following a nationwide trend. The challenge for James Mullins, dean of libraries, was to support the IMPACT program while ensuring the continuation of important library services to the university community and providing as much security as possible to library staff. Mullins worked with other university leaders to develop a plan for a new library-classroom building that would provide space to consolidate many of the science and technology libraries. In addition to new classrooms, the Active Learning Center would provide library space to extend learning from the classroom into nearby study and group areas. It was also meant to support research by providing access to resources and technologies, as well as guidance in using them.

Mullins could already see that students in the transformed IMPACT courses would have different needs because their work practices were different. For example, there was much more use of supplementary resources during class time and much more work on group projects both during and after class. He decided to use the participatory design process to understand emerging library needs in connection with the IMPACT program.

Mullins formed a large team of 13 library faculty and staff members. They received training from Foster and conducted observations, interviews, and design workshops with staff, faculty, graduate students, and undergrads (N. Foster et al. 2013). The analysis of the design workshop drawings and other data yielded findings not unlike those of the University of Maryland project. In both cases, undergraduates expressed a need for space to support varied quiet or noisy activities and individual or group work. In both cases, students looked to the library to help them achieve mental readiness for long periods of hard work.

However, in contrast to the Maryland drawings and drawings from many other universities where the same approach has been used, the Purdue drawings revealed a greater desire for unadorned, utilitarian spaces than for grandeur. For example, only one drawing included large, decorative features; the local team believed this accorded with Purdue culture. Another unusual feature emerged in the staff drawings as well as in conversations at the staff design workshop and in briefing sessions held with staff about the plan to consolidate many existing libraries into the new building: many staff members expressed a strong desire for a private office, even if it could not be "a huge office." Library faculty expressed a desire to be "impressed and inspired... [and] proud to work [here]."

Interestingly, teaching faculty drawings almost completely ignored the library aspect of the space, though they illustrated classroom space in novel ways using interesting new metaphors, such as the campfire (see Figure 14.1, lower left). Use of the library by faculty members at Purdue had already shifted out of the library building and onto computers and related devices. According to librarian reports and interviews with faculty members, the use of library resources in connection with coursework is imagined as a subset of the use of online resources of diverse provenance. Materials are overwhelmingly used in digital formats. It is likely that the new space will not house many books; even so, a faculty member hoped the new building would be "like the Guggenheim for learning, like a museum.... Anyone walking in would say this is a place where learning is occurring."

Both students and faculty members indicated that they would have a considerable need for various digital and communication technologies in the building. Students indicated that they used laptops and other electronics more than anything else to complete their assignments. Faculty members also indicated that the new building should be a technology-rich and technology-enabling environment.

Benefits and Limits of Participatory Design

Ideally, every person or group standing to gain or lose by a design decision would form an equal partnership with each other and engage in a participatory process with those whose expertise was required for realizing the project. In academic libraries, this would mean that librarians, faculty members, students, administrators, architects, and builders would work together to identify needs, design solutions, and build library spaces, services, and tools. It is worth stating the ideal and aiming for it because this ideal contains the possibility of a design process that benefits a very broad range of participants, not just a small group of leaders or a narrow range of so-called experts.

In reality, library participatory design projects are done within the academic hierarchy embedded in larger political and economic systems, and the constraints show. Real projects depend on authorization and support from the library director and are run by the library rather than a broader partnership of faculty members, students, librarians, and technical experts. In addition, these projects may be pressured away from their original purposes to respond to broader external challenges, such as insufficient funding (including stagnant or shrinking state allocations), inflation of costs (such as rapidly increasing journal pricing), or changes in technologies and pedagogies (the emergence of online learning, e-books, and so on). Real projects may stray very far from the ideal. Still, those who use a participatory design process in academic libraries strive toward higher goals, such as improving the dissemination of information or expanding educational access or student success, and these goals are certainly in the public interest.

In the University of Maryland case, for example, student success was a goal from the beginning of the project and remained a touchstone in the participatory design activities. This was often expressed as a desire to support individuals or study groups by improving conditions (providing better lighting, noise control, or space to spread out materials) or by enriching the intellectual atmosphere (exposing students to books and artifacts, connecting them to peers and luminaries in their disciplines, or inspiring them to do better work). Students, faculty members, and staff were able to give significant guidance to the qualitative program in this phase. Moreover, as project planning proceeded, leaders recognized the possibility to create learning opportunities for graduate students through direct participation in developing the quantitative program, conducting the library ethnography, and completing the first phase of architectural design. This served to expand the role of the library in the institution; indeed, it made the library "participatory" in a new way.

In the Purdue University case, the design of the new classroom-library building was explicitly tied to the implementation of "active learning" teaching approaches that aim to achieve greater student engagement and better understanding of the material. Beyond this, the project sought a way to make a major change—a change that evoked a great deal of ambivalence—through a process that would give people a way to grapple with uncertainty, express their highest hopes and worst fears, and do everything they could to ensure that the resulting library would support the needs of the full community. Project leaders explicitly deferred technology choices, focusing instead on teaching, learning, and research needs. Although the technology would be essential, and the consolidated facility would make it possible to pool budgets and buy technology that would be unaffordable to a single department, the project's leaders recognized that tools depend on the work people want to accomplish with them. The participatory process privileged academic goals and activities; the library approached change in a new and effective way.

In both the Purdue and Maryland cases, efforts were clearly focused on providing better working conditions by improving the qualities of the buildings: their material characteristics, their functions and affordances, and the work and other activities they would support. Participatory design posits that this is done best with information from the people who have personal, expert knowledge of the work they do and its requirements. In both projects, faculty, staff, and students were engaged as workers who contributed indispensible expert knowledge to the design process.

Furthermore, both projects went beyond simple design of facilities, technology, and resources by extending participation to address additional needs. The University of Maryland project leveraged further learning opportunities for students, using the project as an occasion to consider an evolving role for the library in a time of quickly changing information forms and uses. The student work in particular drew heavily on visual methods and artifacts, using drawings and images in three separate project phases: development of the quantitative program, interpretation of the participatory design artifacts and report, and architectural design. This process can be glossed as the transformation of participants' drawings and legacy building plans into new architectural renderings.

The Purdue University project gave attention to the work practices of the library faculty and staff who will be based in the new building while developing a picture of the work practices of students and teaching faculty who will use the new building for instruction and research. The inclusion of many more private offices in staff drawings at Purdue than at comparable institutions, signifying a desire for status and respect, is a visible, culturally expressed indicator of the anxiety that an uncertain future causes in some workers in particular. This anxiety could not be eliminated, but it was openly and directly addressed; library workers conducted and participated in a variety of meetings and discussed the connection between the consolidation plan and the survival of the constituent libraries and their own jobs, albeit in changed and possibly reduced forms.

Prospects and Cautions

There are many advantages to participatory design, from supporting greater democracy in the workplace to designing better spaces, services, and tools through collaboration rather than through individual effort. The approach provides a way for applied anthropologists to engage in work that creates shared value rather than extracting value for limited benefit. For academic libraries, participatory design makes it possible for libraries to identify and incorporate better practices while innovating in a thoughtful and informed way. Ideally, participatory design of academic libraries can go beyond finding acceptable ways to handle bad situations since information about how people use academic libraries documents the need for greater public support of higher education.

The most difficult part of the process for the library-based team is the analysis of artifacts and texts. After years of practice, I have learned to provide the greatest support during analysis and interpretation, which are far more challenging than conducting interviews and workshops. I have also learned to help library teams keep the scope of their projects small and to understand that these are design projects rather than research projects, and that they result in better designs rather than generalizable findings.

Numerous libraries now engage students, faculty, and staff in designing and improving spaces, services, and technologies, sometimes with participatory design but sometimes with other approaches. For example, in many libraries a team tests the usability of a prototype or early implemented version of a website or application to be sure the community will find it understandable and workable. Participatory design and usability testing are complementary: the former helps identify needs and develop possible solutions, while the latter supports fine-tuning of the selected solution toward the end of the development cycle. In both cases, the emphasis is on the work that people need to do and how the tool or space will support that work. Even when usability testers speak of "users," they tend to focus on people trying to accomplish certain work tasks.

A very different approach casts students and faculty members as consumers and takes its cues from processes used in the design and exchange of consumer goods. One such approach is what Prahalad and Ramaswamy (2004) call "co-creation." This refers to a tacit agreement in the marketplace whereby a producer provides an explicit opportunity for consumers to influence, customize, or even improve its products and, in return for this opportunity, ensures that consumers loyally buy from them rather than from a competitor, even when the products themselves are essentially the same. It is the "experience" of interacting with the firm that differentiates the product and that constitutes the "value" that the consumer extracts from the production process (Prahalad and Ramaswamy 2004). However, according to a critique of Prahalad and Ramaswamy's work, even when consumers "co-create" the goods, "keeping trumps giving": the firm retains the brand, which seems intangible but may nonetheless be worth billions of dollars (R. Foster 2012). In the co-creation of consumer and commercial goods, the firm seeks to retain the value of the brand and maximize profit, and they will engage with the consumer—that is, offer an enhanced consumer experience—to do so.

Academic libraries, while in the real world and subject to its economic and political forces, are not producers of consumer goods. They are providers of information and related spaces, tools, and services for the advancement of knowledge and the benefit of the many. Academic libraries must manage their budgets, but they are not in business to make a profit. It is right that academic libraries engage the community in design work to make knowledge easier to find, use, and disseminate; that is, to help knowledge workers work well. A risk emerges when those in academic libraries see students and faculty members as consumers and seek to provide good experiences for them through co-creation and related "user experience" processes. The better alternative is to support the communal work of planning and realizing better teaching, learning, and research; greater access; and shared decision-making.

Traditionally, library design was the province of a few technical experts. Nowadays, those experts cannot rely on precedent the way they once could, and they cannot know everything they need to know to break from precedent unless they work in partnership with other kinds of experts. Anthropological methods that form part of a collaborative design process provide the information that allows designers to respond to changes in the world while maintaining or even increasing the value of the library as an institution. New technologies can make scholarly resources more easily accessible to greater numbers of people, and improved facilities can help scholars at all levels do better work, not just for personal gain but for the good of us all.

Acknowledgments

I thank many wonderful project team members at the University of Maryland and Purdue University and am especially grateful to Pat Steele, Jim Mullins, Michael Paolisso, Sandra Vicchio, and David Cronrath for making the projects and this chapter possible.

REFERENCES

Akselbo, Jeppe Lomholt, Lise Arnfred, Sten Barfort, Gina Bay, Tine Bagger Christiansen, et al. 2006. *The Hybrid Library: From the Users' Perspective.* Copenhagen, Denmark: National Library and Copenhagen University Library. http://www.statsbiblioteket.dk/summa/fieldstudies.pdf.

Ehn, Pelle. 1993. Scandinavian Design: On Participation and Skill. In *Participatory Design: Principles and Practices*, edited by Douglas Schuler and Aki Namioka, 41–77. Hillsdale, NJ: Lawrence Erlbaum Associates.

Foster, Nancy Fried. 2013. Designing Academic Libraries with the People Who Work in Them. In *Studying Students: A Second Look*, edited by Nancy Fried Foster, 103–121. Chicago, IL: Association of College and Research Libraries.

Foster, Nancy Fried, Teresa Balser, Rae Lynn Boes, Dianna Deputy, William Ferrall, Michael Fosmire, et al. 2013. *Participatory Design of Purdue University's Active Learning Center Final Report*. 1. Libraries Reports. West Lafayette, IN: Purdue University. http://docs.lib.purdue.edu/libreports/1.

Foster, Robert J. 2012. The Uses of Use Value: Marketing, Value Creation, and the Exigencies of Consumption Work. In *Inside Marketing: Practices, Ideologies, Devices*, edited by Detlev Zwick and Julien Cayla, 42–57. New York: Oxford University Press.

Gibbons, Susan, and Nancy Fried Foster. 2007. Library Design and Ethnography. In *Studying Students: The Undergraduate Research Project at the University of Rochester*, edited by Nancy Fried Foster and Susan Gibbons, 20–29. Chicago, IL: Association of College and Research Libraries.

Prahalad, C. K., and Venkat Ramaswamy. 2004. Co-Creation Experiences: The Next Practice in Value Creation. *Journal of Interactive Marketing* 18(3): 5–14.

Purdue University. 2014. "IMPACT: Mission." http://www.purdue.edu/impact/mission.html, accessed July 1, 2014.

Somerville, Mary M., and Margaret Brown-Sica. 2011. Library Space Planning: A Participatory Action Research Approach. *The Electronic Library* 29(5): 669–681.

Steele, Patricia A., David Cronrath, Sandra Parsons Vicchio, and Nancy Fried Foster. 2015. *The Living Library: An Intellectual Ecosystem*. Chicago, IL: Association of College & Research Libraries.

Strong, Marcy, Kenn Harper, and Mari Tsuchiya. 2013. Learning the Ropes. In *Studying Students: A Second Look*, edited by Nancy Fried Foster, pp. 45–61. Chicago, IL: Association of College & Research Libraries.

NOTE

1 A partial, mapped list of academic libraries where participatory design projects have been conducted is available at http://tinyurl.com/mbhwbpe. For examples of complementary studies, see also work in the Aarhus tradition (Akselbo et al. 2006) and a project that uses a participatory action research approach (Somerville and Brown-Sica 2011).

Caminemos Juntos:
Collaboration, Ethnography, and Design
in Northeast Los Angeles

Elizabeth Chin, Morgan Marzec, Cayla McCrae, and Tina L. Zeng

The road I walk every day,
It's no game, I try to make my way.
People see what they want to see.
That's not me.
Take a look, take a look,
I might surprise you.

> —Lil' Krazy aka Ghetto Boy, "The Road I Walk"

These words come from a song, "The Road I Walk," written and recorded by three homeless youth as part of a community-based research project. Over the course of 10 weeks, MFA students from the Art Center College of Design in Los Angeles visited with clients and staff at Jovenes, Inc., a nonprofit organization that provides support and housing for homeless youth in Boyle Heights, Los Angeles.

Our use of participatory digital methods reimagined engagement in a social context by 1) focusing on process, 2) embracing "fabulous failures," and 3) using digital technology to create and mediate relationships. The result was a suite of interactive design research tools and experiences, culminating in a multimedia installation called *Caminemos Juntos* (*Let's Walk Together*).

By relinquishing authorial control most commonly wielded by designers, we rejected the power dynamics inherent in the conventional design research process. Our work engaged the youths' talents through a carefully constructed, participatory design process that sought to privilege youth voices. We redefined our role as one aimed at identifying and amplifying youths' strengths, rejecting the imperative to provide a product that would solve the problem. Creating an interactive and dynamic physical and social space, rich and unexpected perspectives emerged from the youth as well as us, and from the team as a whole. In discovering that the label "homeless" provides little understanding of the people it identifies, we also learned that as designers, we must seek to dismantle those systems of power that dehumanize those we engage.

If you do a Google image search using the terms "design" and "homelessness," you will find project after project that is either a version of a tent or a shopping cart. In our Google search for example, one designer created a disposable cardboard bed that was intended to make it easy and more convenient for homeless people to carry their houses with them. Another developed a fashionable winter coat that converted into a sleeping bag. We also found a model for the twenty-first-century homeless person's shopping cart, which included sleek, Scandinavian-style storage compartments built into the cart's basic frame. Actual homeless people were absent from nearly every example. The common assumption in these products and solutions seems to be: "If people don't have homes, let's build portable places to sleep!"

For us, this body of work demonstrates troubling patterns in designers' understanding and approach to what is considered "design for good." Focused upon making products that can be mass-produced, the designs objectify people, presenting one-dimensional approaches to complex social problems. Addressing only the most visible aspects of homelessness, none of these tents or carts exhibits a nuanced understanding of diverse homeless populations, or of the status of homelessness. Neither do portable sleeping spots acknowledge the prevalence of anti-homeless laws, on the rise since the late 1980s and aimed specifically at rendering it illegal for homeless persons to occupy public space (Amster 2003; Kawash 1998; Smith 1995).

The notion of "doing good" recently has developed a high profile in design. However, the majority of socially oriented design efforts have brought with them the same product-oriented theory and practice used in commercial enterprise, so much so that some have argued that design must be decolonized before it can hope to actually do much good (Tunstall 2013). Focused upon creating mass-marketable products that solve problems, social design embeds neoliberal and capitalist assumptions from the outset. Thus, the majority of social design implicitly or explicitly promotes what Arturo Escobar calls the "one world world view" (Escobar 2011). In our work, we proceeded from a position that overtly questioned—and often rejected—the idea that design must produce products that solve problems. Drawing from the critical and analytical stance toward development and nongovernmental organizations (NGOs) that has emerged in anthropology, we strove to understand, not to solve (Cheney 2007; Escobar n.d., 2001, 2011; Lister 2003; Schuller 2012). We aimed to provide a platform for the Jovenes youth to articulate and disseminate their own stories, their own perspectives, and thereby to provide a complex point of view on who is homeless, and what homelessness is.

We also used principles from participatory action research (PAR) and feminist research methods to craft our approach (Craven and Davis 2013; McIntyre 2007; Visweswaran 1994). Imagining the aspects of PAR (questioning, reflecting, investigating, developing a plan, implementing it, then refining) in a braided spiral, McIntyre (2007) illustrates the continuous nature of knowledge production in the PAR approach. We identified areas of this process where our design and technology backgrounds could converge and found the practice of creating something based on the youths' input contributed positively to the research, the youths' desire to participate, and overall group morale. The practice of what designers call "making" coincides with a method McIntyre encourages: using creative methods of knowing to undo "what we know" so as to "know anew" (2007, 20). By integrating visual and hands-on activities, relationships between researchers and participants are equalized, especially those "between the marginalized and the self-confident" (McIntyre 2007, 20). Our mode of engagement privileged mutuality and reciprocity, explicitly striving to transform power relationships.

Collaborative Design Sessions

The Media Design Practices/Field (MDP/F) track at the Art Center College of Design takes up questions of social justice, inequality, and complex global systems, emphasizing immersive fieldwork and an understanding of culture and power. Field participants are thus required to develop a self-questioning and reflexive practice in which notions of "good," "help," "development," and "progress" are understood as complex and problematic.

The partnership allowing this work to take place relied on Jovenes, Inc., a nonprofit organization founded in Boyle Heights by Father Richard Estrada in 1989.[1] Jovenes takes a holistic approach to the problem of youth homelessness, providing housing to serve immediate needs and also striving to address the complex systems that produce youth homelessness. The clients Jovenes serves are varied, but are overwhelmingly Latino and African American. They include those whose families have lost their housing, young men who have crossed the border in search of work, transgender youth of color, gangbangers, and youth recently released from jail or who have aged out of the foster care system. Few have ever spent any time on Skid Row or sleeping in the rough. Rather, they have scrounged together a series of strategies that allow couch-surfing with friends or family, use of shelters, and enrollment in residential programs. Jovenes provides three types of direct housing support: the emergency shelter, transitional housing, and permanent housing. Clients are framed as "family," and even when not receiving services, are welcome to participate in organizational activities. Over the course of the class term, more than 30 different clients participated: some for one day only, some for the entire time, and everything in between. Participants came primarily from the emergency shelter, transitional housing, and the "family" groups.

Designers are accustomed to getting a "design brief" at the beginning of a project: think of it like Tim Gunn walking into the sewing room on *Project Runway*, where he presents the designers with a specific task and constraints ("Your challenge, designers, is to make an avant garde evening gown using sphagnum moss and uncooked noodles...") and then challenges them to "Make it work!" A design brief provides specific parameters for the design process and a clearly defined outcome or product. For this project, the design brief was one word: storytelling. Simple as it was, the brief was designed to put students face to face with the specific hurdles they must confront in their first term. The brief was broad and also one that moved them away from typical solution-focused work. Jovenes had a need for a variety of material it could use for its website, marketing, and research initiatives. As student teams pursued their research, they produced huge amounts of audio, video, and photo resources. All the products of our research were organized and shared openly with Jovenes so that it could access and use everything for its own purposes. The trust required on all sides was substantial, and renegotiated on a nearly weekly basis. At its most basic, Jovenes staff had to trust Elizabeth Chin to prepare her students and debrief them thoroughly so that Jovenes needs and interests would remain paramount. Jovenes youth had to trust both Jovenes, Inc., and MDP/F. All involved had to trust that the process would yield something worthwhile, which for some time was very much an open question.

The 10-week engagement involved three-hour meetings on Monday evenings. All sessions included a snack, an important tool in enticing participation and raising energy levels. At the beginning, these meetings took place at the Jovenes facility. Over time, Jovenes participants often came to our program's studio, and eventually some youth became comfortable enough to drop by on their own to work on the project, to attend class, or to hang out. Both Jovenes and MDP/F are situated on the same mass-transit train line, making travel between the two convenient. Jovenes youth were encouraged by staff to attend the sessions, but attendance was always voluntary. Although some were consistent in their attendance, others were erratic. This challenged the MDP/F students to remain flexible by being sensitive to the often-changing group dynamic at each meeting.

Creating Active, Shared Experiences

From the beginning, the changing makeup of participants presented an ongoing challenge for the student designers, who had to structure the collaboration sessions in a way that could create a sense of progress from week to week while allowing enough space for a new participant to join at any given point. The first session was devoted solely to getting to know on another. Simple icebreakers in which people had to learn each others' names while clapping, though seemingly childish, allowed everybody to look and feel awkward and silly. After a few such exercises (in which Jovenes staff and MDP/F professors also participated), we moved on to the main activity. Everyone was divided into five teams and each given one egg, along with plastic cups, cotton balls, pipe cleaners, markers, and tape. The teams then had to construct an outer shell that would protect that egg when dropped from the two-story-tall fire escape in the back of the Jovenes building. This team-building activity is not original to us; one MDP/F student remarked that he had done the same activity as a child at camp.

Many teams reached outside the given constraints and incorporated other materials found around the center: bags of chips, bubble wrap, mouse pads, etc. As teams built prototypes, laughter echoed throughout the center. Teams began naming themselves and their creations. As teams tossed their eggs from the top of the stairway onto the parking lot, we experienced exploding chip bags, and even a rendition of "I Believe I Can Fly!" This exercise helped to soften the social barriers between the youth and designers. It also set the expectation for the coming weeks: the student designers would be working alongside and collaborating with the Jovenes youth every step of the way.

One Jovenes participant, Lorenzo, posed a unique challenge for the group. Charismatic and focused, Lorenzo was intent upon a career as an actor and public personality. Born in an indigenous Central American community, Lorenzo lost both parents by the age of five and found himself on the street. By age 10, he had been brought to the United States by a woman who abandoned him in Los Angeles. Living independently, a college graduate, and no longer homeless, Lorenzo continued to participate with Jovenes consistently. He joined the project with a very specific goal: to produce some videos to promote personal projects important to him. Without a doubt, Lorenzo's capacity for single-minded pursuit of what is important to him has been a key element in his life journey. Negotiating him away from this goal required a very delicate mix of persistence and diplomacy on our part. As Lorenzo became more involved with the group project, he was able to put his personal priorities on a back burner, though he made it clear he never relinquished them.

Getting in Touch: Jovenes Ink

In our second session, we attempted to gather stories, but quickly realized our participants thought our methods were boring. Our focus on homelessness as a topic did little to encourage the youth to open up. As we prepared for the third session, we understood that we needed to move away from using design to explore their homelessness and instead find ways to use design as a medium for creating relationships with the youth. The result was Jovenes Ink, a design intervention in which youth and designers designed temporary tattoos together (Figure 15.1). Many of us already had tattoos, whether Jovenes staff, Jovenes youth, MDP/F students, or professors. We also had seen that many youth would doodle tattoo designs when they had the chance. Asking about their tattoos was a way to get them talking. Building on the youths' passion, we asked: "If you were going to get a tattoo tomorrow, what would you get? Why? Where would you have it on your body?"

We bought temporary tattoo paper, and brought along a computer and color printer so that we could print and apply the tattoos on the spot. The youth and student designers worked side-by-side, drawing with markers on plain printer paper. As people sketched, they talked about what they were making and the meaning behind their designs. Stories naturally evolved, and conversations at one table spilled over to another. One of the Jovenes participants drew a map of California in the shape of brass knuckles as a way of visualizing the violence and harshness of his experience in that state; another drew a large, detailed eye from which dangled a single tear, symbolizing his

FIGURE 15.1: Marlon's tattoo design from the Jovenes Ink activity

own often-unspoken emotions; a third drew suns and moons as a reminder to love himself. After scanning and printing the tattoos, we gave everyone the option of having their photo taken with it beneath a large Jovenes Ink banner.

Applying the temporary tattoos involved cutting out the design, then placing the tattoo and backing on the skin. Next, the paper backing needed to be moistened and the whole thing pressed onto the skin so the tattoo design could adhere. An unexpected element of this exercise was that some of the Jovenes participants needed help putting on their tattoos. As Art Center students dabbed tattoos with wadded-up paper towels, and patted designs onto Jovenes youths' skin, participants came into close physical contact for the first time. Marlon had designed a tattoo of his daughter's name and wanted it to be placed on the side of his neck. Well over six feet tall, Marlon had recently exited the justice system and was living in transitional housing. With several piercings on his face, large plugs in his earlobes, and many dramatic gang-oriented tattoos on his visible skin, he looked intimidating. Tina helped apply his tattoo; as Marlon tilted his head to one side, Tina rose up on her tiptoes to reach his neck, and dabbed away at the paper backing. This is when Marlon explained he had chosen to place the tattoo over his "life pulse" as a reminder that his young daughter is the reason for him to value life. In this vulnerable physical position, he chose to speak to us about matters close to his heart.

Fabulous Failure

For our fourth meeting, the *Caminemos Juntos* team tried to document the Jovenes youths' stories through personal journey mapping exercises. In these exercises, the student designers developed large visual maps with questions and other fill-in exercises for the youth to share their perspectives and personal stories along a timeline. The exercise was a massive fail: using the frame of a timeline, the designers asked the youth to contextualize their experiences as a progression of events leading to their homelessness, but this is not how they would frame their stories.

As we sat through two hours with Jovenes participants who were clearly bored by what we had placed before them, we came to see that our assumptions were simply wrong. Our carefully designed visual tools and creative representations framed the story as one of homelessness, thus claiming power over the narrative. We had inadvertently silenced the youth rather than empowered them.

One participant that day was Greg, who had a commanding but quiet presence. He had a stocky build, wore his hair shaved close to his head, and was proud of his Russian heritage. For Jovenes Ink he had drawn an eight-point star, an icon associated with lieutenants of the Russian mafia. The star held particular meaning for Greg as a symbol of his life's motto: "Kneel to no authority." Greg tossed out our map of homelessness and instead chose use the visuals we had created to begin writing a poem. As he worked he became excited and animated, his voice quickening as he took us through stanzas that had little to do with specific questions on the map, and more about the concept of a path as a metaphor. Greg asked us if he could take the map back to his room. He wanted to post it on his wall and use it to continue working on his poem. Later, he transferred that work to a notebook that he kept on him at all times. Greg's inventiveness subverted and improved upon our failed timeline experiment; from that failure, the team learned the importance of ceding authorial control to the youth.

Engaging with Technology

Like Jovenes Ink, the Pass the Mic exercise hinged upon student designers actively participating alongside the youth (Figure 15.2). It created a shared, collective experience from which the team explored areas of commonality, divergent viewpoints, and hidden biases. In Pass the Mic, the team formed a circle around a video camera placed in the middle; people then rotated around a stool that was facing the video camera. Someone in the group would pose a question, and the person sitting on the stool would answer the question into the microphone while being recorded. He or she would then "pass the mic" to the person to his/her right to answer the same question. The group kept rotating around the stool until everyone felt ready for another question.

FIGURE 15.2: Screenshots of Jovenes youth and MDP students during the "Pass the Mic" exercise

To help the group get a feel for the exercise, we had everyone go through the process first by saying their name, then answering the question: "What did you do this weekend?" When asked their names, everyone gave the standard response, except for one youth, Kevin, who replied: "I'm Kevin, aka Lil' Krazy from the Street with the Hip Hop Revolution."

Kevin moved to Los Angeles from El Salvador. He crashed on friends' couches or slept in his car, a well-maintained and impeccably clean early-2000s Mercedes. He spoke at a furiously fast pace, his words often running into and stumbling over each other. His dress was very considered: for Pass the Mic he wore a crisp white fedora and a plaid collared shirt. His eyes gave the appearance of squinting; he opened them fully only when he was excited or animated. Kevin got involved with gangs when he was six years old. He used to sell cookies to bus passengers until one local *maras*[2] wanted in on the action and began extorting money from him. He turned to another gang for protection. During his teenage years, he spent time in and out of prisons in both Mexico and the United States. He credited hip hop culture for redirecting his life. During the project, it was important to Kevin that we understood that hip hop is not just music, and definitely not just what you hear on the radio: it includes music, dance, graffiti and street art, freestyle competitions, and entrepreneurship. He came to Jovenes for a possible collaboration: he wanted to make a music video to promote his political views and "speak for [his] people."

Kevin infused the group with energy. After the first two warm-up questions, we asked, "What do you think people think of when they hear the word *homeless*?" This was a much more difficult and personal question for everyone to answer, prompting one youth to step away from the circle. We asked him if he was okay, and he said, "Yeah. Living this shit is hard enough; I just don't want to talk about it. Not today." He continued to stay with the group, watching from the sidelines.

No one seemed entirely comfortable in front of the camera. A few participants were flustered when a word failed to come to mind when they got to the stool. People laughed nervously and apologized. As the exercise progressed, the group picked up speed, and there seemed to be a lot of energy in the concepts that people shared. In fact, people built off of each other, and the exercise established a good rhythm.

Following this first run, we formed a circle to talk about the experience. Morgan facilitated the discussion by asking, "So what did you hear? Were there any common themes?" Two themes emerged: 1) homelessness is negative, and 2) being homeless is somehow the person's own fault. Morgan followed up with another question: "Do you feel this represents you or your experience?" The youth were uncomfortable. MDP/F student Cayla stepped up with an answer that everyone agreed with: "No. I mean, some of the answers had to do with being dirty or not taking showers, and that's not my experience with you. I don't think that anyone deserves it."

The group returned to answer a new question: "If you could wave a magic wand and change how people think about homeless people, what would you like them to think?" Here, the exercise continued for many rounds. The group's energy changed and people took longer at the microphone.

The quick-fire approach kept the group's energy up and allowed us to get "pat" or "expected" answers out of the way in a few rounds, pushing through to more meaningful, reflective responses. Originally, the exercise was set up to help get people comfortable talking in front of the camera, but what the team found in the process was something entirely unexpected. The gesture of passing the mic added a ritualistic element to the exercise, signifying passing on authority and community permission to the individual to voice his or her perspective. Passing the microphone was an act that enhanced the feeling of mutual respect and individual empowerment. When we reviewed the video, we discovered that the visual images produced by that moment where two hands met at the microphone were unexpectedly powerful.

Using the technology as part of the process of inquiry created a shared experience, helping to tear down the walls between designers and youth. We used technology itself as a means of knowledge production, which helped us to quickly push through surface answers and stereotypes and onto more reflective responses. The exercise confronted some of the cultural differences and perceptions of the two groups, helping bond the group together.

Design Objects as Research Media

Our team was composed of designers from different disciplines: Cayla had a background in graphic design; Morgan was a poet who built a career in storytelling and organizational culture; Tina studied communications with a focus on hyperlocal journalism. Pooling our strengths, we committed to spend time apart from the youth each week to create a designed object or experience in response to what the youth had expressed in their stories using visible and tangible media. Thus, the Jovenes youths' ideas and expressions appeared in forms that were sometimes surprising: lyrics put onto poster-sized paper and graphically displayed; ideas culled from Pass the Mic presented in the shape of a growing tree. We set aside time during group meetings for Jovenes youth to respond to the designs, often spurring textured, insightful discussions that influenced the ongoing process and final design outcomes.

About halfway through the engagement, Jovenes youth began coming to our studio space in Pasadena for our work sessions. The first week that they came to the studio, we wanted to provide ways for them to feel comfortable in a space where we worried they would feel out of place. To welcome them, and to show them some of the digital technologies we had on hand, we took words we had heard them use to describe themselves in the Pass the Mic exercise—resilient, positivity, original, beautiful, strong, unique—and transformed them into custom key chains. We drew these words in two script styles—"graffiti" and "retro"—and then cut them out of acrylic using the departmental laser cutter. As the cutter worked, youth could watch their key chains being made.

As the project progressed, the group shifted focus to writing and music. To facilitate this transition, MDP/F students reserved a private meeting room where tables were arranged for small group meetings, ensuring sonic privacy from the rest of the larger Jovenes group. The walls were adorned with big, bright, green and orange posters of song lyrics and sketches of ideas for a gallery exhibit that would focus on the work the youth were generating. The meeting location and setup had the desired effect of diminishing timidity about singing and rapping out loud. In a back-and-forth brainstorm and editing pattern, the youth were invited to give feedback on the planned gallery exhibit and refine the emerging rhymes, verses, and rhythms that later became their original song, "The Road I Walk."

MDP/F students put together a pool of ready-made beats, and when the group reconvened, youth tried out their lyrics, practiced rapping over them, and voted on which beat would be best for the song. With the direction of the song agreed upon, we booked time at a small, independent recording studio tucked into the back of a sleepy shopping center in nearby Echo Park. Two engineer/producers and a professional recording artist joined us. After a few nervous takes, each youth took a turn with the microphone and studio monitor headphones, recording as many takes of their original verse as needed to get "the one." As their comfort level in the recording studio increased, each began to contribute creatively, directing the engineers to lay a certain kind of "bleep" over a swear word, rapidly developing and adapting their phrasing to enhance the performance, and even insisting the MDP/F students sing the chorus. The engineer arranged everyone around a microphone and coached us through a group vocal that became a backdrop for the chorus.

Listening to the recording for the first time, the youth were exuberant. Immediately Marlon, typically quiet and reserved, asked to record one more vocal part. He stepped to the microphone and came in on the beat with a punctuated "Life's not over, kid." He asked the engineer to add it to the very end of the song. Later that day, in an uncharacteristically talkative interview, he explained, "My mind was basically about giving a message to young people. Letting them know that there's another way out. It don't gotta be drugs, or gangbanging, or any of that stuff."

Over the course of the day, each of the youth expressed ownership of the song, working to perfect their vocal delivery and contributing to the creative direction generated in the studio environment. The recording session used several strategies MDP/F students had been using in previous meetings (group participation, creating materialized versions of the youth's work, and favoring youth voices); as a result, the whole group had the opportunity to interact in an environment where they flourished creatively and collaboratively while avoiding pitfalls that prevented the youth from participating in earlier sessions.

Materializing New Perspectives

Over the following weeks, the song became the backbone of a community event featuring several material translations of the group's work. The team created an interactive electronic installation in the MDP gallery, and guests were invited to experience it and the other projects from the class. We suspended four sets of headphones from 12 feet up. One set of headphones contained the full song with all three youth voices; in each of the other three headphones, one youth voice was playing. Below each set of headphones we had placed cutouts of feet made of foam core. Underneath each set of feet we had a pressure sensor. When visitors "stepped into the shoes" of a youth by standing on the footprints, the pressure sensor triggered an individual video loop showing images selected by the youth whose voice was playing on the headphones (Figure 15.3). We also created a CD-style booklet with the lyrics and messages from Kevin, Marlon, and Lorenzo, and invited visitors to take these away with them.

Concluding Thoughts

Used thoughtfully and with deliberation, design can offer unique ways to engage voices and perspectives of marginalized people such as the Jovenes youth. Our public installation was especially powerful in providing a platform for Kevin, Marlon, and Lorenzo to take the stage: partway through the evening they decided to perform their song live, and everyone in attendance got to see them deliver their messages.

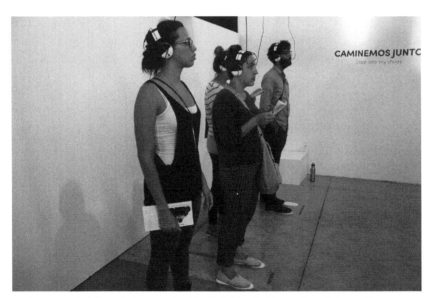

FIGURE 15.3: Visitors to the project installation in the gallery listened to *Caminemos Juntos* on headphones, while "standing in the shoes" of the Jovenes youth, who were singing

Technology and media embed ideologies, and the recognition of this fact allows all of us to subvert or refashion those ideologies. By striving to turn technology away from rote documentation and instead use it to transform social relationships, we uncovered many of our own biases and limitations as designers. Confronting these limitations is what allowed us to move beyond them. It is especially important to acknowledge that failure is likely to be part and parcel of this type of work. Yet failures are key learning opportunities, and if the emergent relationships among those involved continue to be framed within a structure of trust and respect, momentary failures can be overcome.

REFERENCES

Amster, Randall. 2003. Patterns of Exclusion: Sanitizing Space, Criminalizing Homelessness. *Social Justice* 30(1): 195–221.

Cheney, Kristen E. 2007. *Pillars of the Nation: Child Citizens and Ugandan National Development.* Chicago, IL: University Of Chicago Press.

Craven, Christa, and Dàna-Ain Davis, eds. 2013. *Feminist Activist Ethnography: Counterpoints to Neoliberalism in North America.* Lanham, MD: Lexington Books.

Escobar, Arturo. n.d. Notes on the Ontology of Design. http://sawyerseminar .ucdavis.edu/files/2012/12/ESCOBAR_Notes-on-the-Ontology-of-Design-Parts-I-II-_-III.pdf.

———. 2001. *Encountering Development: The Making and Unmaking of the Third World.* Princeton, NJ: Princeton University Press.

———. 2011. Sustainability: Design for the Pluriverse. *Development* 54(2): 137–140.

Kawash, S. 1998. The Homeless Body. *Public Culture* 10(2): 319–339.

Lister, Sarah. 2003. NGO Legitimacy: Technical Issue or Social Construct? *Critique of Anthropology* 23(2): 175–192.

McIntyre, Alice. 2007. *Participatory Action Research* (first edition). Los Angeles: Sage Publications, Inc.

Schuller, Mark. 2012. *Killing with Kindness: Haiti, International Aid, and NGOs.* New Brunswick, NJ: Rutgers University Press.

Smith, Juliette. 1995. Arresting the Homeless for Sleeping in Public: A Paradigm for Expanding the Robinson Doctrine. *Columbia Journal of Law and Social Problems* 29: 293–335.

Tunstall, Elizabeth (Dori). 2013. Decolonizing Design Innovation: Design Anthropology, Critical Anthropology, and Indigenous Knowledge. In *Design Anthropology: Theory and Practice*, edited by Wendy Gunn, Ton Otto, and Rachel Charlotte Smith, 2114–2230. London: Bloomsbury Academic.

Visweswaran, Kamala. 1994. *Fictions of Feminist Ethnography.* Minneapolis, MN: University of Minneapolis Press.

NOTES

1   Our partnership with Jovenes is one for which we are profoundly grateful. Eric Hubbard, director of development, was instrumental in facilitating our relationship with the organization and with Jovenes youth. Many Jovenes staff generously supported this work by participating in work sessions. Our admiration for Marlon, Kevin, and Lorenzo is enormous: they made *Caminemos Juntos* the success that it is. Their struggles, and their successes, continue to inspire us.

2   Maras are an international gang organization with a strong presence in Latin America and the United States.

Games without Frontiers: App Design as Networked Anthropology

Matthew Durington, Samuel Gerald Collins,
and the 2014 Anthropology by the Wire Collective

Introduction

Imagine the following possible scenario for a student enrolled in our urban anthropology field school course, "Life in the City," using a mobile application. They are asked on the first day of class to download the app for the course. The app contains access to all of the multimedia and ethnographic archival material on multiple sites in urban Baltimore produced by students and us in previous research iterations. An essential exercise in conducting ethnographic research is to go "into the field." While the traditional anthropologist would pitch their proverbial tent for an extended time for participant observation, this is not realistic to ask for a semester-long class (although we have always been impressed with students that have attempted to do so). So, how to facilitate a place-based engagement? Rather than meeting on a corner in south Baltimore on a Saturday morning to be led on a walking tour of a historic African-American neighborhood (a task that always leaves many students out due to lack of attention, work, or other obligations), students are told that they will need to unlock four stages in their new anthropology app by the third week of the semester on their own time. They are given the initial site they must visit to begin using the application. Their job as fledgling urban anthropologists is to understand what has come before them, and supplement it with their own work and engagement. This does two things simultaneously: it shows that anthropological fieldwork is never static and that communities are never ossified, but constantly changing.

Matthew Durington, Samuel Gerald Collins, and the 2014 Anthropology by the Wire Collective, "Games without Frontiers: App Design as Networked Anthropology" in *Participatory Visual and Digital Research in Action,* Aline Gubrium, Krista Harper, and Marty Otañez, eds., pp. 259-276. © 2015 Left Coast Press, Inc. All rights reserved.

They journey to south Baltimore and find themselves in front of Ebenezer AME Church, a historic African Methodist Episcopal church on Montgomery Street in Baltimore City. They start the mobile application and are geolocated at the site. The app congratulates them on starting their ethnographic adventure, and the first "stage" is unlocked. Oral history narratives, photographs, short videos, demographic information, and other data previously collected by researchers and former students suddenly appear before them on their smartphone to provide them with immediate context. They use these various forms of data to begin their "assignment" for the site. Their assignment calls for a snapshot of what is occurring in the community at that moment and a structured observation of their surroundings. But this is an open, iterative process. They are also prompted to "remix" one of the narratives they have accessed and provide their own reflection based on contextual material previously offered in the classroom. In addition, they then have to upload pictures and a video. Once these tasks are finished, they have accomplished a two-fold end: first, the contributions of our fledgling ethnographer have expanded the resources and data about this location and field site by adding to archival data to be used by researchers, future students, and the community itself; second, having completed their work, their learning and data collection activities continue as they are directed to the next location in the neighborhood, a row house where a famous member of the community once lived, repeating the process in their "choose your own adventure" ethnographic game. Finally, students (and other users) may contribute to the next iteration of the app in a process where their experience of app-driven fieldwork is itself a form of field-based research.

In the past five years, we've looked high and low for the "killer app"—to use the parlance of our tech friends—for teaching and doing ethnography, a technology that could completely transform the way we do research. We're here to tell you: there is no such thing. The app that will build rapport, conduct participant observation and interviews, and record all the nuances of fieldwork does not exist. What's more, we don't believe it *should* exist. An app that does everything we want to do in our ethnographic research is the result of someone else's ethnography, of their take on the anthropological project. One of the best features of ethnographic fieldwork is that it is tied to the situated perspectives of the individual anthropologist in a somewhat structured discipline. Instead, we look at apps as ethnographic in their own right: as part of the construction of a field site and the collection of multimedia data, together with analysis and interpretation. That is, apps can become part of the ethnographic landscape, and ethnographic practice can use apps. That's the recursive maneuver we find typical of anthropology in a networked world, what we call "networked anthropology" (Collins and Durington 2014). Apps have the capacity for collaboration both in the design process and in the use of various tools by our interlocutors.

In this chapter we explore app development as a form of highly reflexive, ethnographic research in its own right. In our multimedia, collaborative project, Anthropology by the Wire (www.anthropologybythewire.com), we tasked our student researchers with wireframing (designing the rudimentary technical framework) an ethnographic app. Looking back at the design process, we begin to critically reflect on the terms "multimedia" and "collaboration" themselves. At our field site in Baltimore, Maryland, what do these terms mean together? And, where do they begin to break down?

Our inclusion of apps in our research is just one more component of Anthropology by the Wire, a long-term ethnographic project that places researchers, students, and community members in collaborative partnership to create various media. The project itself is meant to create alternative media representations of the city of Baltimore and its citizens to stand alongside aberrant images created through the landmark television series *The Wire*, which gained a massive domestic and international audience. While *The Wire* was brilliant on many levels, it unfortunately reinforced a racial and socioeconomic stereotype of urban Baltimore. The ethos of our project is not only to create collaborative media, but to enhance community-based participatory research for us and our students. Anthropology by the Wire is a complex project that involves three core components: 1) teaching students in a media-intensive ethnographic field school, 2) building long-term partnerships with community organizations, and 3) creating social media connections between those groups in previously unforeseen ways through social networking sites and information communication technologies that are rapidly expanding in the twenty-first century.

When we first started Anthropology by the Wire four years ago, we were using the primary media tools of the visual anthropology toolkit, namely video cameras and supplementary audio-recording devices to make lineal ethnographic documentaries. Our team produced a series of short documentary videos with "rough" aesthetics due to the very guerilla nature of our work, the limitations of fledgling ethnographers and videographers, and a timeline of a few weeks each summer. (View this archived work on the Anthropology by the Wire YouTube Channel.) As we posted student-produced documentary video clips on community social media sites to "share" our work with our collaborators and a wider public, we quickly began to feel constrained by traditional video production. As a community-based participatory project, our goal was to create a networked anthropology in which participants could not only access but also creatively repurpose our project's media and documentation. Our success is measured not by going viral globally with large numbers of "likes," "shares," "views," and "hits," but in small numbers that show the media connections between our research and community networks.

Our students and our collaborators used apps as they conducted their work in the community and played with game apps in their leisure time. We wondered: Why not include the analysis of apps and the user-centered design and construction of apps as another media iteration of the project? At the same time, we joined many other researchers who are thinking critically about games and gamification logics in their curricula and research endeavors. Apps are becoming as ubiquitous as the devices we use in our everyday lives, and research methods now rely upon these mobile programs. Thus, they have an incredible capacity for a participatory ethos alongside other media collaboratively produced by anthropologists and participants. We have witnessed the quick adoption of apps as an element of our project by our student researchers and community partners as we moved from design, to rudimentary programming, to beta testing. And, apps are fun…just ask any millennial near you.

Background

While we appreciate and use traditional ethnographic methodologies, we are part of a new cohort of scholars who are pushing the boundaries of anthropological research through new technological speculations and explorations (boyd 2014; Coleman 2012; Wang 2012; among others). These are not just intellectual exercises: we are also interested in the possible applied dimensions of this work (Pink 2007) and synergies between ethnographic methods and collaborative design. Now in its second decade, design ethnography is a contested terrain where some researchers use the term "ethnography" for exploring and designing information technology (Crabtree et al. 2012), while others use the term for their own idiosyncratic approach to understanding design and culture (Galloway 2013). Exciting and experimental work at the borders of anthropology and design (see Chin 2014; see also Chin et al. in this volume) provokes the question: Why can't design itself be a form of ethnography?

Developing an app once involved a steep learning curve, but that obstacle is becoming less arduous for even the most technologically challenged anthropologist. The apps we are developing through Anthropology by the Wire involve locative, mobile storytelling and collaborative data collection: they allow groups of people to bring together their ethnographic data and display them to an engaged, networked public that can interact with those data in ways that are simultaneously a source of a new data. We envision a body of archival research that is constantly updated as researchers and their collaborators add more layers of data over time. This goes beyond the data collection of a single researcher in a static moment and allows a body of research and understanding to constantly morph and change while enhancing the agency of collaborators as they add their perspectives to anthropological analysis. Essentially, it is the research project that truly doesn't end, and thwarts the ossification that can come when ethnography "leaves the field." In this interactive environment enabled by mobile app development, communities are truly not static, and the complexity of ethnographic engagement is constant and revealed. We think this may be the beginning of a new form of reception and dissemination of anthropology.

Many of the media projects, technologies, and platforms used by anthropologists engaged in participatory visual and digital research can find a life and, perhaps more critically, a way to be analyzed, through app platforms. Research, reception, and collaboration can actually be mapped out and realized through mobile app usage and analytics, as we discuss later in this chapter. While not everyone can (or should) use apps in their research, they are an accessible medium in an era when smartphone adoptions continue to spike across social strata while more conventional forms of ethnographic dissemination (books, journals, films) continue to be paywalled behind increasingly expensive doors. Finally, our engagement of app platforms not only elicits new questions in terms of methodology and analysis, it also forces us to ask (once again) the important question of what we actually mean by collaboration in anthropological research.

Networking Apps and Anthropology

Over the past five years, we have developed a networked anthropology approach involving the collaborative production of multimedia disseminated over multiple social media platforms:

> An anthropology undertaken in the age of multimedia social networks, one in which all of the stakeholders—ethnographers, interlocutors, community, audience—are all networked together in various (albeit powerful and unequal) ways. Networked anthropology generates ethnographic data in multiple media. Here it overlaps with similar advances in different subdisciplines, including visual anthropology, public anthropology and action research. The difference is that a networked anthropology produces data that is simultaneously media to be appropriated and utilized by the communities with whom anthropologists work in order to connect to others (other communities, potential grantors, friends and family). And the opposite is also true—anthropologists are only generating data for their research in the space of their commitments to communities to assist in their efforts to network to different audiences. (Collins and Durington 2012, 8)

In our book, *Networked Anthropology* (Collins and Durington 2014), we take this proliferation of social media as its starting point and build a model of an engaged, participatory multimedia ethnography off of the social fact of sharing.

For us, a "shared anthropology" follows the ethos established by ethnographic filmmaker Jean Rouch in his early musings on his practice, where he anticipated that technological developments would turn the camera over to those collaborators who, up to that point, were solely in front of it as the reified subjects of anthropological speculation and representation. He lamented and attempted to disrupt a power dynamic in ethnographic representation through practice and reflexivity. A networked anthropology facilitates that movement as well, but also creates a mutual reciprocity in real time where the process is just as important, if not more so, than any potential outcomes from ethnographic research.

Networked anthropology is here to stay, whether you like it or not. Even if you recoil at the thought of sharing your ethnographic data on social media platforms, someone is probably already doing that for you: your informants, your students, your grantors, universities, and publishers. We have already disappeared down that rabbit hole. Every time any media you produce is viewed on the Internet, it becomes part of an expanding network that you may not have imagined before. For instance, videos that we have produced and posted on YouTube with our students about communities in Baltimore City are now part of search engine results alongside all kinds of media that we did not produce. The use of metadata such as tagging video posts becomes a path of connectivity to people who decide to tag "#Baltimore" on any video. So your attempt to make a critical video about gentrification in Baltimore is connected to videos of people riding motorcycles in a dangerous fashion down city streets simply because both took place in the same city. It forces anthropology into a multimedia world, and not an insular world where anthropological research too often resides. And, for our colleagues now screaming, "Where are the ethics?!?" let us refer you to the extensive discussion in our book *Networked Anthropology* and the way this new social media reality may actually bolster ethics in anthropology by eliminating boundaries and enhancing collaboration (Collins and Durington 2014, 57–71).

There are many unanswered questions in our research, but one of the most obvious concerns the ways we network our ethnographic media. If a networked anthropology connects text, photographs, audio, and video through social media, how does that work? We continue to explore that through this new possibility of designing apps, using them, and subsequently studying the analytics produced by that usage. While everyone may understand the idea of a connected multimedia, the way material is networked together is still a vitally important concept to understand. Fortunately, the use of social network analytics and other forms of Big Data by social scientists is beginning to provide a roadmap for answering that question, albeit with the cautionary note of using Big Data in an ethical fashion (Parry 2014).

This is especially important for app development. In many ways, apps are the culmination of networked anthropology: our experiences and philosophies given a technological form. While we can imagine apps that support collaborative, geolocationally tagged data collection, sharing, and media, it's unclear how these should all work together. Instead, networked anthropology takes the network itself as a source of data, analysis, and interpretation, building a recursive anthropology on the backs of social media platforms and multimedia applications. The alignment of networked materials in an app is hardly incidental: it instantiates distinct epistemologies and implies specific social relations and practices. We think it is time for apps to be considered recursively along with other elements of a networked anthropology: as data, as analysis, as interpretation and as, ultimately, a collaborative, open design.

Wireframing Anthropology by the Wire

We are seeking to challenge our students, ourselves, and anthropology by designing a mode of research that trains fieldworkers for the twenty-first century with the ethos that comes from community-based participatory research. In doing so, we are furthering the core activities of the Anthropology by the Wire project that combine ethnographic training with production, collaboration, analysis, and novel forms of dissemination that are part of a burgeoning networked anthropology. The integration of gamification and gaming logics are hot topics in higher education (Kapp 2012; Malaby 2009). We have been using gaming logic in the fieldwork component of our courses for quite some time, as students are often on an intellectual journey of discovery and "adventure" in urban Baltimore that they would never have experienced without taking our courses or participating in Anthropology by the Wire. But it is very important to note that this is a progression in which ethical and methods training occur first to facilitate ethnography.

Before departing on their "ethnographic adventure," students are walked through a curriculum that provides background on Baltimore and larger explanatory frameworks for understanding urban life in the United States. The next step is to use multimedia tools for documentation and engagement with Baltimore citizens toward an applied outcome. After years of following this approach we have a very robust set of images, video, text, reflexive statements, and archival research of sites in the city with which we continue to work. These are all the components of an urban anthropology that we practice, but we are also interested in having our next generation of students use this body of multimedia work that has come before them. The nature of our mobile app development is that it "shakes the dust" off of our archive; further research must "remix" and use former research as new data are gathered and collaboration is extended. Rather than simply have them review this material, we want them to "play" immersively with it. We are on the precipice of studying apps as a component of a mediascape of our collaborators in anthropology while also studying and developing these tools as anthropologists. The gaming aspect of this particular form of media is particularly enticing.

The field school app presented earlier is the loose scenario for an anthropology app we challenged our students with in the summer of 2014 in Anthropology by the Wire. In this last iteration of the research project, we divided our cohort into four different groups. Each group was to continue research and multimedia documentation on four ongoing sites where we have been working. Team 1 was assigned to the neighborhood of Sharp Leadenhall, an historic African-American community that has suffered various processes of urban renewal, including the throes of gentrification in the last decade (Durington et al. 2009). Team 1's job was to map out encroaching development while also creating a video for a YouthWorks project tasked with greening and beautifying the neighborhood. Team 2 continued work with a group of HIV-positive "ambassadors" who are public educators in Baltimore. The ambassadors advocate a healthy lifestyle and positive approach to their disease through a variety of platforms facilitated by the JACQUES initiative, an outreach center associated with the Institute of Human Virology. The task for Team 2 was to translate a book of photography (Barrazato 2013) to a gallery setting and make an accompanying video. Team 3 was tasked to revisit a set of collaborators interviewed the previous year made up of former steelworkers recently laid off from their jobs when the former Bethlehem Steel plant at Sparrows Point was permanently shuttered. Their job was to document the movement of these individuals from a manufacturing economy to a service economy in the twenty-first century in the context of postindustrialism. Last, Team 4 worked with a nonprofit organization in Baltimore called Wide Angle Youth Media, who trains teenagers to use multimedia tools as a platform to have their voices heard on a variety of issues.

Each of these groups that we partner with through Anthropology by the Wire is highly engaged in social media themselves in various ways, such as Facebook, Twitter, and other platforms. We are "tagged" constantly on Facebook, and any search of @anthrobythewire on Twitter reveals a multitude of fieldwork moments. These groups have similar goals of sharing their stories, and see the results from our long-term collaboration in the form of media production and other documentation as productive. After all, we want to tell these stories and speak alongside our community partners while simultaneously providing research training for our students and conducting an applied anthropology. Our four groups in 2014 worked within this social media context while also focusing on their primary anthropological fieldwork. Each group that we partner with has engaged the possibilities of a social media presence to disseminate their mission more widely, assist in fundraising, and enhance engagement with the broader community. In this sense, we find ourselves on a similar path because we are attempting to provide our students with ways to demonstrate the impact that an engaged anthropology can have on the world around them.

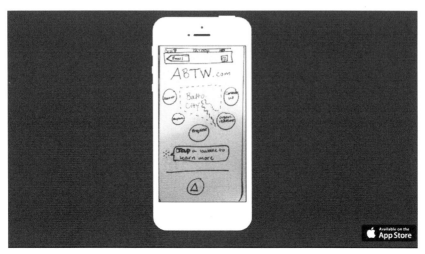

FIGURE 16.1: Screenshot of a wire-framed prototype using http://popapp.in

Each of the four teams had individual "deliverables" for their research, but all were unified in the use of social media to reflexively document their work, including individual blogs, group blogs, image-based social media sites, and connective platforms such as Twitter and Facebook. A couple of weeks into their research, we asked them to draw upon their fieldwork experiences for the development of a mobile app. While this would have been challenging in previous years, new mobile app prototyping tools facilitate this kind of ethnographic exercise. We use a prototyping app called POP (Prototyping on Paper; www.popapp.in) that follows a ridiculously fun workflow. One designs an app on paper, takes pictures of various wireframes, and then simulates the pictures as a mobile app through their smartphones or tablets (Figure 16.1).[1]

We tasked our entire research cohort to reflect on their research design, contextual knowledge of Baltimore, and their projects to design a mobile app for Anthropology by the Wire.

Recursive Analysis through Design

We then analyzed each of the four prototypes for the "flow" between different media, recursively reflecting on the situated perspectives we have assembled over the four years of the Anthropology by the Wire project. How did each student team conceive of the relationship between, for example, archival

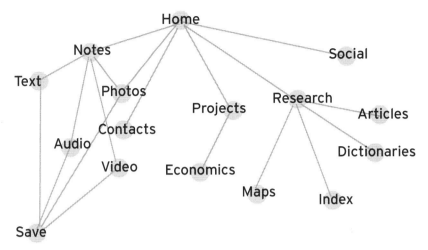

FIGURE 16.2: Group 1 (Baltimore Steel): network diameter, 4; average path length, 2.583

research and neighborhood mapping? Between community collaboration and media production? That is, by tasking them with prototyping apps, we were also asking them to imagine a networked anthropology as a material practice. Our analysis follows two steps. First, each prototype is mapped using a open source, social network analysis program (Gephi) to illustrate the connections between different pages. Second, we examine the path length between different nodes. If it takes just one "click" to go from one page to another, then the path distance is "1"; if we have to go through two pages to get there, then the path distance is "2"; and so on. Finally, that graph is analyzed using "betweenness," a common metric in social network analysis that indexes the importance of a node relative to its neighbors. In the interest of space, we have included only the first metrics table from our analysis to illustrate the issues (Table 16.1). When a node has a high degree (lots of connections) and also lies "between" other nodes in the app (betweenness centrality), then it becomes a high-traffic connector occupying a central place in an app while also providing access to other parts of the app. On the other hand, parts of the app with low density and/or low betweenness lie at the margins: they represent relatively unintegrated parts of the app and, perhaps, areas of networked anthropology that have yet to be effectively connected to other parts (Figure 16.2).

TABLE 16.1: Degree and betweenness
in the Baltimore Steel app

	Degree	*Betweenness*
Home	6	79
Notes	5	33
Social	1	0
Research	5	50
Projects	2	14
Contacts	1	0
Text	2	.25
Audio	2	.25
Video	2	.25
Photos	3	10.25
Save	4	3
Articles	1	0
Dictionary	1	0
Index	1	0
Map	1	0

In this app, the most important node (besides "Home") is "Notes"; the least-connected components of the graph are the "Social" and "Contacts" nodes. The greatest path distance (4) lies between areas of research (articles, dictionary, index) and areas devoted to multimedia (audio and video). The table shows the way the team fit their multimedia materials together and, through that, the way they imagined a public clicking through their app. The Baltimore Steel team had a great deal of archival material provided by the community, which features prominently in their app design. The highest "betweenness" score (after "Home") is "Research." And yet, there seems to be a real division between the archival data and contemporary multimedia of people's lives in wake of the plant closing. In some ways this represents the real divide that former steelworkers face: their lives have been completely turned around. On the other hand, the challenge for the Baltimore Steel team would be to bring these disparate media together to represent those divisions (Figure 16.3).

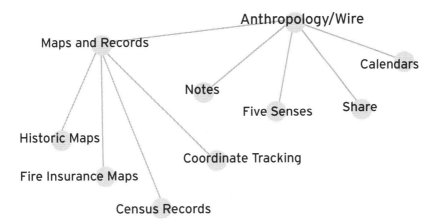

FIGURE 16.3: Group 3 (HIV Outreach Clinic): network diameter, 3; average path length, 2.067

The HIV Outreach Clinic Team worked with a clinic in west Baltimore that takes a more holistic approach to HIV treatment by actively building a community, including clients, caregivers, and supporters. The team embedded this philosophy into the app itself, and rather than concentrate on their analysis of the existing outreach community, chose to build an app that would help people more effectively "connect to care" and stimulate the formation of new communities (Figure 16.4). In this prototype, the most connected nodes outside of "Sign On" are (in terms of degree) "My Communities," "Profile," and "Bulletins." In terms of betweenness centrality (another measure of importance derived from the location of the node in the network), the most important pages are "Map" and "Anthropology by the Wire." The least-connected nodes, on the other hand, are the community sites: "Join a Community," "Start a Community," and "Public Wiki." The greatest path distances are also between the project pages ("Bulletins") and some of the community functions ("Make a Wiki").

The YouthWorks team documented a neighborhood beautification project in a historic African-American neighborhood in south Baltimore. The project combined multimedia documentary with archival materials on the long, embattled, history of this neighborhood. This primary division is reflected in their app design. The most important parts of this app (from the perspective of density and betweenness) are the maps and recordings. The least-connected components are notes, archival materials, and collaborative community functions. These are also the sites with the greatest path distance (3).

FIGURE 16.4: Group 4 (Youth Works): network diameter, 3; average path length, 2.156

The various nodes our participant researchers envisioned for their prototyped apps included several categories: geolocational categories ("Map," "Find Me"), multimedia categories ("Video," "Notes"), research categories ("Articles," "Census Maps") and social categories ("Join a Community," "Contacts," "Share"). How do these prototypes address each of the functions? Would people using this app make the connections between historic inequalities and contemporary efforts to address them? The studied neutrality of something like "neighborhood beautification" needs to be contextualized in Baltimore's African-American history, together with the racist urban policy and development that have preserved a high degree of race and class segregation in the city.

Discussion

In general, "Research" and "Community" functions seem to be the least integrated functions in these application prototypes. If we think about ethnographic research as a linear process, where research is followed by fieldwork, analysis, and dissemination, then "Research" and "Community" would come at opposite ends of the research process. But in a networked anthropology, these functions should work together as integrated, collaborative media that make no distinction between research, analysis, and sharing. Intellectually, we may know this, but it is a difficult, conceptual leap, and each of the prototypes suggests the difficulties in networking anthropology as a form of practice. The challenge for app design in these projects is precisely the collaborative integration of multimedia worlds in the space of practice. That is, apps (unlike other forms of ethnographic representation) demand that we make specific connections between place, representation, and the experience of both. When we find disconnections, or "weak ties" that loosely couple multimedia data, we need to address that to make an app that both reflects the needs of the community and at the same time stimulates critical, anthropological insights in the people using the app.

The challenge for us is to work toward designing app platforms and research methods that would facilitate this collaborative process. While there are apps for ethnographic research (Ethos), apps for mobile storytelling (Baltimore Heritage 2014), and apps for collaboration (Kobits Collaboration, Google Docs), there are no applications (that we know of) that would bring all of these together into a collaborative, multimedia ethnography geolocated in the city. There are tantalizing possibilities: for example, ARIS allows apps that combine geolocational research and notetaking, but these remain unintegrated functions.

That said, the purpose of this exercise was not to "solve" the problems of networked anthropology, but to use app design itself as a form of recursive, ethnographic inquiry. In other words, the act of prototyping an app is also an interpretation of a field site from a multimedia, networked perspective. How do all of the different media we've collected fit together? How do people network with the site and with the community? Apps developed from these prototypes are another step in an iterative process that would next incorporate usage data and interviews to restructure the app to reflect new insights into the field site. Given enough time and resources, we can see this iterative app design process continuing and being more fully integrated with our field research process.

Conclusion: Ethnography and Creative Misuse

An anthropology app has the potential to enhance a networked anthropology that fashions data collection, analysis, and interpretation through a collaborative open design. As we have argued, the idea of using app development as a tool for networked anthropology presents salubrious dilemmas. Problems in app development thus suggest problems with media and participant integration, which ultimately are problems at the crux of our ethnographic practice: apps are where the rubber meets the road in terms of networked anthropology. We see exciting possibilities in the creative misuse of mobile app technology for collaborative, networked ethnography. Jason Farman describes creative misuse as "creatively using a technology in a way in which it was never meant to be used, the results of which offer a thoroughly transformed view of the technology, its place in society, and future practices with the technology" (Farman 2014, 4). For Farman, creative misuse helps individuals "defamiliarize" themselves with their environs and their technologies, which results in a "deeper sense of place and a stronger understanding of our own position with that place" (Farman 2014, 4). We are particularly interested in "misusing" the geolocational possibilities of mobile apps to facilitate interconnections between anthropologists and their collaborators in addition to other interlocutors in fieldwork settings.

By exploring the limits of our understanding and imagination through this kind of app development, we can begin to envision a transformed ethnographic encounter. The popular use of geolocation-based mobile applications presents challenges and possibilities for a discipline that relies upon the authority of being in a space, and deriving stories and narratives that make places. In essence, anthropologists tell deep stories that map onto our field sites and our collaborators in complex ways. For example, the creative misuse of mobile apps would entail using the global positioning system (GPS) capacities of smartphones to enable instant connections defined by one's locational presence in a community. As Sample theorizes, this "goes beyond the check-in" enabled by apps such as Foursquare that instantly connect you with others in a certain proximity. We want to "defamiliarize" the typical fieldwork experience to create a different power dynamic in engagement, albeit between parties that possess smartphones and are app savvy. Each time we prototype, design, and redesign apps, we are simultaneously contesting the boundaries of our field sites and the relationships between collaborators implied by the structure of these apps.

As in the scenario of a field school app we sketched at the start of this chapter, our "killer app" would create a "serious game" environment, with the fledgling fieldworker geolocated in a place where they "check in" to do research. How do we translate what is often trapped in the confines of a classroom to a fieldwork site? How do we avoid the pitfalls of "field trips" that often become tourist walkabouts rather than the walking tours that we hope they will be? As discussed previously, that research could entail structured observation, notetaking, photography, videography, and some social mapping. The app would instantly connect them to a network of individuals both in proximity corporeally in real time, but also through other networked attachments to that location through past research. Our mobile app could enable ethnographic connections to community members on the app platform at that time who are open to an interview or willing to provide some guidance.

What kinds of real-time engagement could a mobile app create through creative misuse? We want our students to connect with members of the community they are working with. Dare we dream of an app that connects our student researchers with potential collaborators and stakeholders in real time? The app also could show our ethnographer what photos are already in the archive for that site that they can use for elicitation or embellish with their own practice to show change over time. The possibilities are endless. As Sample states, "We ought to repurpose Foursquare and similar geolocative apps in order to foster critical and creative misuse of technology, and to encourage serious yet playful (or, playfully serious) chorographic thinking" (Sample 2014, 73). We take this as a clarion call for being playfully serious.

REFERENCES

Baltimore Heritage. 2014. Baltimore Heritage. http://baltimoreheritage.org/ (accessed July 14, 2014).

Barrazato, Cricket. 2013. *Life Don't Have to End*. Sarasota, FL: First Edition Design Publication.

boyd, danah. 2014. *It's Complicated: The Social Lives of Networked Teens*. New Haven, CT: Yale University Press.

Chin, Elizabeth. 2014. The Lab of Speculative Ethnography. https://sites.google .com/site/mdpsummerxterm2014/on-campus-research/project-ec(accessed July 14, 2014).

Coleman, Gabriella. 2012. *Coding Freedom: The Ethics and Aesthetics of Hacking*. Princeton, NJ: Princeton University Press.

Collins, Samuel, and Matthew Durington. 2012. Coming to Terms With Networked Anthropology. *Anthropology News* 53(5): 8, 12.

———. 2014. *Networked Anthropology: A Primer for Ethnographers*. London: Routledge.

Crabtree, Andrew, Mark Rouncefield, and Peter Tolmie. 2012. *Doing Design Ethnography*. New York: Springer.

Durington, M., S. Gass, C. Maddox, A. Rulf, and J. Schwemmer. 2009. Civic Engagement and Gentrification Issues in Metropolitan Baltimore. *Metropolitan Universities Journal* 20(1): 101–114.

Farman, Jason (ed.). 2014. *The Mobile Story: Narrative Practices with Locative Technologies*. London: Routledge.

Galloway, Anne. 2013. Towards Fantastic Ethnography and Speculative Design: Designculturelaboratory. Ethnography Matters (blog), September 17. http://ethnographymatters.net/blog/2013/09/17/towards-fantastic-ethnography-and-speculative-design/ (accessed July 14, 2014).

Kapp, Karl M. 2012. *The Gamification of Learning and Instruction*. New York: Pfeiffer.

Malaby, Thomas. 2009. Anthropology and Play. *New Literary History* 40: 205–218.

Neighborhood Narratives Project. 2008. About Neighborhood Narratives Project. http://www.neighborhoodnarratives.net/ (accessed July 14, 2014).

Parry, Marc. 2014. Recent Big-Data Struggles Are "Birthing Pains," Researchers Say. *Chronicle of Higher Education,* March 28. http://chronicle.com/article/Recent-Big-Data-Struggles-Are/145625/?cid=at&utm_source=at&utm_medium=en (accessed July 14, 2014).

Pink, Sarah (ed.). 2007. *Visual Interventions: Applied Visual Anthropology*, Oxford, UK: Berghahn.

Sample, Mark. 2014. Location Is Not Compelling (Until It Is Haunted). In *The Mobile Story: Narrative Practices with Locative Technologies*, edited by Jason Farman, pp. 68–79. London: Routledge.

Wang, Tricia. 2012. Building Transparency: One Lunch at a Time. *Wired Magazine*, August. http://www.wired.co.uk/magazine/archive/2012/08/ideas-bank/building-transparency-in-china-one-lunch-at-a-time (accessed July 14, 2014).

NOTE

1   We were exposed to the POP app through a workshop at the Human and Computer Interface Lab at the University of Maryland facilitated by our colleague Jason Framan.

Page numbers *in italics* refer to illustrations.

About the Editors

Aline Gubrium is an associate professor of public health and medical anthropologist at the University of Massachusetts Amherst. Funded by the Ford Foundation and the National Institutes of Health, she is working on a digital storytelling-based research project focused on sexual and reproductive health, rights, and justice with young parenting Latinas and a project to design and test a culture-centered narrative approach for health promotion in collaboration with young Puerto Rican Latinas.

Krista Harper is an associate professor of anthropology at the Center for Public Policy and Administration at the University of Massachusetts Amherst. An ethnographer who has worked in Hungary, Portugal, and the United States, she is author of *Wild Capitalism: Environmental Activists and Post-socialist Political Ecology in Hungary* (2006), co-author of *Participatory Visual and Digital Methods* (Left Coast Press, 2013), and co-editor of *Ethnographies of Postindustrialism* (forthcoming).

Marty Otañez is an assistant professor of cultural anthropology at the University of Colorado Denver. Otañez's research and advocacy focus on digital stories featuring viral hepatitis and other health issues, and on the exploitative practices of cigarette makers and leaf-buying companies at the farm level in Malawi and elsewhere. He is also the director of the Coalition for Excellence in Digital Storytelling, a University of Colorado initiative (www.dscoalition.org).

About the Contributors

Darcy Alexandra is a writer, ethnographer, and documentary storyteller specializing in visual anthropology and social documentary practices. Dr. Paul Stoller of West Chester University considers her doctoral thesis, "Visualizing Migrant Voices: Co-Creative Documentary and the Politics of Listening" (2015, Dublin Institute of Technology), "a fine example of the new wave of engaged ethnography." Alexandra has taught digital storytelling in Europe and the United States and conducted research in the United States–Mexico borderlands, El Salvador, Uruguay, Cuba, and Ireland.

Catherine Besteman is the Francis F. and Ruth K. Bartlett Professor of Anthropology at Colby College. She has conducted research on political subjectivity in Somalia, South Africa, and the United States. Her books include *Unraveling Somalia* (University of Pennsylvania Press, 1999), *Transforming Cape Town* (University of California Press, 2008), and *The Insecure American* (University of California Press, 2009, with Hugh Gusterson). She has just completed a book about Somali Bantu refugees in Lewiston, Maine.

Elizabeth Chin is an anthropologist and professor in the MFA program Media Design Practices/Field at the Art Center College of Design in Los Angeles. Working in the United States, Haiti, and Uganda, her focus is on children, race, and social inequality as well as dance and performance. She is author of *Purchasing Power* (University of Minnesota, 2001) and editor of *Katherine Dunham: Recovering an Anthropological Legacy, Choreographing Ethnographic Futures* (SAR Press, 2014).

Samuel Gerald Collins is an anthropologist at Towson University in Baltimore, Maryland. His present work examines the urban as the confluence of people and social media. He is the author of various books, book chapters, and articles, among them *All Tomorrow's Cultures: Anthropological Engagements With the Future* (Berghahn, 2008), *Library of Walls* (Litwin Books, 2009) and, along with co-author Matthew Durington, *Networked Anthropology* (Routledge, 2014).

Campbell Dalglish is an award-winning filmmaker, playwright, published poet, professor, and president of the Plaza Cinema and Media Arts Center. His short film *Dance of the Quantum Cats* (1996) has been screened at international film festivals, and his videos created with marginalized communities of homeless shelters, Indian reservations, prisons, juvenile delinquent centers, and gangland neighborhoods have been used to influence social change.

Matthew Durington is an associate professor of anthropology and director of international studies at Towson University in Baltimore, Maryland. His research interests include urban and visual anthropology in South Africa and the United States. An ethnographic filmmaker, he has produced the film *Record Store* (2008) and is also co-author of *Networked Anthropology* with colleague Samuel Gerald Collins (Routledge, 2014).

Sarah Flicker is an associate professor in the Faculty of Environmental Studies at York University. Her research focuses on youth HIV prevention and support as well as environmental, sexual, and reproductive justice. More broadly, she is interested in community-based participatory methodologies. Her research has informed policy at the municipal, provincial, and federal levels. Flicker and her teams have won a number of prestigious awards for youth engagement in health research.

Nancy Fried Foster is a senior anthropologist at Ithaka S+R and a research associate in the Department of Anthropology at the University of Rochester. She helps college and university libraries design technologies and spaces to support academic work. Her books include *Studying Students: A Second Look* (American Library Association, 2013) and *Studying Students: The Undergraduate Research Project at the University of Rochester* (American Library Association, 2007, with Susan Gibbons).

Gretchen Gano is a research fellow in the Science, Technology and Society Initiative in the Center for Public Policy and Administration at the University of Massachusetts Amherst. In 2013 she managed the Springfield, Massachusetts, site of a National Science Foundation–funded citizen engagement project called *Futurescape City Tours*. This experimental public engagement project features participant photography and a guided walking tour of key urban locations that could soon be enhanced by applications of emerging technologies.

Edward González-Tennant is an assistant professor of anthropology at Monmouth University. He has conducted research in New Zealand, Norway, China, the United States, and the Caribbean. He has authored numerous peer-reviewed articles in international journals, and his first book, *An Archaeology of Intersectional Violence: The 1923 Rosewood Pogrom in Historical Perspective,* will be published in 2016 by the University Press of Florida.

Andrés H. Guerrero is the Viral Hepatitis Prevention Coordinator for the Colorado Department of Public Health and Environment. Andrés' research interests include public health as it relates to incarcerated and formerly incarcerated populations, substance abuse, drug policy, and harm reduction theory. In 2011, Guerrero helped administer the project "Digital Health Stories: Video Interventions for Viral Hepatitis (http://tinyurl.com/cwxzjvd). He is currently pursuing his Master's of Public Health at the Colorado School of Public Health.

Cayla McCrae is a media designer. With a background in social justice and women's issues, her work stems from a convergence of formal design training and ethnography. She is a graduate of the Media Design Practices MFA program at the Art Center College of Design in Los Angeles.

Morgan Marzec is a design strategist specializing in organizational culture and communications. Synthesizing creative technology, storytelling, and participatory methods, she consults for FORTUNE 500 corporations, government agencies, and community-based organizations to design creative approaches for their most pressing challenges. She was selected for Leadership California's Class of 2015, a highly competitive program for women leaders in California.

Charles Menzies, a member of Gitxaała Nation, was born and raised in Prince Rupert, British Columbia. His primary research interests are the production of anthropological films, natural resource management, political economy, contemporary First Nations' issues, maritime anthropology, and indigenous archaeology. He is also the director of cultural and heritage research for Gitxaała Nation and a professor in the Department of Anthropology at the University of British Columbia.

Simona L. Perry is a research director at c.a.s.e. Consulting Services and vice president of Pipeline Safety Coalition. Trained as an environmental scientist and ethnographer, she works in rural and urban places across the United States to document and raise awareness of the interconnections between ecology, psychology, and culture. Current areas of practice include risk/disaster communication, energy-water conflicts, and collaborative long-term ethnography.

Nicholas A. Rattray is an associated health postdoctoral fellow at the Roudebush Veterans Affairs Medical Center in Indianapolis and an adjunct assistant professor of anthropology at Indiana University–Purdue University, Indianapolis. His research examines the cultural dimensions of disability, space, and embodiment in highland Ecuador and among military veterans returning from deployment with invisible injuries.

Jean J. Schensul is the founding director (1987–2004) and senior scientist for the Institute for Community Research (ICR), an organization using participatory research methods to strengthen community voices for change, where she founded its Youth Participatory Action Research Program in 1988 and developed the program's core curriculum. She teaches and writes on participatory methods, including the seven-volume *Ethnographer's Toolkit* series (AltaMira Press, with Margaret LeCompte) on ethnographic methods, now in its second edition.

Cynthia Selin leads the Anticipation and Deliberation Research Program at the National Science Foundation–funded Center for Nanotechnology in Society at Arizona State University, where she is an assistant professor in the School of Sustainability and the Consortium for Science, Policy and Outcomes. From 2014 through 2016, she is a Marie Curie Fellow at the Danish Technological University, investigating energy futures.

Madeleine Tudor is an applied cultural research manager in the Science Action Center at The Field Museum in Chicago. Her research interests focus on understanding how human–environment interaction relates to landscape and place-making, primarily in urban and postindustrial contexts. She has co-curated, developed, and produced anthropologically based visual materials through a variety of public engagement formats, including museum and community-based exhibitions and web-based media.

Natalie Underberg-Goode is an associate professor of digital media and folklore in the School of Visual Arts and Design at the University of Central Florida. She is author (with Elayne Zorn) of the book *Digital Ethnography: Anthropology, Narrative, and New Media* (University of Texas Press, 2013) and more than 20 articles, book chapters, and conference proceedings on the subjects of digital cultural heritage and storytelling.

Phillip Vannini is a professor in the School of Communication & Culture at Royal Roads University in Victoria, British Columbia, Canada, and the Canada Research Chair in Innovative Learning and Public Ethnography. He is author of a dozen books, including the most recent, *Off the Grid* (Routledge, 2014, with Jonathan Taggart).

Alaka Wali is curator of North American anthropology at The Field Museum in Chicago. She has conducted research in both Central and South America and in the urban United States on the human–environment interface and led programmatic efforts to build partnerships with community-based organizations to develop more effective stewardship of natural resources. She is the author of two books, more than 40 articles and monographs, and has received numerous grants for research.

Ciann L. Wilson is a PhD candidate at the Faculty of Environmental Studies, York University. A direct result of her lived experience as a racialized woman, Ciann's research interests include community health, HIV/AIDS, critical ethnic studies, and community-based and indigenous research approaches. Ciann's work is supported by a Canadian Institutes of Health Research Doctoral Award and a Social Research Centre in HIV Prevention Research Award.

Tina L. Zeng is a media designer and creative technologist. Trained in electronics and ethnography, her work is focused on designing from a position of abundance within the community. While still a graduate student, she consulted for UNICEF Innovation Labs in Uganda. Zeng was awarded the Art Center College of Design's Media Design Practices Postgraduate Fellowship based on her thesis work.